Pratish Mistry grew up in apartheid-era South Africa. He has since lived, studied and wandered in over 60 countries, making him truly a citizen of the world. Over the years, he has been happily homed in a variety of colourful boxes ranging from corporate strategy expert and entrepreneur, to poet, award-winning writer and life coach. Pratish has since given up collecting boxes and now focuses on his deepest interests: thinking; meditating; and the ability to play at least one musical instrument without having to face charges of crimes against humanity.

To ask a question, say hello, or share something nice you've done, please feel free to contact him at http://www.mistryworks.com/contact/

By the same author:

THE UNIVERSE & THE MAD BUTTERFLY

Kineosho Learns to Walk by Pratish Mistry was awarded *5 stars* on *Readers' Favorite*:

"This is an exceptionally well written book, with a great voice that will enthrall any reader . . . I hope they make it into a movie"

AUTHOR, ANNA DEL C. DYE

"This style of storytelling offers a wonderful opportunity to share the message of personal growth and inner strength . . . Laughter helps us learn, and Mistry does a wonderful job embedding laughter into the antics of Kineosho"

JANELLE ALEX, PH.D.

"Absolutely loved this novel . . . am always on the lookout for promising African authors and I think I've found a gem in Mistry! The story itself captured my imagination on a number of levels—from an entertaining African fairy tale, to a much deeper allegory about learning to trust oneself."

AMAZON, SIMPHIWE RAMAPHOSA

"I found the spiritual undertones that run through the story, along with the journey of Kineosho, very fascinating and intriguing . . . The story is simple with profound messages."

READERS' FAVORITE, MAMTA MADHAVAN

Kineosho Learns to Walk

By Pratish Mistry

mystic tree

To journeys & adventure

Part I

❦ 1 ❦

Mission Impossible

Once upon a time, in a land where time did not matter, there lived a little lion named Kineosho. He was no ordinary lion cub. In fact, he was the result of a rather extraordinary chain of events that occurred one crisp autumn.

Kineosho's story began in a cosy little cave on the edge of an enormous forest. In the cave lived a majestic lion and lioness, Griffon and Curie. There was freshly imported grass from the savannah scattered abundantly on the floor. The soothing smell of damp earth wafted through the air as the dense, humid jungle hummed and croaked outside the cave. A feather of light from a crescent moon completed the romantic scene for the couple. In fact, it completed it for all the jungle, including the half-blind, asthmatic aardvark who had become quite enamoured of his reflection in a muddy puddle nearby.

Now as romantic as the atmosphere was for the lions, ordinarily the couple would not do anything, well, romantic. In fact, they had successfully avoided doing anything romantic for quite a while already. The pair had long agreed that intelligent and responsible lions should not produce offspring as it was simply selfish. Besides that, the world was just not what it used to be.

The less-than-intelligent conservationists, on the other paw, had been trying for cubs for many moons, but without success: fertility rituals; multivitamin supplements; test-tube cubs; aphrodisiac eggplants—you name it, they had tried it. More recently, they had tried to simulate an environment that would allow the instinctive urges of the regal pair to kick in. After a series of failures, unwittingly, this time they had scored. That night had one special ingredient that nobody had counted on: neither the smart couple, nor the six scientist-types that eagerly watched the video feed of the cave.

The special ingredient lay in the dainty, half-eaten gazelle that was lying in a dark corner of the cave. Poor thing. Not poor because she had just been killed, but rather because she had never managed to resolve those deep identity issues that she was so involved in exploring. The gazelle had been born close to a stampeding herd of elephants, and since then, the very sight of the elephants that caused enormous trauma for mama gazelle, had given baby gazelle a great deal of comfort. So much so, that baby gazelle had simply considered herself a late bloomer, believing that her own trunk would grow someday. So she had happily followed the elephants around as she grew up, oblivious to how strange it all looked. The elephants, of course, hadn't helped matters by befriending her.

Earlier that very day, the friendly elephants had stumbled onto a stash of fermenting marula fruit and decided to have a party. Now there is nothing quite like a bunch of yob elephants imposing peer pressure on a confused gazelle. The animals indulged, and the effects of the marula fruit kicked in. The elephants fell asleep peacefully, and the little gazelle went totally berserk from a marula high. After randomly ramming her head against some trees, she ran around wildly. Then, in what probably seemed a good idea at the time, she madly attempted to leap over a large, fast-moving yellow creature that she had spotted. Much to her surprise, she failed miserably.

As luck would have it, the yellow minibus she had tried to leap over contained some conservationists who were on their way to witness their next lion breeding attempt. They were quite startled by the large thud, and immediately stopped. Initially, they all found it rather amusing to see the gazelle still drunkenly wobbling on her feet making some peculiar, almost elephant-like sounds. When the gazelle glared at them and started trying to flap her ears threateningly, they were practically rolling outside their vehicle with laughter.

They were, however, not nearly as amused with what happened next. The gazelle stormed straight towards them. She headed first for the bewildering fat woman who held the threatening-looking device making the blinding bursts of light that were hurting her eyes. A photo moment if ever there were one.

The gazelle took a flying leap and leading fearlessly with her trunk, she headbutted the lady's stomach. She then began bleating uncontrollably as she shook her head and chewed on the woman's colourful blouse. The lady ran yelling and in tears, allowing one of the conservationists to finally take a clear shot with his tranquillizer gun.

Thud! *Bleat!* Gazelle down.

The conservationists nursed Rosemary, the traumatised wife of their colleague, back to her senses and agreed that they would let the animal recover before deciding what to do. When the fat lady finally managed to speak, she blurted out a string of expletives that would have made the filthiest gutter comedian blush. She then demanded that they feed the deranged creature to the lions. Her colleagues promptly rationalised and agreed that it was a great idea. After all, lions in their natural environment with a fresh kill of their own—what could be more conducive to the successful coupling of two lions than that?

The little gazelle whimpered a confused, low bleat as they loaded her onto the roof of the minibus. They drove for some time and finally delivered her to a feeding area close to the lions' cave. The combination of the tranquillizer and marula fruit resulted in a dozy gazelle totally disconnected from her surroundings. Barely a few minutes later, the gazelle could have sworn that she saw a cute kitty cat leaping happily around her. And then everything went black.

Unfortunately for the lion pair and fortunately for the conservationists, twelve minutes after the meal ended, the special ingredient released a gush of serotonin into the couple's bloodstream. They gazed into each other's eyes and suddenly felt so very warm and happy. No doubt, it was not the first time that recreational edibles had resulted in an unwanted pregnancy.

On a rainy night about four full moons later, the conservationists were huddled in their observation room near the cave once again. They looked more enthusiastic than usual—sure that this was going to be the big day they had been waiting for. Rosemary had prepared herself by wearing an elaborately sequinned dress with a big white hat. She reminded the group of how she had bravely battled the crazed gazelle earlier that year. After all, if it wasn't for her insightful suggestion, they wouldn't be witnessing the miracle of a lion cub birth.

The tension built as the seconds passed—and then finally it happened. Kineosho was born.

The conservationists looked on, anxiously wondering how many cubs would appear. They had expected three kittens based on their research, so were rather surprised to find that only one was born. Of course, they didn't realise that this was because after many years of evolution, lions had adapted themselves to having fewer cubs. Cub-care was enormously challenging for parent lions, and this, together with the lack of predators, drove the genetics behind having fewer offspring.

Swimming in another gene pool altogether, Rosemary waved frantically and yelled at the others to move so she could see the new cub. She looked at the cub, and then annoyingly started tugging at her husband's sleeve, sheepishly suggesting that they name the cub Rose, after her.

Her husband shrugged, and nodded with quiet resignation. His colleagues giggled silently as they had already determined that *Rose* was actually a little boy cub.

The conservationists continued jotting down detailed notes about the rare birth they had just witnessed. Rosemary, in the meantime, ambled around the observation deck wondering what it would be like to pat the little cub and to keep her as a pet. The lion family looked so sweet, gentle, and caring.

Rosemary slowly daydreamed her way to the far end of the deck. There, she spotted an unlocked door brightly labelled 'Feeding hatch—no unauthorised personnel'. "Hmm . . ." she thought, "now that it's stopped raining, perhaps I could get close enough to take a photo and really capture the moment!"

She looked over her shoulder to make sure no one was watching and opened the feeding hatch. She opened the extra security door after it and braced herself to get a closer peek at her new pet. "Oh, such an adventure!" she thought.

As Rosemary slowly tiptoed towards the cave in the moonlight, she stumbled into one of those rather poetic good luck/bad luck situations. It started with a stroke of good luck: she accidentally slipped and fell into a deep puddle, but was completely unhurt. Bad luck: she had just inadvertently splashed away the love of a half-blind, asthmatic aardvark's life. This was once again met with some good luck: aardvarks can't do much damage to humans, except perhaps to slap them in the face with their sticky tongues. Bad luck: the same, unfortunately, could not be said for lions.

The aardvark let out a blood-curdling shriek when he saw his true love in the puddle displaced by a fat human thigh. A few seconds later, Rosemary healthily contributed to the annual statistic of humans getting mauled by a wild animal whilst parading outside the secure area of a national park. The conservationists looked on in horror as Griffon powerfully ripped off chunks of flesh from the potential threat to his new cub.

The distressed aardvark took consolation from having witnessed instant divine retribution. He then blinked sorrowfully for a moment at the big white hat that now covered his lost love before disappearing into the bushes.

The conservationists were still in shock, having just seen a ferocious lion maul their colleague's wife. The only person in the observation room who seemed calm was Rosemary's husband. Actually, the others had not noticed, but he had a slight twinkle in his eye. He was the first to suggest that they return to their distant village for help. The others agreed immediately and they all hurried off to their minibus.

Griffon pawed at the cub and tickled its stomach as he heard the minibus speed off. He sighed deeply when Kineosho gurgled in response. "Never thought I'd say it, but I'm quite looking forward to this," said Griffon quietly. All rationality had slipped out of his mind—there were neither thoughts of leaving legacies, nor intellectualised debate about the pros and cons of procreating. He was overcome with awe by what lay innocently before him.

"You know we need to get out of here, Griffon—we can't stay and risk these idiots coming in and fiddling around with Kineosho—" said Curie.

"—I know," replied Griffon immediately, his eyes still focused on their cub. "We leave tomorrow morning—early. Let's get some rest now . . . it's been a long day."

❧ 2 ❧

Far from prying eyes

Early the next morning, Griffon woke up and scouted around the area to make sure the conservation crew had not returned. The coast was clear.

Griffon nudged Curie. "It's time," he whispered in her ear, and Curie was quick to rise and stretch. Griffon grasped Kineosho by the scruff of his neck and placed him gently on Curie's back. They started walking and neither of them looked back at the cave, their comfortable surroundings for the last long while.

Kineosho was still fast asleep—he had basically been on autopilot since birth, waking up frequently for a feed and then heading right back to sleep.

The family moved at a steady but fast pace, heading deeper into the part of the forest that was still unexplored by the humans. Griffon and Curie were both experienced trackers and were careful not to leave a trail behind them. By sunrise they were deep inside the dense jungle, miles away from the cave. Griffon was single-minded about his destination—it was somewhere far away from humans, where Kineosho could grow up peacefully.

By mid-morning, the pair had reached an old watering hole. Both Curie and Griffon were still quite full from their feast the night before. Griffon's stomach grumbled ferociously as he lapped the fresh water. "Are you okay?" asked Curie.

"Fine," burped Griffon with a sheepish grin, "I just remembered why so few of us become human-eaters . . ."

"Oh . . . *eeew!*" smirked Curie teasingly, "chew on some of the short grass — it'll help the wind settle a bit." Curie had been with Griffon for a long time and she knew him well.

After a short break, they continued towards the end of the watering hole and began walking along the stream that drained into it. The climb became steeper — that was good. The further away and the worse the terrain, the less likely it was that anybody could track them down. By late afternoon, they were both tired. They had covered significant ground, and bar the few stops they had made to feed Kineosho, their pace was relentless. Curie found a cosy, well-protected resting spot and lay down to nurse Kineosho. "Let's rest here for some time," she said. Curie sighed softly as she watched Kineosho. Everything had happened so fast that she had not had time to be overwhelmed.

"Good idea," said Griffon knowingly, "we had better slow it down for a while." They both watched Kineosho sleeping and gradually Curie found herself nodding off into a restful sleep too. Griffon's thoughts slowly drifted to his own childhood, his training with Master Wu, and how much fun it had been to learn new things. He smiled as his thoughts wandered to when he had first met Curie. Griffon watched her sleep, curled around Kineosho, and it wasn't long after that he fell soundly asleep himself.

"*Hmmph* . . . lazy lumpy lions," mumbled a well-groomed female porcupine as she passed the sleeping trio. "And in my spot too," she continued mumbling as she walked a little further. She curled up behind some nearby bushes and soon fell asleep too.

The jungle is a surprisingly peaceful place when you're asleep. It's as though all the quirky whistles and croaks blend in harmoniously to form a smooth, soothing hum. There are certain sounds, however, as natural as they might be, that just jar with the rhythm of the place. One such sound is that of a young creature discovering the ample sonic power it can generate by innovatively using its own armpits. Rest assured, it's not a pleasant sound to wake up to, and neither Griffon, nor Curie, nor the well-groomed female porcupine, were particularly impressed when they did.

There was thankfully a moment's silence immediately after, but it wasn't long before they all heard a very strange, loud sound. "*Eep . . . eep*," it went. "*Eep, eep . . . eep.*"

Griffon immediately stood up on all fours and let out a low, deep growl. Curie stood before Kineosho in a protective stance. The porcupine frowned in disgust and darted her eyes from side to side to determine the source of the strange sound. It seemed to be getting closer.

Griffon could not pinpoint where it was coming from — sometimes it was at ground level, and then it appeared to be coming from the tree branches high above. Seconds later, they heard a rather traumatic *Eep Eep*, followed by a massive *Thud!*

Griffon was squatting, looking about as dazed and confused as the Pope at a Led Zeppelin concert. He was literally unaware of what had hit him. Curie was laughing hysterically at him. Well, not really at him — more at what had just happened. The other animals that had gathered around to see what the commotion was about were all giggling too.

On top of Griffon was a peculiar-looking baby monkey stroking Griffon's forehead in a rapid circular motion, repeating a distressed *Eep? Eep?* It was clear that the little monkey with its long, feminine eyelashes, had no clue what it had done and whom it had done it to. Judging by the pain it had experienced on its behind, the monkey only assumed that what it had hit was hurting like crazy too.

Curie could not stop laughing at this odd little hairy creature with its left arm almost twice as long as its right arm. The baby monkey was holding onto Griffon's mane with its right hand, whilst vigorously patting him with the other, trying to make him feel better.

Moments later, Griffon gathered his senses and let out an enormous roar, spinning around to establish where the attack had come from and how large his opponent was. Griffon's spin sent the little monkey flying across the patch until it slammed head-first into the still laughing Curie.

The disoriented monkey, not knowing what to do next, clutched Curie's ear with its short hand and started rubbing her forehead vigorously with the other. By this time Griffon had realised exactly what had happened, and could not help but laugh at the weird little monkey who was swinging off Curie's ear like a displaced ornament. All the excitement finally woke Kineosho, who although totally clueless as to what was going on, started laughing too.

Griffon gently lifted the strange monkey and put it on the ground next to Curie. It looked rather confused and scared now—understandably so, considering that it had never seen such large creatures with such big teeth before. "*Eep?*" it went, and then burst into tears. Kineosho, seeing the little monkey cry, immediately began to bawl in chorus. Soon, in what could best be described as a wailing wall of dominoes, all the other baby creatures nearby joined in to generate a melancholic group sob.

"All right," roared Griffon angrily at the spectators, "who does *it* belong to?"

The silence was deafening—half the animals had dashed off in fear and the rest remained quivering, unable to move. Even

the wailing wall had mysteriously dismantled itself and disappeared into the bushes.

Finally, a chirpy voice from a branch high above said: "*It
doesn't belong to anyone. I saw its troop leave the baby behind as
it could not keep up because of its wonky hands.*" The little voice
whistled a short melody and flew off.

"No wonder—what an ugly freak," mumbled the well-
groomed porcupine from her curled up position in the nearby
bush. This set off a chain of ugly-freak murmurs from the audience that remained.

"Move along," growled Curie at the remaining animals. They
dispersed immediately. She gently pawed at the strange little
whimpering monkey, trying to console it, and eventually sat it
down next to Kineosho. It was tired from all the excitement and
promptly fell asleep. Griffon and Curie decided to continue their
rest too.

When Curie woke, she stretched her limbs and let out a small
moan of satisfaction. As she turned around, she saw Kineosho
and the strange little monkey cuddled up next to each other.
The baby monkey's long left arm hugged Kineosho's neck and its
other hand clutched his ear. Curie smiled.

"Hey . . . no . . ." whispered Griffon behind her, "we've still
got a long way to go, Curie—it's just not practical."

"I know," replied Curie, "it's a pity our circumstances are not
different."

Kineosho woke up when Griffon began to lift him off the
ground to place him on Curie's back. He looked around a little
dazed and clouted his ear, which was still being clutched by
the little monkey. The monkey looked up in shock and let out a
piercing *Eeeeep!*

It grabbed Kineosho's tail as Griffon lifted him higher,

causing Kineosho to start yelping. The little monkey looked panic-stricken as Griffon parted it from its new-found friend. Griffon snarled, irritated with the game of tug of war. Shocked, the monkey released Kineosho and looked on as Griffon placed him on Curie's back. Its eyes suddenly doubled in size and welled up with tears. "*Eep?*" it asked sorrowfully as the lions turned around to continue their journey.

They had not taken ten steps forward when they heard loud sniffles of anguish trailing behind them. Griffon turned around to find a rather distraught little monkey dragging its long left arm behind it trying to follow them. It was rubbing each eye in turn with its short right arm, brushing away the gushing tears like an overworked windscreen wiper. Griffon paused for a moment and could not help but grin at the sorry sight. He strutted back majestically and stared at the little monkey. The little monkey stared back at him.

Griffon leant forward. "Up!" he commanded.

The little monkey's eyes lit up. It swung its long left arm over Griffon's and clutched his ear with its dainty fingers. It pulled itself up onto Griffon's back and gave him an appreciative hug. Curie shook her head briefly and smiled at Griffon. It was official—the trio had just adopted a new member of the family.

"Do you have a name?" Curie asked the monkey, who had already made herself at home in Griffon's mane.

"*Eep?*" replied the monkey, looking a little confused.

"Kineosho," said Griffon as he pointed his nose at Kineosho on Curie's back.

"*Eep!*" shrieked the monkey excitedly. "Vid . . . di," she said with the most peculiar smile showing her two teeth. "Vid-di!" she said again a little louder.

"Vid . . . di," replied Curie, ". . . sleep."

They walked quietly for a long time. Kineosho and the little monkey had fallen back to sleep on their parents' backs. As they continued their fast pace upstream, the stream became wider and the forest denser. Finally, Griffon heard a waterfall in the distance. "Almost there for today," he whispered to Curie.

When they reached the waterfall, Curie found them a place to rest for the night. She was good at that—finding somewhere safe and quiet, away from wind and prying eyes. Griffon rolled the little monkey off his back and nuzzled her next to Kineosho. Viddi immediately assumed her cuddle position with her new brother. They all slept peacefully after another long day of travel.

❧ 3 ❧

Old haunts

At the break of dawn, the new family refreshed itself at the foot of the waterfall and set off to continue its journey. Both Kineosho and Viddi had enjoyed playing in the water and were quite content to doze off on Curie's and Griffon's backs as they stepped up the pace once more. The journey continued for days.

"It's good to be back here again," said Griffon when they stopped late one afternoon for a break. "Almost forgot what this felt like—being in the wild, I mean. It feels like ages since we moved there to keep an eye on those destructive humans."

"It was a restricted but comfortable life though—calm, peaceful, plenty of food. Except for the odd visits by those obnoxious scientist types," replied Curie. "Nothing to do—"

"—if you enjoy the new," said Griffon, smiling as he completed her sentence.

"*Yenn-Joy!*" yelled Viddi suddenly in an odd accent as she looked at Griffon. She fluttered her long eyelashes like a coy butterfly.

Griffon and Curie both looked at her and laughed. "Yes—enjoy!" they replied loudly in duet.

"Enjoy!" chorused Kineosho shakily a few seconds later, drawing even more laughter. His first word was a good one.

After a short rest, Griffon led the way for the last leg of their trek. The forest was becoming darker and more stifling as they continued. Kineosho and Viddi were awake and silent, both anxiously looking at the numerous eyes staring at them from the trees and undergrowth. After a while, they arrived at a small clearing.

"Almost there," said Griffon, ". . . home for the next while." Griffon nodded at Curie who stepped forward and lifted Viddi off his back. "Wait here quietly. I'll make sure it's secure," whispered Griffon as he cautiously climbed a bit farther above the clearing.

There was a moment of absolute silence and then a huge roar. That was something this part of the forest had not heard for a long time. Even the trees shook. Suddenly fifteen tiny mice scooted from underneath a heap of leaves and broken branches, bumping into everything they could possibly bump into. The one that had bumped into Griffon's paw was not happy. It shrieked loudly and started running backwards, slapping one of its companions repeatedly across its face with its tail. That mouse in turn also started running backwards and stepped on the mouse behind it, which also shrieked. It was chaos.

"Fall back! In line! Cairo!" commanded a small mouse suddenly, in stern military fashion.

Griffon could barely keep track of what happened next. Within seconds, each mouse had rolled on its back, somersaulted forwards, and dashed to the far right of the heap of leaves and broken branches. Two seconds later, they had all stacked themselves up into a pyramid formation facing the lion. The old commander mouse, standing at attention on the top of the pyramid, glared at Griffon. He brushed back his long white whiskers and said, coldly pausing after each word: "Can . . . we . . . help . . . you?"

Griffon smiled.

The mouse continued his piercing glare for a few seconds longer. Then suddenly he relaxed his eyebrows and asked, "Great Banyan Tree . . . *Griffon?*"

"Master Wu," said Griffon, as he bowed his head.

"Griffon!" exclaimed the mouse as his eyes lit up.

"Stand down! Scatter! Kitchen!" commanded Master Wu as he jumped onto a nearby branch. Immediately the pyramid collapsed and the remaining fourteen mice disappeared in fourteen different directions.

"It's been a long time," said Master Wu, twirling his long white whiskers like an actor from a bad 1970s kung fu movie. "Is everything well with you? Aren't you supposed to be keeping guard in the north?"

"Actually, I have a rather large favour to ask," replied Griffon with a smirk on his face.

Master Wu paused, raised his right eyebrow, and grinned. "I thought you had decided you weren't going to have children, Griffon! I remember your long lecture about the sad state of the world and how selfish it would be to bring one more creature into it," he laughed.

"It wasn't exactly planned," smiled Griffon, recalling the conversation that took place many moons earlier near the very spot he was standing on.

"Accidents happen for a reason, you know. Although I'm still trying to figure out what the reason is behind platypus here," said

Master Wu, pointing to a fat, smelly platypus nesting behind some broken branches. "But that's a story for another day. I'm sure yours was a welcome accident." Master Wu paused for a bit, stuck his nose up in the air, and sniffed. "Come!" he called out loudly.

"Master Wu, it's an honour—I've heard so much about you," said Curie with a short bow as she appeared from the bushes a few seconds later. Kineosho appeared next, with Viddi pulling on his tail behind him. Viddi looked up at Master Wu sitting on the branch and opened her eyes up really wide.

"Oh my—identical twins . . . you didn't tell me!" laughed Master Wu. "I see Griffon still hasn't dropped the habit of picking up strays along the way."

"And I thought that was all part of your training Master Wu!" retorted Curie.

"Hardly! Come, let me introduce you to my team and feed you all," said Master Wu as he led Griffon behind the heap of broken branches. The fourteen mice had gathered in another small clearing. They had collected numerous bits of colourful food and arranged them for display in a rather elaborate fashion. "Fall back! Attention! Paris!" he commanded them.

The mice immediately formed two diagonal rows of seven mice, each facing the other. They stood at attention for exactly two seconds and then uniformly kicked up their right legs in Moulin Rouge style and knelt to complete their formation. "Griffon and family—meet the League of Domino Mice," said Master Wu proudly.

Viddi could not help herself seeing this well-choreographed spectacle. She sat up and clapped away, hoping to get an encore of the performance. The mice smiled at each other, pleased to be at the receiving end of an appreciative audience.

Kineosho, in the meantime, had started playing around with two strange balls that looked a bit like cabbages with rabbit ears growing out of them. Master Wu leapt onto one of the balls and said sternly to Kineosho: "We don't play with food."

Kineosho looked at Master Wu, a little shocked at his strict tone. His ears dropped a little and he looked at Curie. Master Wu stepped off the ball and turned Kineosho's head towards him. "What is your name?"

Kineosho looked at him gleefully and replied, "Enjoy!" They all laughed.

Curie came up from behind, nudged him gently and whispered in his ear: "Kineosho."

"M . . . Kineosho?" said Kineosho hesitantly to Master Wu.

"Kineosho—good," replied Master Wu. "And you are?" he asked Curie.

"I'm Curie," she replied. "And this is Viddi," she said pointing to Viddi, who was still staring in goofy-eyed awe at the little Moulin Rouge mice.

"Come, let's eat now," said Master Wu. "Griffon, Curie, these are some fresh cabbits for you—have you tried them before?" he asked, tapping the cabbage-like ball with the rabbit ears sticking out of them.

"No—but I've heard about them! They look so . . . strange . . . is it true that they farm these locally now?" asked Griffon.

"Rocco has a farm about three days from here. All that genetic engineering finally paid off for him. Not too soon either—many an innocent cabbage was sacrificed for the cause. The nutritional value of one of these can keep any animal, herbivore or carnivore, going for days—we all live off them now," said Master Wu, as he headed over to a huge communal bowl of soup. "Monkey, you have some fruit with the cabbit until you grow a bit more," he said to Viddi, pointing at a pair of bananas in the middle of the clearing.

After a filling meal, Master Wu looked up at the moon and said to Griffon, "Rest well tomorrow — I have some work to take care of. We start at dawn the day after next."

Viddi yawned and put her long arm around Kineosho. She could not believe how her life had changed so quickly. She reached out with her short arm to hold Curie's ear and smiled as she touched it. Even Kineosho felt oddly settled in his new surroundings. That night, they all slept as soundly as a new moon on a dark night, secure in the promise of the next day.

❧ 4 ❧

The birds and the bees

The time between the third and seventh full moons of a lion's life is critical for both its physical and psychological development. Ability to learn is at its peak during this period—a cub would absorb everything. Where some animals would just see a tree with leaves after a second of observation, a lion cub is able to observe each leaf's orientation, subtle differences in colour on the bark, and little bugs parading up and down the tree. It would even be able to observe the pair of sparrows on the second highest branch having a domestic squabble. In this particular instance, it was an angry female sparrow who was scolding her partner about his constantly wandering eye when ostriches were present.

Kineosho did not observe this, however. He was too busy playing with a cabbit he had found behind the bushes. He whacked it with his paw and watched it roll off in the funny way cabbits roll until it wound up in one spot just bobbing to and fro like an upside down pendulum with rabbit ears.

Viddi was up much earlier than Kineosho that morning—she had secretly watched Master Wu and the League of Domino Mice perform their ritual morning exercises. She had also seen them depart at dawn carrying an antique wooden trunk on the back of a large bird. She spent an hour wondering what was in the trunk before she dozed off hanging from a branch with her long left arm. The thumb of her short hand was still in her mouth as the last remnant of her pensive pose.

She tilted her head forward to bow when her dream transported her to being the main attraction in the League of Domino Mice performance. She pictured herself doing some of the complex rhythmic gymnastics she had witnessed earlier that morning. Viddi swung from the branch as she dreamt of twirling up to the top of the pyramid. Then she gripped the branch with her teeth and hung with limbs and tail spread out wide as she fantasised about carrying three mice on each of them. Master Wu was sitting on the very end of her tail, applauding in awe.

Viddi began to swing around the branch with her teeth, in preparation for her final dismount in the dream. She swung around once, twice even faster, and then a third time even faster still. Her momentum was intense. It was just about as intense as Kineosho's last strike of the cabbit, which was hurtling towards Viddi. In fact, had it not been for the chain of events that happened immediately afterwards, the moment when the hurtling cabbit was accelerated forward when Viddi's feet hit it would have been a moment clearly remembered as an intensely poetic meeting of imagination and reality.

The hurtling cabbit continued to hurtle through the air with the tremendous momentum it had gathered from Viddi's kick. Little animals watched it from the ground. "Is it a bird?" a little badger asked its mom. "Is it an insect?" asked another enthusiastically. "I don't know," replied the mommy badger, looking confused, ". . . it looks like a flying cabbit to me."

As the flying cabbit was about to reach the fastest speed any cabbit had ever experienced, it found itself being suddenly lifted and shaken violently by its left ear. It had managed to get itself hooked onto the talon of a low flying eagle who was trying to get it off by swinging it fiercely from side to side. The eagle flew higher and higher as he flapped his wings harder trying to get the cabbit off. The animals below looked on in awe as the flying cabbit became smaller and smaller.

Back on the ground in the meantime, the shock of kicking the cabbit at the peak of her dismount had woken Viddi up instantly. Dizzy from her mad spin, she had released the branch from her jaws and went flying through a forest of branches yelling her signature *Eeeep!* Eventually, she landed on the head of the fat platypus. The platypus was not happy.

He became even unhappier when Viddi applied her own traditional pain remedy by vigorously rubbing his head. Confused and highly irritated, the platypus started quacking, not even sure if that was the sound he was meant to make. The deranged quacking attracted a flock of ducks that had been flying above. They descended immediately and all began to quack in total discord around it.

A plump female duck aggressively scolded Viddi and pecked threateningly at her hands, which were still furiously rubbing the platypus's head. Viddi retreated with tears in her eyes, overwhelmed by the noise and a little embarrassed at the number of animals that had gathered around her little accident.

"Quack, quack?" asked the plump female duck to the platypus after the cacophony had settled down a bit.

"Quack?" asked the platypus.

"Quack quack!" replied another duck.

"Quack, quack!" said the platypus.

"Quack, quackity quack?" asked a smaller duck.

The fat platypus tried to move. "Quaaack" he groaned as he strained to move one of his fat webbed feet. When he succeeded, the ducks looked at each other in silence and then turned their attention back to the platypus.

Suddenly, each duck thumped its left foot on the ground in unison and yelled "Quackity!" The platypus looked at them and began breathing heavily as he lifted his other foot forward and landed it securely. "Quack!" exclaimed the ducks, this time thumping the other foot on the ground. The platypus moved. "Quackity!" exclaimed the ducks again after that, each thumping their left foot once more. For the next two hours, the chanting and foot thumping grew louder and the forest echoed with rhythm. The gap between the ducks' *Quackity!* and *Quack!* grew increasingly shorter as the platypus moved faster.

By the time the platypus was close to the riverbank, Master Wu had returned with the League of Domino Mice. Curie told him how Viddi had fallen on the platypus and what happened thereafter. Master Wu looked at the platypus and the ducks, and smiled whilst shaking his head, bemused at the spectacle.

Moments later the platypus reached a small crater filled with twigs and leaves next to the riverbank. By this time, the frenzy of rhythm was intense. The *Quackity! Quack! Quackity! Quack!* seemed to be perfectly synchronised with the thumping feet. Even the spectators had started clapping along to the beat. At the height of the frenzy, the platypus raised his front webbed feet and let out an enormous conclusive *Quaaaack!* before he collapsed into the crater. The ducks thumped their feet in cheer as did the audience in support. Everyone was happy. But mostly the platypus — he was ecstatic. He was tired, but ecstatic. In the space of a few hours, he had found his home, new friends, and a renewed sense of purpose.

Master Wu sighed as he looked at the platypus. "Our destiny always has a way of finding us. It never ceases to amaze me that there is no escape," said Master Wu, fondly patting Viddi on her head. Not quite understanding what Master Wu was going on about, she smiled and wasted no time in asking what had been on her mind all day: "What in the box? What in the box?"

Master Wu laughed. "Come!" he called out to Griffon and Curie. They all walked back to the clearing where the platypus had been vegetating. "Thank the Baobab he's moved on—he was really beginning to reek quite badly!" He sniffed the air and paused a moment before yelling out: "In line! Box! Fall back!"

The League of Domino Mice quickly assembled, brought the antique box to the centre of the clearing, opened it, and took out several paw-shaped imprints and a large broom made of straw.

"What that? What that?" asked Viddi excitedly before anybody else could even open their mouth.

"We take these out to the very far edges of the forest and make track imprints away from here to send nasty poachers on the wrong trail. The broom we use to wipe out our own trail . . . it's been working for years," Master Wu explained proudly. "They're not too bright, thankfully!" They all laughed.

That night the forest exchanged stories about almost everything that had happened that day. They spoke about how the mice had made a large circle with the prints to fool the daft poachers, how amazing the platypus's choir was, and how Viddi's funny collision had started everything off. Everyone had been so caught up with the day's events that they had forgotten all about the flying cabbit. It had been having an adventure all of its own since it had been picked up by the eagle.

Besides being the fastest cabbit that had ever lived, it had also become the highest-flying cabbit of all time. The third record it broke, however, was the one that made history across species. After being hooked to the eagle's talon for a couple of hours, the mad shaking and flapping finally dislodged it. The cabbit plummeted to the earth, cabbage-end first. Then it happened: it became the fastest object to ever hit a large beehive directly.

If cabbits could feel anything, this particular one would have been in trouble. Fortunately, it did not feel a thing as it smashed into pieces when it hit the hive.

The first reaction of the bees as their hive was sent flying towards a peculiar sheet was not pleasant. In fact, they went bonkers. The first reaction of the poachers, who were resting in the tent that the hive had fallen on, was even more animated when they realised what had happened. They ran. The bees followed. They ran through the bushes. The bees followed. In their anxiousness, the poachers ran in a completely different direction to the trail that they had been tracking. They had not been to that part of the forest before and they did not care. They just wanted to get that swarm of bees away from them. Shouts and screams accompanied every sting until there was a large splash, and finally silence.

The poachers had run through some pretty dense forest and wound up jumping off a low cliff into a river. They kept as much of themselves as they could underwater until the bees eventually buzzed off. They had run quite a distance and the hobble back to their campsite by retracing their own steps was a soggy, painful journey.

Dinner finished early for everyone that evening. The birds, the bees, and all the animals were very tired after a rather eventful day. The poachers were tired too. They picked out their bee stings after much cursing and went to bed, praying that the next day would be a less painful one.

5

First day of school

Master Wu was up early the next morning. As always, he completed his daily meditation about an hour before sunrise. Then he mentally jotted down a few planning notes for the day ahead. Master Wu had trained all sizes and shapes of animals over the years. He had come to realise that while there were common themes and techniques he could use, he had to do some tailoring to cater for the individual nuances of his students.

He walked around, silently observing Griffon and Curie. Then he paused to think, and climbed a nearby branch. From there he looked down on Kineosho and Viddi. Viddi had become quite accustomed to sleeping with one arm around Kineosho and her short hand clutching his ear. "Hmm . . ." thought Master Wu pensively. He climbed down and walked up next to Kineosho. He picked up a twig and carefully used it to stroke the underside of Kineosho's paw, testing for a reflex response. Kineosho's small claws fanned outwards. "Good," thought Master Wu, "he's sleeping well."

At the first hint of sunrise, Griffon awoke. He stretched

and walked over to Kineosho and was about to wake him when Master Wu leapt in front of him, finger to lip and whispered: "*Shhh* . . . Wait—just a short while." Curie woke up a minute later and they all gathered around Kineosho and Viddi, and watched them sleep without a care in the world.

When they awoke, Master Wu led the way to a nearby clearing. "Griffon, Curie—please wait there," he said, pointing to a large tree at the edge of the clearing. "You two, come with me," he said to Kineosho and Viddi as he walked them to the base of a large baobab tree at the opposite end of the clearing. Viddi hung on to Kineosho's ear. Kineosho kept trying to shrug her off until he eventually got irritated and slapped Viddi on the head with his paw. She yelped in pain and Master Wu glared at them both. "You are no longer two days old—best you behave like it," he said coldly.

Kineosho and Viddi both felt a little uncomfortable and looked cautiously at Master Wu. "Over the next few days I am going to teach you some very important things you must practise daily. It will help you become strong—both physically and mentally," said Master Wu.

"Like them?" asked Viddi, energetically pointing at the League of Domino Mice that had assembled in single file nearby.

"Yes—like them," said Master Wu. "It will also help you find your place in the jungle later, but you will not understand the importance of that right now. For now, I need you both to stay focused and do exactly what I say—is that clear?" he asked.

Kineosho nodded as Viddi continued to stare in awe at the mice.

"Now then," said Master Wu, "today we will learn about discipline and building physical strength. First let us clear our minds and prepare for the day." Master Wu flicked his long white eyebrows back before sitting in the lotus position in front of the large baobab tree.

Kineosho and Viddi made themselves comfortable in front of Master Wu. "To start with," said Master Wu, "you'll find it quite difficult to control your mind, however with time and practice it will get easier. Close your eyes and simply relax your mind. If a thought or image enters your mind, it's okay. Just observe it, and let it pass. I want you to focus on your breathing . . . as you breathe in, and out . . . in, and out . . ."

Griffon and Curie watched as Kineosho twitched about and peeked to see what Viddi was doing. Viddi on the other hand was surprisingly calm, she barely moved at all. After a few minutes that seemed like an eternity to Kineosho, Master Wu instructed them both to open their eyes.

"Now let's get you fuelled up for the day," said Master Wu. While Kineosho and Viddi had been meditating, the League of Domino Mice had set aside quite a spread for breakfast. They all gathered in the clearing and ate with gusto. Griffon was quite surprised at Master Wu's enormous appetite. "What?" asked Master Wu loudly while pointing at his stomach, "A mouse has got to eat. After all, remember the old adage, breakfast like an elephant, lunch like a jack rabbit, and supper like a grasshopper!"

When everyone had had their fill, Master Wu called Kineosho and Viddi. "Come, let's go for a walk," he said as he pointed towards a narrow path leading out of the clearing. Master Wu led the way with a wooden cane in one hand. Kineosho and Viddi followed closely.

"I cannot stress the importance of a routine when it comes to maintaining your well-being. So, what I teach you today, you both need to continue daily . . . perhaps not in the same form but at least in principle. Wake up each morning, take a moment for yourselves and clear your minds. Have a good, healthy breakfast to give you energy for your day ahead, go for a short, meditative walk . . . Make sure you take some time for yourself each day," said Master Wu. He stepped up the pace as the path broadened.

"And now, let the fun begin!" said Master Wu when they arrived back at the clearing. He pointed at the League of Domino Mice who were practising a new formation. "Fallback! In-line! Load harness!" commanded Master Wu.

Within seconds, the League of Domino Mice had strapped harnesses and individual wooden carts onto both Kineosho and Viddi. "*Eep?*" said Viddi, a little confused.

Master Wu led them both to the riverbank. "We need to build your strength starting from today's training session, and fortunately I have the perfect opportunity to get you started."

Kineosho tried to shrug off his harness as they walked but it was too firmly strapped on. When they reached the riverbank, they found four enormous wooden rafts and a group of rough-looking beavers. One beaver in particular stood out—despite being a little smaller than the others, he had quite a presence. "Must be those blue dungarees he's wearing," thought Kineosho.

"Rocco, meet our new trainee labourers—trainee labourers meet Rocco," said Master Wu. "That's quite a cabbit crop you have there this time Rocco—I think it'll last us all for many seasons to come."

"Yes," replied Rocco, "and with my latest genetic modifications this lot will last for years if coated with my special turtle wax. I've also introduced six new flavours including a wildebeest-flavoured carnivore cabbit which is sure to be a hit with the cats!"

"Ah, Rocco," said Master Wu, "what a genius you turned out to be. When I trained you years ago, I never dreamed you'd achieve so much. I still remember the days when each animal had to have its own synthetic food supply created . . . so inefficient. We did not even imagine the possibility of having a food source that automatically releases the correct nutrients based on the animal eating it."

Viddi looked up at the huge mountain of cabbits that the beavers had already offloaded from the rafts. Kineosho frowned at the small cart behind him as he quickly realised what was to follow.

"Load and lock!" shouted Master Wu as he clapped his hands.

A pair of mice loaded five cabbits onto Kineosho's cart and three cabbits onto Viddi's. Kineosho and Viddi then followed a few cabbit-laden mice to the faraway tunnel entrance of a large underground bunker.

When they arrived, another pair of mice unloaded the cargo, and passed the cabbits into the tunnel. Then the mice led them both back to the river.

Viddi had turned into quite the drama queen on their return journey. As she limped back, she dragged her longer arm behind her, knuckles down as though it were dead. Her other hand kept wiping her brow as small grunting noises emanated with each step forward.

"*Hmm*," said Master Wu, grinning when she arrived, "perhaps we need to try something different for you." He whispered something in the loader-mouse's ear who nodded promptly in reply. For the second trip, the mice loaded seven cabbits for Kineosho and reduced Viddi's load to just one.

When they reached the unloading area, one of the mice took Viddi by the hand and led her to the entrance of the dark tunnel. There, he introduced her to a rather happy-looking turtle named Gita, who escorted her inside.

Much to Viddi's relief the darkness did not last for very long.

The first lit chamber they entered was a storage chamber. "We store the cabbits here while they are prepared for their turtle wax preservation treatment," explained Gita cheerfully. Then she led Viddi into another chamber that smelt like fresh strawberries. Pairs of gophers and turtles were working together to apply a special wax to each cabbit.

While a gopher lay on its back, its turtle partner fetched a cabbit from the storage room and rested it, ears-up, on the gopher's four paws. The laid-back gopher then began to spin the cabbit with its feet, all the while repeating: "Wax on!" The turtle then smeared wax onto the cabbit using a quick circular motion with its flippers.

After some time, the gopher would start chanting "Wax off!" repeatedly. Its turtle partner then proceeded to take a cotton sheet and shine the cabbit in the same circular motion as it continued to spin around. A few moments and a shiny, coated cabbit later, the gopher on its back would shout: "Next!" The production line continued with the processed cabbit moving on to the final storage chamber.

Viddi was mesmerised by the sequence of events and the fast, rhythmic chanting of *Wax-on — Wax-off*. Gita tugged at Viddi's hand and asked her if she would like to try. Viddi nodded excitedly. As soon as she heard "Next!" she immediately threw herself on her back and grabbed the next cabbit that was being brought in. Gita, the gopher and its turtle partner looked on in surprise.

Viddi skilfully balanced the cabbit on her hind feet and began rotating it. She then used her long arm to gather some turtle wax and started applying it to the cabbit in unison with the chanting of *Wax-on!* by the gophers. When the chant changed to *Wax-off!*, Viddi snatched a lonely-looking cotton sheet and began to polish her cabbit. On the shout of "Next!" she kicked the cabbit directly into the hands of a mouse standing at the entrance of the storage chamber. Gita was already waiting for her with the next cabbit.

After the first three cabbits, Viddi joined the gophers in their entrancing *Wax-on — Wax-off* chant. She could not imagine being happier. The mice, Gita, and the turtles transporting the cabbits were stunned — Viddi was a natural waxer like they had never seen before.

Kineosho, in the meantime, had returned to the riverbank to collect the next batch of cabbits. His load had varied each time until Master Wu determined his optimal capacity for that day to be twelve cabbits. By the time he had reached that stage the platypus and his duck choir were passionately singing the Rocky theme tune as encouragement. Kineosho felt more motivated than ever to push ahead.

By day's end both Kineosho and Viddi were exhausted. Except for a lunch break and a few stops for water, they had been active the whole day. They could both feel their muscles ache, but they felt satisfied.

Griffon and Curie looked on as Kineosho and Viddi could barely keep their eyes open when they arrived at the clearing. "It's changed quite a bit since we were trained, hasn't it?" Griffon asked Curie.

"I guess it has to change with the times," replied Curie.

"Indeed it does," whispered Master Wu, sitting on a branch directly above Griffon. He climbed down and sat next to Curie. "It's good that there is so much opportunity to tailor training based on the individual now. It's the only way to allow them to realise their full potential in the long run, you know. In our day we all just had to cart buckets of water from the river to the reservoir."

"Now *that* I remember," laughed Griffon.

They ate a small meal and rested. Kineosho was so tired that he could barely think about what the next day was going to bring. Viddi threw her long arm around Kineosho and clasped his ear gently as she passed out into a deep sleep.

❦ 6 ❦

Graduation

An hour before the first cock's crow the next morning, Master Wu sat in a tree above Kineosho and Viddi. He stroked his whiskers pensively, then looked down at Kineosho, and etched out something on the branch he was sitting on. When Griffon and Curie arrived below, he instantly leapt down in front of them, put his finger to his lips and whispered sternly: "Wait!"

"Come with me . . ." whispered Master Wu, as he led Griffon and Curie away from the sleeping beauties. When they were out of earshot, he said: "Recently, I've been studying patterns in sleep cycles to help animals optimise their days . . ."

"Sleep cycles?" asked Curie.

"Yes. Sleep cycles . . . It seems we all have our own rhythms — and especially so when sleeping. If you wake up before a cycle has properly ended, you could feel even less refreshed than before you fell asleep. Have you ever noticed how energised you feel when you wake up naturally? And how grumpy you can be if you are woken abruptly?" asked Master Wu.

"Yes, indeed," replied Curie, rolling her eyes accusingly at

Griffon. "But how do we know when their sleep cycle is up?"

"Well typically, it's after a phase of deep sleep ends — it's almost like they wake up temporarily before they fall asleep again into their next cycle. In the case of our twins over there, it seems that their sleep patterns have aligned themselves quite well," said Master Wu.

They returned to Kineosho and Viddi, and watched them for a while. As they both tried to turn at the same time Master Wu touched Kineosho very lightly and whispered, "Good morning". Both Kineosho and Viddi awoke in an instant and smiled after a satisfying stretch.

Over the remainder of that lunar cycle, they built on their new routine. Kineosho's concentration improved slowly through their morning meditations, as Master Wu gradually increased the meditation time each morning. Viddi and Kineosho both thoroughly enjoyed the physical activity too.

Two days before the next full moon, several mountains of cabbits had been moved from the rafts, and Rocco had made his way back to his farm. Kineosho managed to increase his optimal carrying load to 48 cabbits in a cart six times the size of the one he had started with. Viddi had become quite a hit with the underground community as she helped step up the pace of the entire waxing operation by using her tail as a metronome.

"In two days there is a full moon and you've both worked very hard over the last little while. You should rest and play over the next couple of days, but don't forget to do your meditation each morning," said Master Wu, as Griffon and Curie looked on proudly. Kineosho and Viddi looked at each other and for a moment almost didn't recognise who they saw. The strenuous physical activity had had a dramatic effect on their bodies. They both looked and felt different. Viddi flexed her biceps to show

Curie her achievement. They all laughed as a giant ball of muscle suddenly popped out from an otherwise skinny arm.

After their meditation the next morning, Kineosho and Viddi explored the forest, and tested their new-found strength on anything and everything they could find. It was all good fun until they decided to test their strength on each other. Viddi, with all the *Wax-on-Wax-off* training, discovered that she was now strong enough to lift Kineosho, lie on her back, spin him around on all fours, and use her tail to slap him in the face each time he spun around. Of course, having the League of Domino Mice cheer her on as she did it was really not very helpful for Kineosho. When Viddi booted Kineosho off as part of her grand finale, the crowd roared with laughter.

Kineosho angrily uprooted the nearest small tree and bashed Viddi over the head with it. The two sparrows whose nest had been in the tree and was now on Viddi's head, flew anxiously around her.

Griffon pounced on Kineosho, who was still laughing at the cartoon moment, and pinned down Kineosho's head with his paw. Griffon roared, silencing the forest. Even the League of Domino Mice disappeared into a nearby thicket. "Play nicely, you two," growled Griffon in a deep, low tone as he looked at them both. He lifted his paw and pushed the tree trunk off Viddi. Kineosho and Viddi stood next to each other and looked at Griffon shamefully. Viddi swung her longer arm around Kineosho and fondly clasped his ear, grinning sheepishly. Curie, who had only just arrived at the scene of the commotion, could not contain her smile. She nudged Griffon aside and said to Kineosho and Viddi, looking at them each in turn: "You heard your father—don't fight. Why don't you both go make some new friends together?"

Over the course of their physical training, the animals in the forest had warmed to them both. Even the strange hedgehog family, who were typically very cautious, found themselves considering letting their own children play with them. For the rest of the day, Kineosho and Viddi wandered around the forest and made some new and interesting friends: there was Twigs, the lanky giraffe who made Viddi collapse backwards while trying to look at him; a team of wild dogs who completed each other's sentences; a herd of rather dumb but playful wildebeest calves; and last but not least, they also befriended Specs, a large white barn-owl with peeping Tom tendencies.

Specs had two large black marks around his eyes, which he insisted were birthmarks. Only Specs, four woodpeckers, and an old oak tree knew the real story behind those marks. Despite his curious habits though, Specs was worldly wise. Early on the night of the full moon, he flew up to the highest branch of the tallest tree in that part of the forest. As expected, he found Master Wu sitting there silently, gazing into the cosmos.

"Master Wu," whispered Specs. "I think you should know that on my last flight to the edge of the jungle, I noticed that the poachers weren't following their usual path—you know, the one we create . . . I think we should be concerned."

Master Wu remained still for a minute. Then he nodded the briefest of nods without saying a word, and Specs flew back down to join the festivities.

The atmosphere down below was a lot more raucous than above with Master Wu. It was Kineosho and Viddi's first full moon festival with their extended jungle family and they loved it. The League of Domino Mice had put on a splendid display of acrobatics and the young of a variety of forest animals took turns entertaining the audience. There were acts ranging from wildebeest karaoke to other more exotic talents that were definitely more acquired tastes. The platypus and his new duck choir were one of the highlights of the show that evening. Griffon and a slightly teary-eyed Curie sat next to each other and watched happily. "I missed this, Griffon, the whole jungle—our family. I understand why we had to make the sacrifice to keep an eye on the humans, but I really missed this," said Curie.

Later that evening, Master Wu joined the festivities in a joint performance with the League of Domino Mice. Viddi was entranced. For her, the demonstrations appeared more and more miraculous each time. And it's not to say that they weren't. Master Wu was a talented veteran, incredibly strong, and fearless. After a climactic opera rendition by the platypus choir, Master Wu closed the evening. Before retiring, he whispered a personal message to Kineosho: "Rest well now, our training continues tomorrow."

When things had quietened down somewhat, Master Wu climbed up to his secret spot and gazed at the moon, pondering over what Specs had told him earlier. "I wonder," he thought to himself, "how long we've got."

❦ 7 ❦

The Mental Ninja Mice

During the course of their training, the initial few minutes of silent time had more than quadrupled. Kineosho, who had struggled to concentrate at first, now felt more comfortable with the process. After their meditation that morning, Kineosho and Viddi had breakfast with Master Wu.

"Is Rocco bringing more cabbits today?" asked Kineosho, eager to get going.

"No," replied Master Wu. "That part of your training is over now. You'll both continue with some daily exercises to maintain your strength and grow it slowly."

"Oh," replied Kineosho, a little disappointed. "So no more cabbit carts?"

"No more cabbit carts, for now . . ." said Master Wu.

Viddi, in the meantime, had not absorbed a word of the banter. She was quite enjoying her breakfast banana and cabbit.

After breakfast, they followed Master Wu. As they walked, Master Wu said: "You are both physically strong now. In order to survive though, you need to be able to apply your strength wisely depending on your circumstances. For this, you need to have control, and discipline. This is more difficult than pulling carts or polishing cabbits—you will be training something that you cannot see, but which is significantly more powerful."

Kineosho nodded, although he wasn't quite sure what Master Wu was talking about.

After walking for some time, they arrived at a different part of the forest—one that they had not seen before. It was dense and a deep, dark green. "First, we will have to sharpen your reflexes, and then we'll work on your concentration," said Master Wu. Kineosho and Viddi's attention moved to some rustling in a nearby bush. When they turned around, Master Wu had disappeared.

Somewhere from the treetops, they heard his voice: "Protect yourself!"

Viddi looked at Kineosho and let out a confused "*Eep?*"

A creepy silence followed. It was disturbed only by the same rustling that they had heard earlier. Neither could pinpoint its source until suddenly there appeared, as though by magic, a pyramid of ninja mice—all dressed in white and masked to the hilt.

Viddi instantly sat and clapped, anticipating a show from the League of Domino Mice. Kineosho sensed something else was going on—he had noticed that not only were there almost twice as many mice as he had seen in the show the night before, but also that each of them held an ominous, long wooden stick.

Before he could stop Viddi clapping, eight ninja mice from the top of the pyramid lunged forwards onto them. They both tried to slap them off wildly, but to no avail. The ninja mice painfully whacked and jabbed Kineosho and Viddi, who were soon manically slapping themselves trying to get the mice off, causing even more confusion.

The attackers did not hold back. In fact, they seemed to become even more aggressive and started beating them harder with their sticks. Kineosho and Viddi were yelping in agony.

"Stop!" yelled Master Wu suddenly.

The ninja mice immediately disappeared off them and regrouped into the pyramid.

Kineosho and Viddi stared at the pyramid in silence, quivering.

Master Wu floated down on a leaf from a nearby tree and landed in front of Kineosho. He flicked his white eyebrows aside and asked bluntly, "Now tell me what just happened?"

Kineosho and Viddi were both still in a state of shock. Master Wu turned around, waved at the ninja pyramid and snarled: "Leave us!" The pyramid vanished into the thicket almost instantly.

Kineosho relaxed a little. Viddi was in tears. Master Wu asked in a calmer tone: "Now tell me, what just happened?"

"Well, they attacked us, and started beating us all over with those . . . those sticks!" said Kineosho.

"I told you to protect yourself, did I not? Why did you not stop them?" asked Master Wu, maintaining his calm tone. Viddi said nothing—her eyes were welled up, and she was still trembling.

"I tried. But they were all over, and too fast. When I tried to slap them off they moved and I wound up slapping myself, like this . . ." said Kineosho, as he slapped himself on the side of his head, looking at Viddi from the corner of his eye. Viddi smiled nervously, and uttered an acknowledging *Eep!* in support of Kineosho.

Master Wu remained silent for a moment. Then, he said: "You are going to experience many such challenges, where the attack on you is going to come quickly and from all angles. In these cases, your physical strength will rarely be enough to defend yourself.

"To survive and emerge victorious from such battles, you need to conquer your mind," said Master Wu in his best New Age kung fu master voice. "All things, living or not, contain a certain energy—you need to feel, and understand that energy. See it for what it is. When you can do that, you will know how best to interact with it."

Kineosho and Viddi nodded hesitantly, neither of them fully understanding what Master Wu had just said.

"Observe!" said Master Wu as he sat in front of them in a meditative lotus position. He inhaled slowly as he brushed his long white whiskers aside. Then he closed his eyes and remained absolutely still. Seconds later, he raised his hands slowly and began to levitate in front of them. Suddenly, the earth trembled violently. Viddi, who had had quite enough trauma for one day, leapt onto Kineosho's back, clasped his ear, and shut her eyes tightly. To Kineosho's surprise, the incredibly large tree behind them was now hovering above him in mid-air.

He could smell the earth from where the tree had been uprooted, but he could not believe his eyes.

Master Wu waited a while. Then, he slowly lowered his hands and the tree resumed its original innocuous position.

"This is not something you will learn over a lunar cycle or two, and you will first need to experience your own energy fully. I can only teach you the basic principles, and the rest you will figure out if and when the right time arrives," said Master Wu.

He climbed up to Viddi who looked like she was practically in a coma now on Kineosho's back. "Hmm . . . I think perhaps it would be better if you sat this one out," he said softly as he patted her eyebrow.

Master Wu continued talking to Kineosho as they took the scenic route back to their clearing. "It will take some practice, but the next time you're overwhelmed with such an onslaught, first slow it all down in your mind. Observe each part of the attack in turn, until you can see clearly that they are a collection of smaller individual attacks, rather than one big overwhelming one. Then, focus on how to best defend yourself against each of the smaller attacks."

"What about the tree?" asked Kineosho. "Can I use the tree?" he said as he gestured using it to beat the ninja mice.

Master Wu laughed. "Slowly, Kineosho, slowly . . . first you have to learn to walk! For starters, you don't even understand how *you* work."

"Oh?" replied Kineosho curiously.

Master Wu continued: "Your mind takes input from your senses — sight, smell, hearing, balance, touch, motion, taste, to name a few. It processes them, and right now reacts subconsciously to each of them. Suppose you enjoyed the taste of your wildebeest cabbit. Then the next time you see one, your mind will remind you of that enjoyment. That's why you want to eat the cabbit again . . . to repeat the experience of that yummy taste.

"You may not realise it now, but that is a vicious trap. If you consistently yield to your mind, you will be a slave to it, and to your senses. To realise your true power, you need to detach yourself from your senses, and the desires they help create. When you have total control of your mind, *that's* when you will have realised your full potential."

Kineosho found Master Wu's voice inspiring. Although he did not fully understand what Master Wu meant with his long lecture, he wanted to be able to do what he just saw Master Wu do. Master Wu, of course, knew this already.

That afternoon, Master Wu asked Griffon and Curie if they would coach the pair on some basic logic exercises as he had some work to take care of. Viddi had calmed down since her morning adventure. In fact, curiously, she behaved as though it had never happened. Kineosho had the image of the floating tree above him burnt into his mind along with Master Wu's words, even though he did not grasp them fully yet. His thrashing at the hands of the ninja mice was already a distant memory.

Master Wu returned on Specs's back later that evening, looking quite concerned. He called Griffon, Curie, and three elderly animals together for a meeting. "Walk with me," he said softly, as he led them down the path he had taken with Kineosho that morning. "I flew with Specs to the border and it seems something peculiar is going on. I don't have a good feeling about it."

"Are the poachers not following the fake tracks you laid out?" asked Curie.

"Worse—we don't know where they are. Their camp site is nowhere to be found and we can't even find a trail to see what direction they're moving in," replied Master Wu.

"Perhaps they gave up and left?" said the old wildebeest.

"Perhaps," said Master Wu, "but I doubt it. We need to investigate the situation in more detail. Griffon, I'm afraid we are going to have to delay our training schedule."

"Does this mean we need to go back to . . ." asked Curie hesitantly.

"—I'll go back north to the conservation area and scout around. You stay here," interrupted Griffon. Curie could feel the lump in her throat. "Don't worry," he added quickly, "I'll be back soon."

"Specs and I will cover the south and investigate further from where we last saw the poachers. We'll leave a fresh set of prints leading in another direction while we're down there. Curie, you can stay here, as there is no path east from the river. Dada, can you take your herd to the west side and take care of any issues?" asked Master Wu, looking at the fierce bull elephant. Dada grunted.

"What about us?" asked the wildebeest.

"You need to stay here to protect the other animals and our supplies," replied Master Wu. "Let's rest this evening and leave first thing in the morning."

Both Kineosho and Viddi sensed the tension in the air when the elders returned to the main clearing. Griffon explained the situation to the other animals in the forest and the need to keep calm while they investigated what was happening. That night, dinner was a quiet one. Kineosho couldn't understand the sense of impending doom, particularly after he had seen what Master Wu was capable of. "Why couldn't they all just stay and defend themselves?" he thought to himself. Later that evening he asked Griffon that same question.

"It's not only a question of defending ourselves Kineosho," said Griffon. "This environment that we have created—where we all live peacefully together like this—has taken generations to build. We have used genetics and technology to our benefit and still preserved our natural lifestyle. We created the space for ourselves to appreciate the universe on a deeper level, without having to worry daily about our survival. If there is a war now, this delicate balance will be lost. Even the strong who survive would never be able to live the way they were living before—free."

"I want to come too—can I come with you?" asked Kineosho eagerly. Griffon was silent for a moment. He recalled how he too, many years ago, had asked his parents that very question. That was the last time he had seen them.

"No, Kineosho," he replied softly. "There is still a lot for you to learn about yourself. I also need you to help protect our family here. Your mother, and Viddi too . . . okay? I will not be able to do it while I am away." Kineosho nodded solemnly.

Griffon looked at Curie who had been listening silently behind them. He walked over and lay down beside her, resting his head on her front paws. A cloud of uneasy silence covered the forest that night.

❦ 8 ❧

Friends and acquaintances

The atmosphere the next morning was surprisingly more upbeat, and the goodbyes held a certain optimism about them. Master Wu and the League of Domino Mice set off southbound with Specs and two other birds. Griffon and the bull elephant, Dada, left soon after.

After Kineosho and Viddi completed their meditation, Curie explained that Master Wu's training would be postponed until he returned. Then she said, "I'm going to be working with some of the other parents to create a life-skills curriculum over the next few days — so in the meantime, consider yourselves on vacation!"

Viddi jumped around happily, having already apparently forgotten that Griffon, Master Wu and the League of Domino Mice had only just left. She bounced around Kineosho and eventually jumped onto his back and clasped his ear.

"Don't wander too far away and whatever you do, keep away from the river — it can be very dangerous there," said Curie, as Kineosho debated which path to select out of the clearing.

Kineosho whacked Viddi's hand off his ear and the pair

wandered down a path that they had not been on before. The forest was abuzz with lively energy as many of the other younger animals were also free and running around.

After some time on their path, they bumped into Twigs, the giraffe. Viddi dashed up and gave him a big hug, almost causing him to collapse backwards. "Where are you going?" asked Twigs curiously.

"We're exploring the jungle," replied Kineosho. "Want to join us?"

"Why not?" replied Twigs. "But I have to be home by nightfall."

"We too!" shouted Viddi as she yanked Twigs's ankle, almost toppling him as she tried to lead the way. "Where are the others?" she asked. "Can you see them?"

"Wait a second," said Twigs as he took a deep breath and extended his long neck to almost double its already long length. Kineosho looked up in amazement, trying to stretch his own neck but to no avail. "*Umm* . . . I think I see Ish, Kish, Mish, Tish, and the other baby wildebeest over in that direction—they're playing with the dogs . . . shall we join them?"

Twigs exhaled slowly and retracted his neck back to its regular length. Kineosho continued to stare in amazement. "What?" smiled Twigs. "My mom takes her stretching exercises very seriously!"

Viddi tugged hard at Twigs's ankle again and they set off towards their wildebeest friends. Since there was no easy way to cut across the forest, Kineosho leapt ahead and led the way back to the main clearing.

There, Curie and a few others were engaged in fervent debate about the content of the life-skills course. The discussion was rather animated. An elderly female deer complained that the others were not paying enough attention to the importance of jumping for survival. The enormous female wildebeest, in turn, whinged about how deer were just anorexic. She stated that if deer simply ate a bit more, they would be able to defend themselves quite effectively by their size and number, rather than by having to hop around like rabbits. The nervous-looking rabbit immediately took offence to that. Curie tried desperately to keep the peace and stressed the importance of having each animal play to their individual strengths.

Kineosho and the others sneaked around the outside of the clearing and took the appropriate path. After walking briskly for quite some time, Kineosho asked Twigs, "So how much farther are they? I thought you said they were just a short distance away."

"Not too far now," replied Twigs. "I guess objects seen with an extended neck are further away than they appear," he giggled.

Viddi in the meantime was having quite a relaxed ride. She had made her way up to Twigs's neck and had been half dozing off to the gentle rhythm of his walking. When Viddi had actually dozed off, her hand instinctively reached up for Twigs's ear. Unfortunately, what it happened to clasp was a nearby branch instead.

Within seconds of waking, she found herself dangling from a dizzy height while Twigs had moved on. By pure instinct, she swung herself and reached out for the nearest branch. Quite remarkably, Viddi instantly rediscovered that she could swing from tree to tree using her strong arms.

In her excitement, she went higher and higher into the branches. Neither Kineosho nor Twigs could figure out where that strange *Eep! Eep!* was coming from, and why Viddi was nowhere to be seen. That is, until Viddi lost concentration while trying to catch Kineosho's attention.

She missed a branch and went plummeting through the air

until she bounced off Twigs's head, and landed straight onto Kineosho's. Kineosho and Twigs both toppled over in surprise. When the sore Kineosho saw Viddi, he was furious. He snarled at her and pushed her aside. She had never seen Kineosho that angry before and she began to cry. Twigs was still suffering from his own mild concussion and was trying desperately to figure out what was going on.

"Why don't you just go play by yourself?" growled Kineosho to Viddi coldly. He nuzzled Twigs back up to his feet and kept him moving on the path. Viddi looked at them sadly as they walked away—Kineosho's glare and harsh tone had really upset her. She followed them quietly from a distance, not knowing what else to do.

A short while later, Kineosho and Twigs reached the herd of baby wildebeest and the pack of wild dogs playing together. They were running around quite madly after each other and a small group of dogs had just leapfrogged over another small group of dogs after suddenly changing direction.

"What are you playing?" asked Kineosho.

"*Team-tag!*" replied an excited out-of-breath little wildebeest named Tish. "You have to touch someone on the other team with your nose and then they are *it*. Once a team is tagged they need to chase the opposing team and do the same."

"Sounds like fun! How do you win?" asked Kineosho.

"Win?" asked Tish, a little confused. "I don't under—"

"—It's not that type of game," chuckled a dog before Tish could finish. "It's just fun."

"Oh," replied Kineosho, a little puzzled.

"Hmm . . . it would be difficult to play with you two on our teams in any case—you don't really blend in all that well. Perhaps we can try a different game?" asked another of the wild dogs.

"Hide and seek won't work either," laughed another dog, staring up at Twigs. "How about playing Secret Treasure?"

The dogs and the wildebeest looked at each other and they all nodded enthusiastically.

"Okay, so here is how it works," said the dog. "First, one of us needs to hide something—a treasure—that the rest of us need to find." He went behind a nearby tree and rolled out a tennis ball-sized golden egg. "We can use this as the treasure," he went on. Then he pointed to the dog that was most recently tagged as *it* and told him to start.

"Okay, now everyone face me and close your eyes while Hinds hides the ball—and no peeking!" said the wild dog. Then he started counting aloud backwards, "100, 99, 98, 97 . . ." By the time he reached 50 some of the wildebeest had already dozed off and were snoring loudly. The dog with the egg was nowhere to be seen. The counting dog turned around and shook his head. Then he shouted: "Okay, let's go look for the secret treasure!"

Within seconds, all the animals dispersed in various directions. Kineosho went to the spot where the dog had rolled out the golden egg and sniffed around trying to get its scent. Viddi looked keenly down from a nearby tree and clapped in encouragement. Kineosho turned around, glared at her, and ran in the opposite direction.

About half an hour later, still nobody had found the egg. Even the dogs with their keen sense of smell had been running around in circles. Half the wildebeest that were still awake had lost interest in the game and had decided that singing karaoke would be much more fun instead. Kineosho and Twigs were not having much luck either and were it not for a rather peculiar sight, they would have quite likely stopped too.

Kineosho discovered a large, strangely shaped grey boulder that seemed to have escaped the eyes of the other animals.

He was convinced that the dog had hidden the secret treasure under this boulder—particularly because it appeared to have an unusual attachment, which had marks in the sand around it. Kineosho took a deep breath and pushed the boulder as hard as he could but it would not shift. Twigs arrived at the scene not long after and tried to help Kineosho. The boulder would just not budge.

"Perhaps we should try pulling it," said Twigs, pointing at the boulder's peculiar appendage. Kineosho grabbed it and pulled with all his might. Within seconds, the boulder rolled backwards and let out a mammoth yelp. Before Kineosho and Twigs realised what was happening, they found themselves being haphazardly smacked about by the muscular trunk of a small elephant. A crowd of hysterically laughing dogs and wildebeest gathered at the scene.

"How dare you disturb my meditation!" yelled the baby elephant at Kineosho as she slapped him across the face again with her trunk.

Kineosho roared at the baby elephant, hoping to scare her into not hitting him again. The baby elephant glared back, inhaled deeply and made a loud noise with her trunk that sounded rather like a flatulent trumpet. For a moment there was silence, and then it seemed that the entire forest burst into laughter.

"I'm sorry," whispered Kineosho softly. "We thought you were, well . . . a boulder—and we were trying to find the golden egg . . . we really didn't know—"

"—It's okay, and I'm sorry I hit you both," replied the small elephant. "My name is Uma, by the way," she said as she smiled and extended her trunk to Kineosho.

While all this was going on, none of the animals had noticed that the wind had picked up quite a bit. There was an ominous thick, black cloud above them and a piercing chill in the air. Suddenly, there was an eerie rumbling in the sky and flashes of lightning appeared from all directions.

"Quick, stay close together and let's head back to the clearing," said a wildebeest.

"Follow me—I know a shortcut around the side of the mountain!" yelled one of the dogs as he led the way. Kineosho, Uma, Twigs, and all the other animals followed anxiously. It began to rain heavily as the animals ran.

The mud along the mountainside got thicker and as luck would have it, Kineosho fell victim to it. Whilst running, he had stepped on a spot above a network of mole tunnels and the entire network collapsed. Kineosho slipped helplessly down the steep, muddy mountain and barely managed to hang on to a protruding tree root with one paw. The mud made it too slippery for him to climb up and the fall below him would be fatal. He shouted out for help as he desperately kept himself from slipping into the abyss below.

The few animals that were close by gathered around the top of the mudslide and offered Kineosho advice. "Don't struggle!" yelled one voice. "Just wait till the storm settles," squeaked another. "Try to jump out on that side!" shouted yet another. None of the advice was of much use.

Uma and Viddi, who had been lagging behind the others, also arrived at the scene. Suddenly, there was a bolt of lightning not far from the animals and the branches of a nearby tree burst into flames. Some of the wildebeest and dogs jumped in shock and immediately stampeded away. Kineosho shouted desperately for help but the only response he received was even harder rain. After another unnerving bolt of lightning, the rain morphed into hail. Most of the animals that remained above hesitated only for a few seconds before dashing for their own safety. In fact, only two of them remained — a little monkey and a big baby elephant.

Viddi desperately extended her long arm in an attempt to reach Kineosho and pull him up. But it was of no use — Kineosho was too far down to reach her hand. As the hail pelted down, Viddi tried to take shelter under Uma's ear. Then, she had an idea. Kineosho saw Viddi whispering to Uma, who immediately extended her trunk down the side of the mountain. Viddi climbed down the trunk and gripped it tightly with her shorter right arm. The hand of her longer arm was now within Kineosho's reach. Kineosho stretched and grabbed at it, but unfortunately Viddi's hand had become so slippery with the mud that Kineosho could not hold on.

"Use your claws!" shouted Viddi as she held on tightly to Uma's trunk. Kineosho hesitated for a second, but his grip on the root was weakening. He closed his eyes, focused all his energy and leapt, digging his claws into Viddi's long arm. Viddi pulled with all her might — not knowing which was worse, the pelting hail or the pain of sharp claws tearing into her arm. Kineosho went flying up and just about managed to grip onto a tree root near the edge. By the time he climbed to safety, the hail had almost miraculously been reduced to a drizzle. Kineosho, Viddi, and Uma looked down the slippery side of the mountain in silence.

"We had better head back to the others," said Uma. Kineosho looked at Viddi, not knowing what to say. Without a word, she climbed onto his back and put her long arm, now covered with bloody claw marks, around his neck. Viddi clasped his ear and fell asleep as they walked back quietly.

By the time they arrived at the clearing, the weather had already improved. When the other animals saw Kineosho they animatedly gave their versions of what had happened in the storm and how they had tried to help him. Kineosho just heard voices and collapsed.

Curie, who had been out looking for them, was relieved to see them when she got back. Uma told her how Viddi had bravely rescued Kineosho from what would have been a certain death.

Both Kineosho and Viddi slept for hours and hours, and then some. When Kineosho finally woke up, he found Viddi still sleeping nearby. Her long arm was covered in a dressing of large yellow leaves. Kineosho nudged her gently with his nose. "I'm sorry I was mean to you, Viddi," he whispered in her ear. Even though not quite awake yet, she smiled.

❧ 9 ❧

Survival of the smartest

While Kineosho and Viddi had been out on their adventure, Curie and the other grown-ups had finally concluded their debate on the approach to teaching life-skills. They had decided to split up for the survival skills training since each animal would need different skills depending on its capabilities. They would then reconvene after a few days for more generic individual and group skills training.

The elderly female deer was quite happy designing her course on how to leap deceptively. She was glad that she wouldn't have to induce bulimia in her fawns to suit the wildebeest. The hefty wildebeest parent was equally content because she wouldn't ever have to jump more than a couple of inches off the ground. Curie was just glad that she didn't have to deal with the other parents that day.

The following morning Viddi's arm looked much better. After they completed their daily meditation and exercise routine, Kineosho and Viddi headed deep into the forest with Curie.

As they walked, Curie explained the importance of observing a regime with respect to their meal times and diet, in addition to their current routine. Kineosho and Viddi both listened attentively.

After some time, they arrived at a watering hole surrounded by tall grass. Neither Kineosho nor Viddi had been there before. Curie stopped in the middle of the tall grass.

"Today, we're going to learn about survival skills in the forest. Now you're both quite strong already because of your physical training, but often that will not be enough to get you out of trouble," said Curie.

"I know — like with the ninja mice," said Kineosho, recalling Master Wu's very similar words.

"Exactly," replied Curie. "It's important to break down larger problems into smaller, more manageable ones. Today, we're going to build on that by teaching you some of the other essential survival skills. Now, crouch down like this and follow me," continued Curie. She crawled forward with her firm belly touching the ground. Kineosho and Viddi struggled along behind her in what they found to be an uncomfortably low stance.

"What you need to develop to survive is something that's inherently part of your make-up. For some it's naturally stronger than for others, but regardless, every creature in the forest has it. What I'm talking about is a combination of your instinct, natural curiosity, intuition, and an understanding of your own capabilities and potential. If you can use those together effectively, then you can be your own guide to surviving any challenge that you face," continued Curie.

Just then, a small jackal crouching down low right next to Kineosho nodded his head and smiled confidently. Kineosho looked at him, a little startled as he had not noticed him there just a second ago. "Where did you come from?" whispered Kineosho.

The jackal shrugged and looked a little confused. "Where did *you* come from?" he asked Kineosho in return.

"We just came from the clearing where Master Wu lives. Who are you?" whispered Kineosho.

"I'm Basho," whispered the jackal. "Who are you?" he asked curiously in return.

"I'm Kineosho," replied Kineosho, still a little surprised.

"Are you paying attention back there, Kineosho? We're talking about intuition here," said Curie sternly, hearing the mumbling behind her. Kineosho quickly crawled forward next to Curie.

Curie stood up and walked towards the watering hole. Kineosho and Viddi followed. When Kineosho turned around to introduce his new friend to Curie and Viddi, Basho was nowhere to be found. He looked around a little puzzled, and then shrugged and continued listening to Curie.

Curie had taken care to make the course as practical and engaging as possible, and she had succeeded. Both Kineosho and Viddi were engrossed in the lessons. They were fascinated to see how their bodies and senses reacted to different stimuli and how the forest reacted to them when they did different things. Curie taught them how to identify different types of tracks, scents, and sounds. She also trained them to recognise the telltale signs of danger, and what to do in different circumstances.

Later, on the way back to the clearing, Curie told them how she divided each day into three parts: the time for her chores and other duties; her leisure time; and finally the time for sleeping. She told them that they should strive to balance those times because they were all equally important.

"Much harder than just the balance, is to be happy during each of those parts of the day," continued Curie, as they arrived at the clearing in time for dinner.

"Then you'd be happy all the time!" said Viddi excitedly.

"Exactly!" replied Curie with a smile.

One morning after completing their routine, Curie led them to a clearing close to the river. A tall, dainty heron and a number of younger animals, including some baby wildebeest and a quirky leopard cub, were already there.

Soon after, an ocelot, four fawns, and two large, rather slow hillbilly-looking crocodiles arrived to join them. When all the young animals finally settled down, the dainty heron explained what they were going to do that day.

"Today we're going to learn about shapes, sizes, colours, creativity, and sand," said the dainty heron in a chirpy voice. The young animals burst into cheers immediately. Most of them had no clue about shapes, sizes, colours, or creativity. But sand—they knew all about sand, and they loved it. None of them ever understood why their parents did not allow them to play with it. After all, there was tons of it next to the river and in so many different colours and textures too.

"To make things even more fun, after you learn about all the different shapes and colours, we're going to have a sand art competition this afternoon," continued the heron. The animals had begun to bounce around uncontrollably with excitement and the heron was grateful that some of the parents had remained behind to help her out.

The young animals persevered through the boring morning lesson about shapes, colours, and perspective. In the afternoon, it was the grown-ups' turn to persevere through shrill yells and coloured sand being plastered in the most inconvenient of locations. The heron had assigned each youngster an area in the clearing where they had to create an original sand artwork that included the various shapes, sizes, and colours they had learnt about that morning.

Viddi worked quietly and happily on her little beige box containing bright purple and white bubbles. Both Curie and the heron were surprised at her attention to detail. The wildebeest had difficulty remembering more than two of the shapes. The ocelot had even tried to help a couple of them out but soon stopped in frustration. Kineosho worked on a unique piece that encompassed every shape they had learnt about. He created an abstract but beautifully symmetrical design. Each shape looked measured to perfection and he used the coloured sand with surprising skill to give it a three-dimensional effect.

Towards the end of the afternoon, the quirky leopard cub with green eyes had almost completed her sand art masterpiece. She created what looked like a stained glass image of the forest using various shapes cleverly overlapping each other. As she worked on the finishing touches, the larger of the two crocodiles stood back and admired his own work.

Actually, both crocodiles only looked a little slow, but they were not. In fact, they were both quite bright, although each had more than his fair share of mental issues. Neither their parents nor the grown-ups present had realised it yet, but the larger of the two suffered from a serious anger management problem, and the other experienced bouts of kleptomania.

Confident that he had created a winning artwork depicting a beautiful bonsai in the centre of a Zen garden, the larger crocodile ambled around looking at the other pieces. When he saw the leopard cub's masterpiece, he suddenly did not feel as confident. He looked around suspiciously and then quite deliberately tripped over his own feet and fell on his back. He pretended to struggle to get up and waved his huge tail around frantically. In the process, he conveniently wound up slapping the little leopard cub and completely spoiling her artwork before managing to turn himself over. The quirky leopard cub immediately broke out into a dramatic bawl.

What the crocodile had not counted on was Kineosho witnessing exactly what had happened, and being quite prepared to do something about it. Kineosho bounded across the clearing, stood in front of the leopard cub and roared angrily at the crocodile. Although Kineosho was strong, he was still a young cub, and the crocodile was much larger. The crocodile pretended to be flustered and turned around clumsily, deliberately slapping Kineosho across the face with his tail. Kineosho was furious. He leapt back on to his feet and bravely swiped at the crocodile's head, delivering a hard smack. By this time, Curie, the heron, and the crocodile's father had rushed to the scene to break things up.

The little leopard looked thankfully at Kineosho, but soon began to bawl again when she saw that her sand artwork had been transformed into a messy stained glass depiction of a forest hit by several tornadoes.

By this time, the heron had decided that she had had quite enough. She praised all the students for their efforts and complimented their artwork, no matter how hideous she thought some of it was. At the end, with the exception of Viddi and the leopard, they all waited expectantly when the heron announced the winner of the competition. It was Kineosho.

He was thrilled. The large crocodile with his bonsai tree and Zen garden felt slightly calmer when he took second place. Of all the animals Viddi was probably the saddest that she could not take her little box of purple and white bubbles home with her. Kineosho waited with her as she wished her bubbles goodbye. He wandered the clearing and browsed the other pieces in the meantime. When Curie went to get them, she noticed Kineosho sneering at the baby wildebeest pieces, which all contained exactly two shapes and two colours.

"You know, by their own standards those are actually very good," said Curie, walking up behind him. "They'd probably feel the same about your running if you ever competed against them in an endurance race," she laughed. "Well done on winning the competition in any case — your piece was beautiful!"

Kineosho smiled proudly.

Curie was up early the next morning and she wondered if Kineosho would fare as well in the group skills course. When they arrived at the course venue, Kineosho and Viddi helped her spread a large white sheet on the ground. Soon after, a different group of animals from the previous day's students arrived. This time, Kineosho and Viddi knew quite a few of them. They were both happy to see Twigs, a few more of their baby wildebeest friends, and the pack of young wild dogs. Gita and two other cheerful turtles were also present.

"Today we're going to work together as a team to create a lovely *pawcollage*," said Curie. "Each of you needs to contribute your paw prints to this large canvas to create the scene I'm going to describe to you. You can dip your paws, hooves, hands, or flippers into any of the colourful natural powders over there for effect." Curie went on to describe a lovely scene including trees, a river, and some animals playing on a sunny day in the forest. Then she told them to begin and stepped back without another word.

She watched as Kineosho, one of the dogs, and the largest of the baby wildebeests battled to take control of the situation. Even Twigs tried to take charge initially. His tall presence certainly helped, but the others soon drowned out his voice. In a bid to win some authority, Kineosho proudly explained how he had won the sand art competition the day before. After much debate though, the group voted that the leader of the dogs had the best plan. Even Kineosho had to admit sulkily that it was more practical than his was.

The teamwork of the wild dogs was superb. It seemed as though they were all connected in a supernatural way. They were even able to effortlessly finish each other's sentences. The leader of the wild dogs extended his influence to the other animals as well, and both Curie and Kineosho were left in wonderment at his ability to coordinate everyone.

Viddi, the wildebeest, Gita and the two other turtles were quite happy dipping their hands, hooves, and flippers into the playfully tempting powders and placing them exactly where they were told to on the canvas. The dogs tapped Kineosho's skills of depth perception to its maximum and they seemed to welcome suggestions from anybody who offered them.

Once Viddi, Gita, and the other two turtles had completed *pawcollaging* their blue sky, they sneaked off to a quiet corner behind Curie. There, they jokingly chanted their *Wax-on — Wax-Off* mantra, remembering their cabbit-waxing days. Then, they happily proceeded to paint each other completely blue.

Towards the finishing stages, Kineosho noticed that Twigs had backed away from the activity and he encouraged him to join in. He prompted the dogs to let Twigs put some of the final prints on the canvas and they were glad to let him do so. Twigs happily placed some rocks beside the river, albeit a little clumsily. As he was about to place his final imprint for the last black rock of the team masterpiece, he lost his balance. Everyone looked up at him as he wobbled around madly. The more everyone stared, the more Twigs wobbled until he started falling forwards onto the canvas. He quickly regained his balance but by that time, there were little black giraffe hoof marks all over the blue sky of their landscape.

Twigs hung his head down, flustered and embarrassed. Kineosho glared at him in frustration, the dogs with disappointment, and the wildebeest just laughed at his clumsiness. Noticing what had happened, Curie quickly came to the canvas.

"Wow, that is one of the best *pawcollages* I've ever seen!" said Curie. "I love how you've created the trees and how you've captured the little animals playing, and the sun . . . it's simply beautiful!" she continued. She glanced at each of the animals, including Twigs, and then turned her head to face the dogs with a final nod of praise. The laughter and the disappointed looks, with the exception of Twigs's, vanished around the canvas.

After observing what Curie did, Kineosho realised another goal of the exercise that day. When he looked up at Twigs, he could see the look of sad disappointment. He looked down at the canvas and immediately added: "I think Twigs's impromptu finale is definitely the best part — after all, what would the forest be without birds in the sky?"

They all gazed at the colourfully expressive canvas and the leader of the wild dogs was equally quick to cast a pleased look at Twigs and voice his agreement with Kineosho. They both noticed the sadness lift from Twigs's eyes as his usual happy smile returned. By then, the three blue turtles and a very blue Viddi returned to the party and added to the group cheer.

Curie smiled and nudged Kineosho in acknowledgement as they walked back to the clearing. Although he was still a young cub, for the first time Curie felt that he was growing up so fast.

❧ 10 ❧

Safe and sound

Over the next while, the young animals practised their weakest skills. Curie proved to be a tough taskmaster, and Kineosho and Viddi were very disciplined with their daily routine. Even when they were not training, they spent a lot of time with her learning all sorts of interesting facts about the forest.

One evening, after a day of learning about which plants to use for healing and which ones to avoid, Kineosho, Curie and a very itchy Viddi made their way back home. As they approached the clearing, they could hear some loud noises, grunts, and anxious shouts followed by a long trumpet. Curie hoped that another awful domestic squabble hadn't broken out in the hippo household again.

Much to her surprise when they arrived at the clearing, the trumpet had belonged to Dada, the fierce bull elephant who had just returned from his journey. Alongside him was a ragged-looking Griffon carrying Master Wu on his back. Specs and four other birds who had accompanied them sat on a branch above. There was even more noise when the rest of the elephant herd and the members of the League of Domino Mice entered the clearing. Curie was in tears with relief.

Both Kineosho and Viddi rushed to greet Griffon who was equally thrilled to see them.

When all the survivors had entered the clearing, Griffon roared the crowd to a silence. "Tired, battered, and victorious!" he said, passionately punching his powerful paw in the air. Hundreds of creatures had gathered around and they all broke out into a positive frenzy.

That night the weary heroes rested well. They spent most of the following day relaxing and recovering from their ordeal. Late that evening, the animals gathered in a large circle and eagerly waited to hear the tale of their adventure. Master Wu, Griffon, and Dada, however, had gone off for a walk into the forest late that afternoon and had not returned yet.

Many in the circle of eager ears knew Specs to be an articulate storyteller and prompted him to introduce the adventure. He happily obliged.

Specs described how he had first detected that something was amiss on one of his routine reconnaissance flights to the far edge of the forest.

"I didn't know where the poachers were, only that they were not doing what they normally did," continued Specs. "So I flew Master Wu there to investigate further. When we returned, he was very concerned for the safety of everyone here. He immediately called a meeting of the elders and they decided on a plan to figure out what was going on. They wanted to solve the problem once and hopefully, for all . . ." Specs had the full attention of the circle. Even more animals had joined in to listen.

Specs went on to describe how he had helped Griffon to avoid what would have been a wasted trip to the conservation area. He explained how all the humans had migrated to their villages in the south for a bizarre festival of some sort.

"So my reconnaissance colleagues and I sped off to inform the elders who had dispersed in their agreed directions. They were quick to decide and move towards gathering at one of their secret meeting points deep in the forest. I cannot get that area out of my mind . . . from above it looked open and innocuous and I could not understand why Master Wu had suggested that we meet there. But—" continued Specs.

"—credit for that special meeting place goes to Griffon's father," interrupted Master Wu as he arrived at the clearing on Griffon's back. Dada followed soon after and the crowd broke out into wild raucous shrieks. A battered-looking Master Wu leapt off Griffon's back onto a nearby branch. He wobbled a bit on the branch at first and settled before stroking his whiskers in his signature kung fu style.

Master Wu described how many moons ago Griffon's father had led an enormous army of ants and moles to dig an underground network of tunnels from a cave near that special meeting point. The largest of the tunnels led to the closest human village to the forest. He explained how the elders had long known that the time would come when easy access to the humans would be tactically advantageous. When he had discovered that the poachers had found the river that would eventually lead them to their home, he knew that that time had arrived. So, they gathered at the cave and planned their attack.

Dada added how Specs's recon team had bravely flown fast and low over the other three nearby villages, giving them an accurate lay of the land. The crowd was riveted.

"The cave was filled with vials of a non-lethal biological weapon that Rocco's father had created. Because of an antidote he had also created, it was relatively harmless for us but caused a horrific disease in humans —" continued Dada.

"— a highly contagious mutation of bubonic plague with some fun side effects, to be exact! And that was before he dedicated his life to genetically modified food sources and taught me everything he knew," chipped in Rocco proudly as he arrived at the circle. The audience clapped joyfully, adding to the already buzzy atmosphere. It was as though everything just came together with perfect timing, even in the storytelling.

Dada explained how he and the elephant herd went off to make an example of the poachers near the river. His comical story of what happened when they tracked them down had the circle rolling uncontrollably. He went on to describe how the herd then built a formidable wall of logs and agreed with the Queen of the bees to build hives all over them. They also laid some treacherous traps in case any other humans ever dared to venture that way again.

Griffon took the reins thereafter and described in dramatic detail how he led Master Wu and the League of Domino Mice through the dark tunnel to the first village. He explained how their mechanism for releasing the disease was accidentally crushed when they had to dig the last part of the tunnel to get out. He added a dramatic pause and the audience stared at him and murmurs of "What happened then?" spread in the circle.

"Then, Master Wu and the League of Domino Mice decided to go old-school. They broke the vials and bravely drank the diseased formula," said Griffon with a look of terror on his face.

The audience responded with shocked expressions and lots of *Oohs!* and *Aahs!*. Even Kineosho found himself clawing the ground with anticipation.

"Since the village was large and it was going to be sunrise soon, I knew the only way to succeed was for me to carry Master Wu and the mice across the village myself," continued Griffon.

"—and so he did," interrupted Specs. "I could see Griffon from above bravely running around and dodging all sorts of dangerous things that were being thrown at him—there was everything from flaming torches to furniture. Master Wu and the mice leapt on and off and went on a crazy biting spree in the village. Griffon had sustained serious injuries but still he continued without hesitation through the village." The audience roared and cheered in acknowledgement.

"Wow . . . he is really amazing . . . I can just see him running super-fast, ducking and diving, battling them bravely," whispered the little jackal sitting next to Kineosho as he punched his paws in the air.

"That's my father!" replied Kineosho proudly, a little startled at how Basho the jackal had managed to sneak up on him again. He had not seen him since that training day near the watering hole.

"I would love to battle like that and be an awesome hero someday!" said Kineosho, digging his claws deeper into the earth with excitement.

"Soon," continued Specs, "almost the entire village was infected and the side effects of the vial started kicking in. It was crazy! The women in the village literally went quite mad and started hopping up and down and beating the men with rolling pins for no apparent reason. The men responded by laughing hysterically—causing the women to hit them even more! And so it continued as we flew low and led Griffon to the next village. We all waited till nightfall and wreaked havoc there too before moving on to the third village."

By this time, the females in the circle were leaping about making mock head-bashing strikes on the males. The young animals were rolling around like deranged marbles at the surreal scene.

Griffon explained the adverse effect that the direct ingestion of the disease had had on Master Wu and the League of Domino Mice. It had maimed, and even killed several mice in their daring mission because they had not been able to administer enough of the antidote in time. He told them how even Master Wu had lost a leg, and was now sadly blind in one eye.

At that moment, Master Wu interrupted, and the crowd quietened down immediately. "The important thing is that the humans now believe that much of the forest is infected with this strange disease. They now know for sure that it is even more dangerous than they had already believed it was. Our sacrifice was necessary and even though so many of the League were lost in this gruesome battle, it was certainly worthwhile to secure our future," said Master Wu confidently.

"Our home and lifestyle are now secure for a long while to come. The good rains have also enabled us to harvest and store enough cabbits to last us for years. We all have fine shelters, and we want for no basic needs. Finally, my friends, finally . . . we can all live peacefully, as one happy family in the forest!" said Master Wu with an eloquence that would have made Martin Luther King Jr proud.

The circle stood up in ovation and all the animals shouted out in joy as they hugged each other and celebrated. Master Wu and Griffon did not say much after that. They reflected on their adventure and silently appreciated the courageous few that had not made it back. They knew, better than most, that the price of freedom was one that had to be paid.

❧ 11 ❧

The call of the wild

The celebration continued for a few days and ended with another entertaining full moon festival. When things returned to normal, Griffon gathered the animals and gave them various responsibilities. He explained that it was necessary to maintain the order of things in the forest.

Griffon gave the job of chopping cabbits into assorted sizes for different creatures to Kineosho. He knew that his own agility had largely been responsible for their victory and was determined to ensure that Kineosho was also adept at moving fast, in case the threat from the humans ever returned.

All the animals accepted their roles and over the weeks that followed, they swapped jobs with each other until they settled into their individual niches. Kineosho found that he was very good at most of his roles. He also found that he got bored quite quickly once he learnt how to do something. When he did get bored, Griffon was always there to nudge Kineosho to take on roles that would improve his agility.

Many moons passed and Kineosho grew to be a strong, diligent lion. Somehow, he lost touch with many of the friends he had made as a cub. Some had found partners and others became involved with raising their own families. Others simply seemed to have disappeared. Even Twigs, Uma, and the wild dogs with whom he had spent much time earlier were nowhere to be found. Kineosho assumed that they had just taken on new roles on alternative paths out of the clearing, and did not think much of it.

He still spent much time with Viddi, who was thrilled with her job of braiding hair. She was one of the few animals who had not changed their role since they had received it.

One evening, Viddi was playing with Gita on the riverbank when Kineosho walked by. They were both throwing leftover cabbit ears as far as they could across the water. Kineosho and Gita both laughed at Viddi's silly sequence each time she threw a cabbit ear. Her eyes would squint and her tongue would hang out from one end of her mouth as she worked on her build-up. When she finally released the ear, she would spin at least three times to recover from the momentum of the throw. To her credit though, Viddi threw the farthest. As they were about to leave, Viddi requested an opportunity for a crowning throw.

Her build-up this time was even more intense than usual. Gita was almost in tears with laughter. Viddi's incredible power and precision when she released the ear saw the ear rise gently and then suddenly propel itself all the way across the river. As the ear was about to land on the opposite bank, a red bird swooped down to snatch it. They all looked on in wonder at the bird as it flew gracefully back across the river. When it plonked the cabbit ear onto Viddi's head, both Gita and Viddi began to laugh like lunatics and started dancing around with the ear.

"That was weird!" laughed Basho as he walked up behind Kineosho along with a few other animals who had witnessed the event. Kineosho nodded, glad that he was not the only one who thought the whole chain of events was quite bizarre. Although he had often walked along the shore, that was the first time he really became curious about what was on the other side of the river.

The following day Kineosho walked along the riverbank when he completed his duties for the day. There, he met Basho, who was sitting casually and staring across the river.

"Did you see that?" asked Basho suddenly.

"What?" asked Kineosho.

"There's something glittering across the river, over there . . ." said Basho, pointing excitedly. "It's like a little sparkling ball, or something," urged Basho.

Kineosho looked but could not spot it. Then just as he was about to say something to Basho, he saw a glimmer across the river. "Yes . . . I think I just saw it too! It's probably nothing though — only a reflection from the river."

That evening he asked Griffon about the other side of the river. Griffon replied irritatedly that there was nothing there, and that Kineosho should focus on his duties. Not satisfied with the reply, Kineosho asked many of the other animals if they knew anything. To his surprise, they all gave him spectacularly different replies. They ranged from total paranoia about the river from a hedgehog family to funny stories about how naughty young animals got sent there for punishment. One duck even told him that the other side of the river looked exactly the same as the side they were on and that it was quite boring really. Kineosho was intrigued.

A few days later, Kineosho asked Griffon about the other side of the river again. This time Griffon told him that it was dangerous there and that many animals that crossed never returned. He added that of those that did return, many of them came back mad. Once again, he told Kineosho that he should forget about the river and focus on his responsibilities to the community. However, Kineosho continued to ask around. The less everyone was able to explain consistently about the other side, the more his curiosity grew.

The following day Kineosho tracked down Master Wu in the forest and asked him about it. At first, Master Wu brushed him off and did not say much.

"Father said it is dangerous there and that animals return mad — is it really that scary?" prompted Kineosho.

Master Wu looked at Kineosho with his good eye and twirled his long white moustache. "What your father said is true — many of the animals who venture across never return. Those who do — well, he is right about that too.

"Once there was this ostrich . . . she was fine when she went across but many moons later she returned completely mad. Each night she sneaked around and tied animals' feet together while they slept. Then the following morning when the animals woke up and tripped over themselves she ran around shouting *Whee! Whee! Free! Free!* Needless to say, she didn't last long here behaving like that. Now, why do you ask about the other side of the river?" asked Master Wu.

Kineosho explained his curiosity after what he had seen with Viddi and Basho. He told Master Wu about the conflicting accounts he had heard from the other animals. Master Wu remained silent for some time. He knew that Kineosho's journey across the river had already begun.

"The rules on the other side of the river are very strange, Kineosho. Anything can happen and in fact, most of the animals who venture there, *die* there," said Master Wu eventually in a sombre voice.

"Then . . . why do they go?" asked Kineosho curiously.

"Why do they do anything?" replied Master Wu with a cynical laugh. "Because they want something that they don't have!"

In the days that followed, Basho did not help the situation. The little jackal took every opportunity to tempt Kineosho to the riverbank in the hope that they would spot the magical glittering they had witnessed before. One day, when Kineosho felt particularly tired and bored with his current role, he went down to the river and sat next to Basho.

He gazed across the river for quite some time, wondering what role he could take on next. Then he threw a cabbit ear into the water in frustration and in that very instant, the strangest vision appeared across the river. There was no sparkling light or angry bird as he had seen before. Instead, this time, he saw the blurry image of what looked like an elegant female leopard. She seemed to be signalling him with her paw to come across.

Just then, Curie called out to Kineosho: "Come home!" To Kineosho the sound seemed to come from all around him. He rose and looked around frantically for someone to validate what he had just experienced. But there was nobody there—not Viddi, not even Basho, who he was sure had been sitting right next to him only a moment ago. There was not a single creature in sight. Suddenly Kineosho felt very light headed and collapsed. Within seconds, Viddi and a few of the other animals hiding in the bushes burst out guffawing like crazy.

Curie ran to the riverbank when she heard the mad laughter. She sniffed at Kineosho for just a second, turned around and scowled at the laughing animals. "Hand it over right now!" she scolded as she approached them.

An edgy beaver squirmed and pointed snitchfully at Viddi from behind.

"Viddi . . ." said Curie, "hand it over right now!"

Viddi sheepishly handed over a small bunch of purple mushrooms wrapped in leaves. "And the cactus water . . ." said Curie sternly. Gita slowly handed over a coconut shell filled with a milky liquid, looking as shamefully guilty as a turtle could possibly look.

They returned to the clearing with Curie and helped Kineosho recover with a foul smelling plant root. When he finally came back to his senses, he insisted that he had seen a vision from across the river beckoning him.

"You just can't leave good enough alone, can you? I told you that we need you here right now, did I not?" said Griffon angrily. "Forget about the other side of the river!" he added fiercely.

Later that evening Kineosho told Master Wu about what he had seen. He asked him if he could swim across the river, just for a day to see what was there.

Master Wu looked at Kineosho and silently stroked his long whiskers. After some time he said: "That's not how it works, Kineosho. If you go across, you may never return the same way . . . even if you find things you cannot bear there. The path back is treacherous and it is far from as easy as going across."

Kineosho nodded. Master Wu frowned pensively for a while longer. "Leave me now—let me think," he said bluntly.

The following day, Master Wu called Griffon and Curie aside to a private corner. "I think the time has come for Kineosho to continue on his journey," he said.

"Master Wu, you know that vision he saw was only because of the crazy purple mushroom cactus concoction that Viddi and the others put into his drinking water . . ." said Curie.

"That may be. But the seed had been planted a long time ago and it was just a question of the right catalyst. You knew this day was bound to come—" replied Master Wu.

"—but what about his duties here, the forest will need him in case the humans ever return!" interrupted Griffon.

Master Wu looked at Griffon and shook his head ever so slightly. They all remained silent for a while.

"Did you tell him that he would not be able to return as he is?" asked Griffon, almost visibly trying to suppress the lump in his throat.

Master Wu said nothing further.

That night there was an awkward silence in the clearing. After dinner, Curie called Kineosho and sat him aside.

"There are a few things you need to know before you cross the river . . ." said Curie before pausing. "Ah, I just wanted you to know that I will miss you," she continued softly.

"I can go?" asked Kineosho excitedly.

"Yes, I think it's time," replied Curie, with more than a hint of sadness in her voice. "I have a little gift for you before you go," continued Curie as she handed Kineosho a soft brown sack. "This is a magic sack containing some mementos I kept for you—like this—the cabbit ear from the first one you ever ate, and the pebble you took your first step on, the clump of hair Viddi accidently pulled off your tail when you were playing . . . and many more." Curie explained that the magic sack immediately shrank anything that was put inside it.

"Keep it safe and look after yourself, Kineosho. Go see Master Wu now . . ." said Curie, bravely holding back the tears.

"Thank you! You know I'll be back soon though—I just want to see what's over there and I'll be right back!" said Kineosho enthusiastically.

Curie nodded, but did not say a word.

Kineosho went to Master Wu who was sitting on a branch a short distance away. "I have a gift for you before you leave," said Master Wu as he handed Kineosho a black bandana. "There will be times when you have too many thoughts in your head, clouding your intuition and preventing you from moving forward. This may come in handy to clear your mind and deal with the clutter."

"How do I use it?" asked Kineosho, wrapping the bandana around his paw and punching the air with it.

"You can figure it out when you need to," laughed Master Wu with a devious kung fu style laugh. "Now, go and see your father. He is waiting for you by the river and he is quite upset that you will be leaving." Kineosho thanked Master Wu and left for the river.

"Good luck, and let's hope curiosity doesn't kill the cat," whispered Master Wu to himself as Kineosho walked away.

When Kineosho arrived at the riverbank, he found his father staring pensively at the other side. Griffon looked sad and said nothing.

"I'll come back, I just can't stop thinking about what's there," said Kineosho. "I'll be back soon!"

"Nobody comes back," replied Griffon with a sigh. "Never the same, at least. Anyway, I suppose you have to do what you must. Before you leave though, I have a special gift for you." Griffon patted Kineosho on the head and handed him the five shiny gold coins that his father had given him many moons ago. That was the last time Griffon had seen him.

"Are they magic coins, like the sack mom gave me?" asked Kineosho excitedly.

"No," laughed Griffon. "They just turn out to be quite useful at the oddest of times and well, they were quite lucky for me and for your grandfather too."

Kineosho accepted the coins proudly. He still could not understand the fuss and melodrama around such a short journey. In his mind, he thought no more of it than an exploratory day trip to satisfy his curiosity.

"Rest now, and you can leave in the morning," said Griffon after a long pause.

Kineosho was excited about his trip, but he slept well. Griffon and Curie said their goodbyes quietly as he slept peacefully under his favourite tree in the clearing for the last time.

The next morning Kineosho rose early and completed his daily exercises with Viddi, as usual. Then, for the first time, he felt a little nervous about crossing. Although he still did not view the journey in the same way as his parents, or Master Wu, the air of finality about it all began to sink in.

After breakfast, Kineosho placed the black bandana and five gold coins into the magic sack that Curie had given him and slung the sack over his shoulder.

Master Wu said his goodbye in the clearing itself. "Don't forget your daily routine, no matter where you are!" he scolded playfully as he twisted Kineosho's ear slightly. Kineosho smiled and the excitement of his impending adventure returned to replace his nervousness.

Griffon, Curie, and Kineosho slowly walked down towards the riverbank. The water was unusually calm that morning.

"Where's Viddi?" asked Kineosho, looking around.

"She probably doesn't understand that you're leaving, or is too upset to acknowledge it if she did," replied Curie sadly. "I'll tell her that you wished her well. By the way, I've put a few cabbits in your sack . . . they should last you for quite a while."

Griffon did not say much but Curie could see the concern in his eyes. For him, this was the most challenging experience ever—even more so than his recent adventure with Master Wu. Curie knew it as she faced the same challenge.

"Go well son," whispered Griffon, before he walked away. Kineosho smiled at Curie one last time and dived into the calm water.

Part II

Part II

❧ 12 ❧

The rude awakening

Kineosho swam through the peaceful, warm water and he reached the other side much sooner than he had expected. When he arrived, he shook himself dry and immediately looked across the river. The scene was peculiar in that the opposite bank looked very familiar — in fact, it looked identical to the view from the opposite side. When he turned around though, there was no doubt in his mind that he was somewhere else.

The colours were brighter, the trees looked taller, and the sensation of the earth underneath his paws was unlike anything he had experienced before. He felt as though he were floating. Even the scent of the riverbank there seemed pleasantly intoxicating. For a moment, Kineosho regretted not having made the journey much sooner.

He wandered along the bank and then into the forest, experiencing the full wonders of his senses. Everything felt more intense on that side of the river. By evening, he had walked quite far into the forest. He laid his head on his magic sack and fell asleep peacefully.

Kineosho woke up the next morning with the sound of sweetly twittering birds and Basho's paw poking him repeatedly on the head, urging him to wake up.

"Hey, I didn't see you yesterday—I didn't know you had swum across already! Isn't it wonderful here?" mumbled Kineosho as he opened his eyes. As soon as he did, Basho pointed at the three crocodiles squabbling with each other nearby and dashed off to hide behind a large tree.

"We haven't seen one of those before—why does he have so much hair?" asked one of the crocodiles to another curiously. The largest of the three promptly bashed him on the head with a wooden club.

Kineosho stretched, and went to greet his first friends on that side of the river.

"Who are you?" asked the smallest of the three crocodiles.

"I'm Kineosho, son of Griffon," replied Kineosho proudly.

"Oh . . . okay—whatever—," replied one of the other crocodiles.

"—So, what's in the bag there?" interrupted the largest crocodile inquisitively.

Kineosho looked at Basho hiding behind the tree. He was waving frantically at him trying to get his attention.

"Just something my mother gave me," smiled Kineosho. "Anyway, if you'll excuse me now I have to complete my morning exercises," he said as he started walking towards Basho's tree.

The largest of the crocodiles leapt in front of him, blocking his way. "Wait . . . don't go just yet. We're your new friends here.

You don't want to be rude to your new friends now, do you?" he asked Kineosho.

"Yeah, c'mon tell us what's in the bag," interrupted the smallest crocodile without giving him a chance to reply.

"Yeah—tell us. What's the big secret?" asked the medium-sized crocodile, pushing Kineosho a little from behind. "How can you keep secrets from your new friends?" he asked, as he nudged him again.

Only seconds later, the largest crocodile pushed Kineosho against a tree and relieved him of his magic sack. He opened it as eagerly as a rabbit in heat, and started shaking the sack vigorously upside down. Out fell lots of mementos including a twig, a tooth, one of the ninja mice sticks, a couple of cabbits, and some mud from the mudslide. Each item reminded Kineosho of something, but his immediate situation was getting increasingly out of hand and he could not focus.

The crocodiles seemed very upset with the items that were coming out of the bag and they became rougher with him. Soon, they began beating him as hard as they could in frustration, asking him why he was hiding everything from them. Kineosho tried to fight back but they were strong and one of them had pinned him against the tree. They started asking seemingly irrelevant questions like "Tell us where the tree is?" and "Why are you holding out on us—are you protecting the pig?" Each time they asked Kineosho something he honestly could not answer, they beat him even more. It looked like they were enjoying themselves. Basho peered from behind the tree and was unable to move. He wanted to help, but just couldn't.

Eventually, one of the crocodiles snatched the sack from the ground and shook it in anger before he beat it against the tree behind Kineosho. To everyone's surprise, a rather dazed-looking

Viddi with a sheepish grin fell out of the bag, as did three of the five gold coins that Griffon had given him.

The largest crocodile snarled as he snatched the three shiny coins off the ground. He gave Kineosho one final kick in the ribs before he called the others to leave. The smallest looked around and warned them both to keep some better stuff in their sack for the next time. Battered, bruised, and bleeding, Kineosho blacked out in front of the tree.

Viddi was panic-stricken and not knowing what else to do, she started yelling loudly for help. Fortunately for her and for Kineosho, it wasn't long before an armadillo heard her plea and scurried over.

"What happened?" the armadillo asked Viddi. He looked at Kineosho, who lay unconscious beside the tree. Viddi just looked at him in shock, unable to reply.

"Well you're lucky I was walking this way—it looks serious," said the armadillo sombrely as he examined Kineosho more closely. He took a few things out of his pouch and proceeded to create a dressing of large leaves. He coated it with a yellow paste and applied it to Kineosho's wounds. After that, he mixed a strange concoction of herbs and gave it to Viddi. "Give him this when he wakes up and make sure he drinks lots of water. And don't worry, he'll be fine, okay?" said the armadillo reassuringly.

"Thank you," replied Viddi, with tears in her eyes. She slowly opened her hands and offered the armadillo the two gold coins she had been tightly holding onto since she had been thrown out of the sack. The armadillo smiled and not wanting to offend Viddi, took one of the coins.

"You can keep that one, and don't worry, I'll stay with you till he wakes up," said the armadillo calmly. Viddi felt relieved for the first time since she had come out of the sack.

"Thank you—," she began before she realised she did not know what to call the armadillo.

"—Milo," he smiled.

Over the next two days, Milo changed Kineosho's dressings twice between wandering off to seek more herbs to store in his pouch. Viddi waited patiently at Kineosho's side and made sure she gave him plenty of water.

On the morning of the third day, Kineosho woke up looking visibly better. He was still groggy when Milo left and it took him a short while to remember what had happened. He felt much better that both Viddi and Basho were with him, but his initial enthusiasm for that side of the river had all but disappeared. The colours still seemed brighter and the landscape more beautiful, but he felt a nervousness that he had not experienced before.

"Well, I think it's been fun," he said to Basho. "We should probably head back home now." Both Basho and Viddi agreed instantly. Basho led the way back to the river after Viddi happily leapt onto Kineosho's back.

When they arrived at the river, Kineosho looked across and the distance seemed farther than when he had crossed. Confident that he could still easily swim it though, he put his paw into the water, looking forward to the comfort of returning home. As soon as he did so, however, the current suddenly became incredibly strong. Kineosho immediately withdrew his paw and looked confusedly at Basho. Viddi held on tightly as he tried again. This time the current was even stronger and he almost lost his footing on the riverbank. As soon as he withdrew his paw, a sinister dark cloud formed above them.

Basho tugged at Kineosho's mane and pointed anxiously towards the forest. "We had better run before the sky bursts!"

said Basho. Kineosho looked across the river, distraught. It had finally dawned on him that Master Wu had quite literally meant that he would never be able to return the same way.

A deafening roll of thunder abruptly disturbed his realisation. It began to pour and Kineosho followed Basho's lead back into the forest. The rain soon turned into hail and they ran deeper for cover. Basho hoped to find somewhere they could take shelter, but for a long while they found nothing. They just ran.

Suddenly, Viddi spotted the entrance to a cave and they dashed inside. Kineosho was not sure how long it poured down for. His mind had drifted back to Griffon's words and he regretted not heeding the warnings he had received.

13

Reversal of fortune

The next morning, Kineosho was glad to wake up next to Basho and Viddi. He was even gladder to see that the hail had finally stopped. When they left the cave, they found the entrance flooded with water. There were a number of paths leading away from the cave and the water had made it impossible to figure out which one they had arrived by.

Kineosho was wary and unsure which path to choose so Basho took the lead and chose one. Kineosho and Viddi followed him deeper into the jungle. Soon, the waterlogged area passed and they entered a beautiful part of the forest filled with lovely scented trees and prismatic flowers. The walk was serene and Kineosho felt calmer. Slowly, the sensations and experiences of the first day returned to him. The smell of the damp earth was comforting. There were no crocodiles or other voices to be heard—just the calming chirp of insects. By this time, Basho had run on much further ahead and neither Kineosho nor Viddi could see him.

Just as Kineosho began to feel relaxed, he heard the sound of galloping paws in the distance. He sniffed the air and said to Viddi, "Something is not right — quick, get behind that large tree!" He rushed there after her. They both breathed as lightly as they could.

After some time, they heard the frantic rustling of what sounded like a small pack of animals hunting for something. Then there was silence.

"Is it the crocodiles?" whispered Viddi anxiously.

"I don't think so, they smell very different," replied Kineosho, as he peered cautiously around the tree. "Do you see anything?" he whispered to Viddi.

Viddi did the same on the other side of the tree. "No, I think they're gone," whispered Viddi.

"Are you sure?" asked a peculiar voice from what seemed to be a pair of bright white cabbit ears that seemed to have magically appeared under Kineosho. Viddi and Kineosho looked at each other and were both silent for a moment, a little concerned about the owner of the unusual voice. "And do you mind moving a little, you're squashing my back, Hairy," said the cabbit ears.

Kineosho hesitantly pulled the cabbit ears out from under himself and to his surprise, they didn't belong to a cabbit at all. "*Whoa!* Easy on the ears!" scolded the strange animal at the top of his voice, startling them both.

"Who are you?" asked Kineosho.

The animal quickly rubbed down his soft white fur. "I'm the Dark Overlord of the North, don't you recognise me?" he replied. He fluffed up his chest fur and straightened his ears. "I've been travelling across the forest with a secret potion that can take you anywhere you want to go in an instant. Look at my eyes — they are red because I have amazing powers bestowed upon me by the great wizard Jang Tse Long himself!"

"Wow . . . really?" replied Kineosho excitedly.

"No, you idiot!" he replied, shaking his head in disbelief. "I'm a fat white rabbit trying to escape from a bunch of angry foxes. What are you doing here anyway, and why are you hiding from them?"

"We're trying to find our way back across the river—can you help us?" asked Kineosho hopefully.

The rabbit laughed hysterically until he started coughing. "You . . . you . . . want to go back? You can't, Hairy. Didn't anybody explain the rules to you? Once you've passed a certain point you cannot go back—well it just wouldn't make sense to anyway because nothing would be the same."

Kineosho and Viddi stared at the rabbit, quite confused.

The rabbit looked at them and let out a huge sigh, still shaking his head in disbelief. "Okay, okay . . . look, you probably saved me from the foxes even though you don't realise it so I guess I owe you something."

"The magic secret potion?" asked Viddi curiously.

"No!" laughed the rabbit, shaking his head even more theatrically. "Let's find a safe place to hide and I'll explain a few things to you. I'm Lucky, by the way—follow me."

The fat white rabbit limped ahead and led them to a small clearing. There, he explained a bit about that side of the river, confirming again that there was no easy way back.

"Things are not always what they seem here. You really need to trust yourselves in order to survive. Don't worry, though—you can have a pretty good time here if you play your cards right," said Lucky sadly as he paused to look down at his missing left foot.

"Anyway, as I was saying, there is a much nicer part of the forest than this. To get there though, you need to pass through the underground talent show. *Ooh!* That's tricky. If you fail too often you'll just disappear into nothingness! It's tough—really tough!" said the rabbit, shaking his head and speaking quite quickly.

Viddi looked at Kineosho, concerned.

"Where do we find this underground talent show? And how come you're in this part of the forest, and not in the nicer bit?" asked Kineosho.

Lucky gave them both a disappointed look and sat down to tell his story. He explained how he had been taking part in the show as a magician pulling foxes out of a magic hat that an uncle of his had given him. What he had not counted on was the rotten foxes using him to get into the talent show and then trying to use him in *their* act. By this time Lucky was quite flustered and speaking very fast. Viddi could barely keep up with what he was saying.

"They were going to use me for their own *spin the rabbit and throw knives at it* act—can you believe that! As soon as I took the first fox out of the hat, he grabbed me and released the entire pack. Then they started tying me up to a disc. Luckily, some rhino about to break some big weightlifting record distracted them all. In the few seconds I had, I gnawed off my foot and dashed out. They chased me and even threw a couple of knives at me but I managed to escape . . . they're probably waiting for me now at the entrance of the talent show cave—no way I'm going back there! I'd never get in there again anyway, not without my lucky foot," said Lucky sadly as he sighed in despair.

Viddi tried to console the unhappy rabbit and Kineosho suggested that they find a safe place to rest for the night. Curie's survival skills training proved very handy.

The next morning, Kineosho woke up to the sound of Basho's voice: "If the nice part of the forest is safer than here, then we should definitely try to get there," he said. Basho then whispered something in Kineosho's ear with a sneaky smile. Kineosho nod-ded in reply.

When Lucky woke up, he was still reluctant to lead them to the talent show. In fact, he was determined never to go anywhere near there again.

"Well, we could always tie you up to that tree and ask the foxes how to get there when they find you. Either way works for us," said Kineosho calmly. The rabbit's face drooped into a disgruntled frown before he hesitantly agreed to take them.

They walked for quite a distance before they arrived near the entrance of the cave. Lucky explained that Kineosho would have to win a game of backgammon with the large hippo at the entrance in order to gain access to the talent show. He looked sadly at his missing left foot and wondered if he would ever be able to get in again.

"You have to be careful though, he's a real gambler and a big cheat too!" said Lucky. "Do you know how to play?"

Kineosho shook his head.

Lucky drew a backgammon board in the sand, removed the pair of dice hanging around his neck, and taught him how to play. Kineosho picked it up easily and by their fourth practice game, he had worked out the logic and was quite enjoying it. Then Kineosho thought for a while and devised a plan to get them all into the show. The rabbit was quite excited at the pros-pect, although he was not entirely sure how he would ever get out of the talent show without his act or his magic hat.

Kineosho set his plan in motion. He told Viddi, Basho, and Lucky to climb into his magic sack and to hang on as closely as they could to the top. He then strutted up confidently to the hippo and asked what he needed to do to enter.

"Win a game and you're in," sneered the hippo.

The game was on. When Kineosho laid his bag on the ground, he opened it enough for Viddi's long arm to sneak out. The plan was that if he needed help, he would tap the bag lightly with his foot. Viddi was then supposed to tickle the hippo's feet to distract him before Kineosho's turn to throw the dice. Kineosho would then help the dice along to just the right combination they needed for that throw.

To Kineosho's credit, the plan worked well. For the most part Kineosho did not need any help, as he was lucky with the dice rolls. Then the hippo started cheating. He miscounted his own moves and shuffled around some of Kineosho's pieces refusing to move them back to their rightful places. The first couple of times Kineosho tapped the bag with his foot Viddi was quick to lend her hand and tickle the hippo. The plan worked like a charm.

Then for some reason, when he really needed a final good roll to win the game, Viddi did not respond to the light tap on the sack. So he kicked a little harder and there was still no response. Kineosho coughed and kicked the bag really hard. Viddi let out an enormous yelp, much to the surprise of the hippo and Kineosho. When Kineosho looked down, he saw Viddi's hand trapped under the hippo's foot from the last time she had tickled him. Her other hand was angrily rubbing her head, which Kineosho had just kicked.

The hippo had not even realised that he was standing on Viddi's hand. She had been successfully muffling her mouth with her shorter hand until Kineosho put it to better use for consoling her head. The hippo grabbed Viddi and snarled angrily at Kineosho.

"You're trying to cheat me?!" he growled.

"Wait, wait . . . how about we go double or quits . . . look, I need a double six to win. Anything else and I lose . . . those are pretty good odds for you, right?" asked Kineosho.

The hippo looked at Kineosho, paused for a bit, and dropped Viddi. "Fine. You lose and I get to sit on your back for the next ten full moons," said the hippo with a sneer.

"And if I win we both get to enter, right?" asked Kineosho.

"Sure!" replied the hippo confidently. He was quite looking forward to a softer bench to sit on.

"Blow on the dice, Viddi," said Kineosho nervously. She blew. The rabbit, who had been listening from inside the magic sack, started rubbing his right foot anxiously against his head. Then he felt a light tap on the bag and he could hear Kineosho's dice rattling.

"What are you waiting for? Throw the dice!" said the hippo.

Kineosho looked at the hippo who just glared back at him, totally focused. No distraction arrived. Kineosho closed his eyes for a brief moment and rolled the dice. There was absolute silence for a couple of seconds.

When the hippo finally registered the double six, he slammed the board and swiped it off the table angrily. "GO!" he snarled, "Before I change my mind!"

Kineosho looked at him, surprised. He had hoped Lucky would have taken his cue and done something to distract the hippo but it turned out that he didn't need it anyway. He quickly grabbed Viddi, closed the magic sack tightly and headed towards the entrance of the cave.

There were two much friendlier bouncer cranes waiting there. They inspected their ears and behind Viddi's ear they found a peculiar birthmark. After consulting each other briefly, they told Viddi that she could come and go as she pleased. They tapped some sap from a nearby tree and gave it to Kineosho to drink. He felt a little woozy after a sip and the cranes hurried them both inside the cave.

☙ 14 ❧

Who's got talent?

A short while later Kineosho recovered and let Basho and Lucky out of the magic sack. There were animals of all types in the cave and it was very noisy. Everything about the place seemed to be chaotic and odd. Besides the feeling of rush hour in a giant sardine can, the animals looked quite strange. There were some elephants the size of mice—in fact, most of the animals there appeared smaller than their normal size.

"That sap they gave you when you entered," said Lucky, "is a magical one."

"You're just joking again," smiled Viddi, pleased that she was not falling victim to the rabbit's humour again.

"No, it really is magical," said Lucky nodding his head. "When you do something that is judged by your panel, you either grow or shrink in size depending on how much the judges enjoyed your performance."

"Panel? Judges?" asked Kineosho, looking confused.

"Up there," said the rabbit, pointing to the rotating platforms suspended above dozens of stages in the cave. "Nobody on the floor can access the judging area. They usually include some of the most respected members of the forest and the panels vary for each animal here."

The judges, to Kineosho's surprise, included some strangely familiar faces including Griffon, Curie, Dada, Master Wu, and some of the other elders with whom Master Wu was often seen discussing things. Kineosho looked at them excitedly and shouted out to them. He had no idea how they had got there but he was pleased to see them. They appeared not to hear him.

"Why don't I have a word with them?" asked Basho, as he disappeared into the thick of the animals. Only seconds later Basho appeared sitting next to Master Wu, much to Kineosho's astonishment.

Lucky tugged at Kineosho's mane as the noise became overwhelming. "I'll show you how it works, but first let's head to somewhere a little quieter," said Lucky. He walked away and Kineosho and Viddi followed closely.

As they made their way through the crowd, Kineosho's attention was unexpectedly captured by an elegant female leopard on the other side of the cave. He could have sworn he had seen her before but could not recall when. He tried to think back to the blurry image of the leopard he had seen across the river but the noise made it too difficult to concentrate on anything. When he looked again for the leopard, she was gone.

"Are you okay?" asked Lucky, once they reached a slightly quieter area.

"Yes," said Kineosho hesitantly. "I just thought I saw . . . never mind."

Lucky shrugged and then explained how the underground talent show worked. Each participant had to perform an act that his or her individual panel would judge. As soon as the animal took to the stage, its judges would immediately be able to see it from their rotating platform above.

"I know it's noisy in here but it's easier if you focus on one performance. Otherwise, it gets quite overwhelming," continued Lucky. "Come with me, I'll show you one in action and it'll all become clearer . . ."

They followed Lucky as he skilfully manoeuvred through the crowd like an eel on steroids. Kineosho kept an eye out for the mysterious leopard but he did not spot her again. After some pushing and shoving, they finally arrived near a stage on which there were three slightly shrunken ferrets preparing for their performance. Lucky explained that whenever any animal or group of animals was ready, it stepped onto a stage and performed. The judges would then evaluate the performance and depending on their applause, the magic sap that the performers drank would make them grow or shrink.

Suddenly, one of the ferrets on stage coughed and then clapped loudly. Their audience quietened down immediately. Kineosho could see the other animals still bustling about and yelling but for some reason right there in front of that stage, it was quiet.

"I'd like to sing you a song that we call . . . The Dark Side — *hit it Rosco!*" said the ferret as the drums began in the background. After a short musical introduction with what looked like a miniature red bass guitar, the lead ferret punched his fist into the air and started his rap.

> *On a journey*
> *in my mind,*
> *seekin' that*
> *I cannot find,*

all my stuff
now left behind,
time to me
been so unkind

demons 'tacking me
all at once,
from the east
I run and pounce,
to west
I cry and bounce,
north I see
many enemies

Comin' closer
from the south,
seein' 'em frothin'
at the mouth
wild 'n' angry
they be hungry
murderin' me
without a doubt!

But one by one I fight and tear them off,
my deepest fears wiped out, from every pore
Till thundering behind I hear an evil roar,
shakin' me down to my soul's very core

Then from behind,
you burn me . . . those fiery eyes

piercing through the moon's pitch black sky
Finally I turn, and what do I see?
Nothing . . . but a nasty reflection of me;
reflection of . . . me . . .

The audience broke into a frenzy as the drummer ferret embarked on his solo. Kineosho looked around and saw that everyone there was as enthralled by the performance as he was. Then the lead ferret continued his rap.

So deep down
in my mind,
I'm stuck
and oh so blind,
needing mercy
of some kind,
an intervention
so divine

For what to do
I do not know,
don't know how
my cards he knows
"Show your hand,"
I say, no fear,
"Going home
or dying here . . ."

So what happens now to poor, dear old me?
Am I stuck here now for all eternity?
Then that nasty devil said to me:
"There ain't no ending for you, oh so twee."

"To win this game, you simply cannot play
for there's no way for you, this beast to slay . . ."

The song ended with a dramatic drum roll and both the judges and the audience screamed. The louder they cheered, the larger the ferrets grew until they reached their normal size. Not long after, a fight broke out in the audience and things started to get seriously rowdy.

"*Err* . . . I think we had better move on from here before I lose another foot," said Lucky as he hurried them off to a quieter spot.

"That was really mind-blowing, but what if their judges hadn't liked rap?" asked Kineosho.

"Then it gets a bit tricky," replied Lucky. "The judges are always those who are important to that particular performer. So, they would either have to add or change their judges, or change their act. Either way, enough members of their selected panel have to think they're good enough, otherwise they'll never be able to leave!"

"How many is enough?" asked Kineosho, becoming increasingly concerned with the complexity of the rules.

The rabbit shrugged uncomfortably. "Sometimes it can be as few as one, or as many as a hundred—there are no rules about that."

Lucky then led Kineosho and Viddi through the crowd to another stage. There was a small moose on it preparing for her act. "Take this lassie, Chocolate, for example—she was here when I was here last time. I thought she had a class act but her judges were really not very impressed. It looks like she's added a few judges to her panel this time."

Just then, Chocolate tapped her hoof loudly and the audience around that stage fell silent. She counted to three and began her tap-dancing routine. The tapping tempo was slow at first but it soon escalated into a breath-taking beat. Many in the audience and even some of the judges began bopping to the pulsating rhythm of Chocolate's tempestuous tapping. At the end of her performance, Chocolate leapt into the air with dramatic flair and landed on her knees in front of the audience.

"Wow . . . that was as spectacular as the first time I saw her!" said Lucky, looking quite smitten. "Look up there at the new judges," he continued, pointing to Chocolate's panel. Some of them were giving her a standing ovation. Even Lucky began to applaud and holler in support. The fat white rabbit looked quite wonky trying to clap with a foot missing but he knew that every little bit would help her. Soon the rest of the judges, including two elderly moose on it, also started to cheer. It was like a chain reaction. Chocolate let out an obviously emotional smile as she suddenly began to grow.

When Chocolate had grown to her full size, the judges descended from their panel and led her to another part of the cave.

"Quick, let's follow them," said Lucky. They witnessed Chocolate's emotional exit ceremony in which she stood with one foot on a coconut. One of the elderly moose judges then stepped forward and marked the back of Chocolate's ear with a small spot of red paste. The other elderly moose approached her too and they both said something to her before she smiled broadly and bowed her head. Chocolate then proudly strutted out through a heavily guarded exit, with everyone present at the ceremony cheering at full volume.

"She's going out!" said Lucky excitedly. "See, *that's* where we need to go!"

They ambled around a bit in the cave and Lucky asked Kineosho whether he knew what kind of act he was going to perform.

"I don't know . . . I definitely can't rap or tap like either of those acts," replied Kineosho.

"What are you good at? If you don't have a talent it's going to be pretty tough to take part in a talent show, if you know what I mean!" said Lucky.

"Well, I'm good at lots of things. I know I'm very strong and agile," said Kineosho. "I can pull a cart filled with over fifty cabbits!"

Lucky shook his head. "You know the rhino I mentioned — the one who distracted the foxes when he was breaking that record? He lifted over five hundred cabbits without blinking an eyelid! *Erm* . . . so what else can you do?"

"I'm an expert cabbit chopper?" replied Kineosho, not knowing whether that would even qualify as an activity.

"Cabbit-chopper? There's a cabbit-chopping showdown with Leggs just over there — you should go — but quick — the odds are almost in!" said a plump hamster wearing a chequered hat who rushed past them. He was carrying a stack of leaves with scribbles on them.

Lucky grabbed Kineosho by the mane and speedily followed the hamster.

"What's a showdown?" asked Kineosho.

"It's like a competition and if you win, you're outta here!" said Lucky. "This is your chance!"

Kineosho stepped onto the stage. For a moment, there was a flurry of activity below them as the plump hamster shouted out lots of numbers. Others raised their hands and yelled back at him. The hamster then scribbled some more on his stack of leaves and rushed around handing them out.

Suddenly Kineosho heard the sound of knives clanging and

the noisy crowd quietened down. He looked around and saw the platform with his panel of judges suspended just above his audience.

"Arm yourselves!" shouted a loud voice.

A giant tarantula at the other end of the stage walked towards the centre and picked up six knives. He looked a little awkward standing on two feet. Kineosho walked to the centre and picked up two knives. He still wasn't sure what to expect, but the look of daggers from the tarantula was not a welcoming one.

"Friends, I present to you the defending champion—Leggs! Chop on the count of three!" shouted the loud voice again. A bright spotlight shone on Leggs and the audience counted down: "Three—Two—One—Chop!"

As soon as they said *Chop!*, three cabbits were thrown in turn towards Leggs. He leapt up and with an astounding display of skill, juggled two of the knives whilst using the remaining four to chop the incoming cabbits into perfect little cubes at lightning speed. As the chopped cabbit cubes landed on the stage, Leggs deftly arranged them into the shape of a pyramid. After the final cabbit was chopped he dramatically tossed up all six knives. They landed in a perfectly straight line at the foot of the cabbit cube pyramid. The audience roared and the plump hamster winked at Leggs.

"And our contender tonight is . . ." said the loud voice.

"*Erm* . . . Kineosho," replied Kineosho.

"*Erm* . . . Kineosho!" repeated the loud voice. "Chop on the count of three!"

The audience counted down and Kineosho braced himself. He was still in shock with what Leggs had just done to the three cabbits in a matter of seconds.

When he heard *Chop!*, the first cabbit came hurtling towards his head. Kineosho chopped as fast as he could and he had barely finished before the second cabbit arrived. The third cabbit almost hit him on the head and had the audience roaring with laughter. Within seconds, Kineosho shrank to half his size. He was shocked.

The hamster dashed past him and chuckled. "Better luck next time, pussycat," he said as he collected the leaves with scribbles and handed out some others.

Kineosho stepped off the stage, embarrassed to the core. "I'm never going to get out of here!" he whispered to Lucky, feeling quite distressed. Viddi looked at Kineosho, a little confused at what had just happened and puzzled at how he had suddenly become so much smaller. She could not help but giggle at him.

"It's not funny, Viddi!" snapped Kineosho angrily.

"Take it easy, that was just your first try at something," said Lucky. "You know, I saw you bolt towards the tree when the foxes were chasing me—you were pretty fast. Perhaps you should try the Great Rat Race—many of the animals try that out when they first get here," he continued.

Kineosho nodded anxiously and Lucky led them to the far end of the cave. There were lots of different animals gathered near the entrance of a massive circular track that seemed to extend along the entire perimeter of the cave. There were many more animals already running on the track.

"Why do they call it the Great Rat Race when there are so many other animals in it?" asked Viddi curiously.

"Don't know—I think it's because the rats always seem to win," replied Lucky with a shrug of his shoulders.

"But why do they enter if the rats always win?" asked Viddi.

"Don't know—I think it's—," replied the rabbit.

"—because they're not sure what else they can do," interrupted Kineosho with a hint of cynicism in his voice. "I'm sure

I can win this. There is no way I'm going to be beaten by a rat!" said Kineosho as he walked off to the starting sideline.

There were dozens of animals including lots of rats around Kineosho waiting to join the race, and hundreds more already in it. As groups of animals dropped out of the race, stewards allowed new batches onto the track from the starting sideline. It was not long before Kineosho's batch took to the track. He started strongly, but the rats seemed to work in teams to trip up many of their competitors and often themselves too.

The scene from the sidelines was quite sensational. Besides the tripping up, the rats were leaping forward to bite the backs of those ahead of them. On top of this, there were competitors who thought they could win the race by running in the opposite direction to everybody else. None of these strategies seemed to work well though. Apart from generating some entertaining comedy for the spectators, they all seemed to be pointlessly running around in a huge circle. Both Viddi and Lucky were hopping around with laughter.

When Kineosho completed a few laps and passed them on the sideline, he asked how anybody there knew that they had won if they just kept running around in circles. Lucky shrugged, honestly not knowing what to reply.

Soon Kineosho became tired. He had started by growing a bit when he was full of energy, and was doing well. As he tired and fell behind, he started shrinking again. A short while later, he thought it would be better to fall out of the race than to risk becoming much smaller than he already was.

When he stepped off the track, he felt depressed. His initial concern about getting out of the cave had evolved into a practical certainty in his mind. He pushed Lucky and Viddi aside, and wandered overwrought around the cave. Everywhere he walked, he could see creatures of all sorts performing magnificent acts. When he saw how happy they were to leave, Kineosho became even more upset.

He even tried sneaking out behind one of the larger animals who was about to exit the cave, but the hippo guards promptly caught him and threw him back in. There was no escape.

Kineosho continued to wander around aimlessly for some time until he wound up watching a funny knitting showdown between a ladybug and a radiant toucan. Suddenly, he spotted the elegant female leopard watching another performance nearby. This time he did not take his eyes off her. He barged through the crowd until he finally managed to step up beside her.

"So . . . what are you trying in the cave?" asked Kineosho after a slightly mousy pause.

She smiled and tilted her head to show Kineosho the red mark behind her ear. "I'm just waiting for someone before I leave. What are you going to try next?" she asked in the softest voice, continuing to watch the performance and not looking down at Kineosho.

"I'm not sure what to try next—I haven't had the greatest start here," shrugged Kineosho.

Then she crouched down beside him. "Try something that you feel comes naturally to you—that's always a good start," she said as she smiled. Her deep green eyes had an oddly familiar look about them.

"Was this the blurry leopard I saw from the other side of the river?" thought Kineosho to himself. Before he could ask anything further, the leopard excused herself and disappeared into the crowd.

Kineosho resumed his aimless wander, pondering over what the elegant leopard had said. He did not ponder very long before he saw Viddi and the fat white rabbit leap, hop, skip and trip right in front of him. The foxes, who had since tricked their way back into the cave, were chasing them at full speed.

Seconds later, one of the foxes pounced on Lucky and held him up by the ears. He dragged Lucky onto a stage which had a large revolving wheel on it. The fox promptly mounted Lucky on the wheel with the help of his colleagues. This time there were no distractions. Lucky's happy reunion with his little left foot that he had gnawed off was all too brief. He squealed anxiously as he saw the foxes prepare their sharp throwing knives.

Kineosho, who had followed them through the crowd, leapt onto the stage. He stood squarely between the foxes and Lucky. For a moment, he had forgotten how small he had become. The foxes were only too glad to remind him of it as they strutted forward and glared down at him. As the foxes taunted him and debated loudly amongst themselves whether they should mount him on the wheel too, Kineosho felt his anger mounting.

Suddenly, Kineosho roared at them as deeply as he had ever roared. Then he roared again and there was silence for a split second in the cave. The judges on his panel looked down curiously at him. When he stepped forward and roared once more, the foxes scampered off terrified and the audience cheered at the power of the roar. Kineosho really didn't think much of it but he roared again and this time the judges cheered too—both at his roar, and at his bravery. As the applause echoed through the cave, Kineosho slowly grew back to his full size. He looked at the panel and they all looked impressed—all with the exception of Basho, who just yawned and went on filing his nails.

Then Kineosho glanced at the audience and he spotted the elegant green-eyed leopard. She too had witnessed the commotion and cast him an enigmatic smile before disappearing into the crowd once more.

To Lucky's surprise, he also grew larger and fatter until he reached his original size. He looked at his judges and they were apparently sufficiently impressed that he had managed to influence a lion to come to his rescue.

Kineosho untied Lucky and called Viddi down from the ceiling where she had been hanging with his magic sack. Lucky immediately untied his gnawed-off left foot and rushed to the knitting showdown stage. There, he whispered something sweetly to the ladybug who promptly fluttered her eyelashes and stitched his foot back on.

Kineosho felt relieved. Griffon, Curie and Master Wu descended from their platform and led him to the exit ceremony. Griffon proceeded to mark his ear with the red paste. When Kineosho took his right foot off the coconut shell, he was overwhelmed with emotion. In the excitement, he did not even notice that Master Wu no longer walked with a limp and that his eyes were just like when he had first met him.

As they walked towards the cave exit, Kineosho asked Master Wu: "Does this mean I get to go home now?"

"You have only just earned your right to begin the journey, Kineosho," said Master Wu with a laugh as he patted him on the head. "You still have a lot to learn — to get home, you have to know a few things: when to be stupid; how to be smart; when to be strong; and that it's okay to be wrong . . . but be patient with yourself, and it will all come when it's time."

"You've done well to earn such respect," whispered Griffon proudly with the briefest of bows.

Kineosho smiled and with a blink of his eyes, Griffon, Curie, and Master Wu vanished.

Kineosho took the magic sack from Viddi and put a stone from the cave into it. As Viddi climbed onto his back, Basho ran up next to them. Kineosho nodded proudly at the hippo guards who nodded in reply and let him out. As they stepped out of the cave into the dark quietness, all three of them felt calm but very tired. They barely took a few steps before they all fell sound asleep.

15

Shangri-La

Kineosho opened a well-rested eye, trying to spot the source of a sweet melody. After a satisfying stretch, he looked around a bit more, but the creature proved elusive. The smell of the air made Kineosho recollect how he had felt when he had first arrived on that side of the river. The colours were as vivid and the landscape as breathtaking. Everything seemed truly spectacular—he felt like he had woken up in paradise.

Kineosho was keen to explore this new part of the forest. Lucky, who was nowhere to be found, had raised expectations while they were in the talent show and the first signs were that the rabbit had not exaggerated at all.

There were a number of paths to begin their exploration. Kineosho was quick to choose one and to suggest it to Viddi and Basho. As they walked, Kineosho asked Basho: "Don't you think it was strange that there were so many familiar faces in the cave? It's almost like we had never left home."

"Very strange indeed," replied Basho.

"It was great though—when I roared I really felt like I

owned the stage . . . That everyone was paying attention to me," continued Kineosho.

"You did. We were! It was great!" exclaimed Viddi cheerfully, recalling the events from her aerial view.

"Yes, you must be proud—you certainly did very well in there," added Basho.

They walked on a little further. "I noticed you did not cheer as much as the other judges though . . . did you really think I was good?" asked Kineosho.

"Ah, I was just tired," replied Basho, following at some distance behind. "You were great."

Kineosho smiled and continued ahead proudly. After some time, they reached a small pond and decided to relax there for the rest of the day. Viddi was quick to dive into the water and it wasn't long before she started a water war with the resident pond frogs.

That evening, the friendly and rather psychedelically coloured frogs invited them to see an entertaining show starring the infamous Braying Mantis. Kineosho learnt that he was apparently on a tour of all the watering holes in the forest doing his hilarious animal impersonations.

"I often get asked why I'm called Braying Mantis," said the mantis as he strolled onto the stage that evening. "All I say in response to that is *ee-aw ee-aw!*" The crowd let out some muffled laughter, a little disappointed with the poor impersonation. The mantis looked at the audience and shrugged his shoulders. "What?" he continued. "Were you expecting me to be a donkey, or something? Then I'd probably sound more like this." The mantis turned around, paused for a second and turned back to face the audience with a totally distorted face. Then he brayed loudly. He sounded more real than a donkey itself.

The crowd immediately exploded with laughter. The donkey impersonation was the funniest thing that Viddi had seen on that side of the river and she could not control her guffawing. Kineosho and Basho were rolling on the floor too.

The impersonations continued and the Braying Mantis spared no animal. The classic one of Master Wu in which he leapt around madly twirling his antennae whilst doing a mock kung fu mouse accent had the audience in tears.

Towards the end of the show, the Braying Mantis mentioned that he had just seen Kineosho in the talent show and was in awe of his performance. He then took a deep breath and replicated his roar. It sounded even louder than Kineosho's and the audience, including Basho and Viddi, laughed out loudly and cheered the mantis on. Kineosho, however, was shocked. He barely managed to let out a politely muffled titter.

When the show ended, they all talked about it enthusiastically. Well, everyone did, except for Kineosho. Suddenly he felt as though his achievement was not as great as he had originally thought.

When the mantis's roar came up afterwards, Viddi recounted the full story of the talent show to the frogs. She clearly made Kineosho out to be the hero, and he felt a little better. Still, as they were falling asleep that night, Kineosho found himself wondering if that was the reason why Basho seemed indifferent to his performance.

"It was more than the roar anyway. I was very brave to face those foxes like that," he told himself as he drifted off into sleep.

❧ 16 ❧

Trouble in paradise

An excited Viddi sneaked off with Kineosho's magic sack early the next morning and went to visit her colourful new frog friends at the pond. After a few laughs with them, she enthusiastically collected a few suitable mementos that would remind her of their evening together and the superb Braying Mantis show.

When she returned, Kineosho and Basho were both ready to continue exploring. Not long after they set off, they came across a rhino pushing an enormous boulder that was easily five times his size. They all stood and stared at him in amazement.

"Do you think that's the rhino that Lucky was telling us about?" asked Viddi curiously.

Before Kineosho could answer, they heard the rhino suddenly burst out sobbing. As though by pure reflex, Viddi immediately leapt onto the rhino and began to rub his head. This tickled the surprised rhino and he laughed hesitantly.

"Why are you crying?" asked Kineosho. "You must be the strongest creature in the jungle!"

"So what?" replied the rhino sadly. "Big deal . . ."

"So, you can move mountains!" said Kineosho, pointing at the huge boulder.

"So what?" replied the rhino, shaking his head despondently as he looked off the path into the forest. "I need to find the Angel's Trident and it seems I've been walking around in circles for days now."

"The Angel's Trident?" asked Kineosho curiously. "What's that?"

"I don't know, but it's obviously very secretive and powerful," replied the rhino. "Before I went to the talent show, I met a calm creature who seemed to know a lot about this place. She told me that she was going to find the Angel's Trident so she could get all her questions answered. We left the talent show many moons ago but I didn't have any questions at the time, so I didn't follow her to look for it. Besides, I was quite happy enjoying the splendour of the new forest."

"So what happened then?" asked Kineosho. "Did you see the Braying Mantis show near the pond?"

"Or the frogs?" added Viddi enthusiastically.

"Braying Mantis? No. And no frogs either," replied the rhino, a little confused. "One day though, I saw these ants — lots and lots of ants. I was just walking about as usual and I accidentally tripped. When I was on the ground, I saw these ants marching towards their anthill. Each ant was carrying something — nuts, leaves, stones — all different things. I thought it would be funny so I put my foot in their path but they just went around it. Well, all except for one ant. He leapt up onto my horn and started scolding me.

"'You think you're strong so you can just do whatever you feel like, you big lunk?' shouted the ant from the tip of my horn. He was still carrying a relatively large stone. I remember replying yes and arrogantly laughing at him. And that's when he said some things that have been tormenting me ever since."

"An ant brought you to this state?" asked Kineosho in disbelief. "What did he say?"

"Well, first the ant said that he was much stronger than I was — to which I, of course, simply laughed. Then the ant looked up at the stone he was carrying, smiled and said: 'Firstly, this stone may look small to you, but it's about 50 times my own body weight — there's no way you could even lift half of that! And secondly, even if you were as strong as me . . . *so what?*'

"That question has been haunting me ever since," continued the rhino. "So I've got to find the Angel's Trident . . . and soon, before it drives me spiking mad," he said as he turned around and began to wander back into the forest.

"Wait!" shouted Basho suddenly behind him. Kineosho followed with surprising urgency and repeated the call. Then he darted in front of the rhino and said, "We're exploring the forest, why don't you join us and perhaps we can . . . help you find it?"

The rhino paused for a moment and agreed. He had been roaming alone for quite some time already and he hoped that the company would help. Viddi leapt on his back with her usual eagerness and Kineosho felt curiously calmer than he had been since the comedy show at the pond.

"What's your name?" asked Viddi, clearly delighted that the rhino was joining them.

"Rhino," replied the rhino.

"Just Rhino?" asked Kineosho.

"Yes — and why does everyone keep asking me that?" asked Rhino, sounding a little irked.

Kineosho asked Rhino if he knew anything about where the Angel's Trident was so that they could continue their journey in the correct direction.

"Well, before we entered the talent show, she told me it's on the way to a beautiful waterfall and that all animals find it when they need to — that's all I know. I've asked a number of animals already but I keep getting pointed in different directions," replied Rhino.

"Let's continue on the path we're on — we know it's not behind us otherwise we would have noticed it," suggested Basho.

Rhino agreed. He felt a little less upset now that he had found some company for his mission. The troop continued for a long time without encountering any animals who knew about the waterfall.

The following morning, Kineosho woke up sometime before dawn and found Basho still awake and busy filing his nails. Basho kept repeating softly to himself: "Hmm . . . *so what* if you're so strong? *So what?* How interesting . . ." Kineosho hushed Basho and went back to sleep.

Later that day, when they continued on their journey, Viddi got bored walking and happily began picking small flowers by the wayside. She carefully braided them into her hair all the way down to her tail.

"You look very jazzy!" laughed Rhino.

"Thanks!" said Viddi and immediately leapt onto Rhino's back. "Wanna smell, wanna smell?" she insisted, waving the end of her tail around the rhino's nose.

Rhino tried frantically to avoid Viddi's tail getting into his nostrils. Finally, it was just too much. He rose uncontrollably on his hind feet in build-up, and let out a gargantuan sneeze. It launched Viddi flying high into the air.

While in mid-flight, Viddi's attention was distracted by some gorgeous colours radiating off the side of a mountain. She then tumbled down to the ground after bouncing off a couple of trees and landed squarely in front of Kineosho and Basho. They were both laughing themselves silly.

"There are all these pretty colours exploding out of that mountainside!" said Viddi passionately after she had recovered and everyone had collected themselves. She clasped Kineosho's ear and tugged at it, pointing in the direction of the colours.

"What kind of exploding colours, Viddi?" asked Kineosho.

"Well, I remember there was red, then orange, then yellow, then green, then blue, then — *ummm* . . ." replied Viddi.

"That sounds like a rainbow!" said Kineosho.

"And it's a clear day out — I think we may well have found our waterfall!" said Basho. "Let's head towards the exploding colours!"

Viddi pointed again and Rhino charged off the path into the forest, making a trail for the others to follow. Eventually, they reached an already-formed path in their direction and they decided to follow it.

Whilst walking, they encountered numerous animals who were already on the path or were about to join it from different directions. There were animals travelling solo, some in couples, and even some with their young. Kineosho asked some of the animals what they had done in the talent show, and how they wound up walking in that direction. The stories of their achievements fascinated him and their accounts of how they ended up looking for the Angel's Trident seemed even more incredible.

As they continued, Kineosho wondered about the logistics of it all. How big was the trident? Did each animal get to ask it a question and then pass the trident on to the next animal? Would there be a powerful creature protecting it? Could he only ask one question? He wondered if there would be a deep, mysterious voice answering each question, or whether it would be a squeaky one. Despite the slew of unanswered questions, the fact that he was heading towards something made him feel like he had a sense of purpose. He felt peculiarly happy, as did the rhino.

❦ 17 ❧

The Angel's Trident

After a couple of days of walking through mountainous terrain, the animals were weary. Late that afternoon, they heard the waterfall, and that encouraged them to press onward.

As they did, Kineosho heard some rustling in a nearby bush scarcely off the path. Then he heard something whispering at him: "*Pssst* . . . hey cat!" Kineosho looked at Basho who just shrugged his shoulders in reply.

"Who's there?" asked Kineosho.

"I know what you're looking for . . . and I can help you!" said the somewhat unpleasant, yet familiar sounding voice.

Kineosho looked at the others and signalled them to follow as he approached the bush. When he was close to it, a dirty hand grabbed his paw and pulled him behind the bush.

"You! What—what—do you want?" stuttered Kineosho nervously when he saw that the scaly hand belonged to the largest of his crocodile initiators.

Three heads immediately popped up around the bush to see who had Kineosho spooked like that.

Viddi and Basho looked equally spooked but Rhino simply glared at the crocodile and bellowed: "Yes, what do *you* want?"

The crocodile visibly cringed and backed away a little. He was obviously concerned that he had misjudged the situation. "Wait, wait—I've changed, I swear. I know I was mean to you before but I just want to make up for it—honest. I know what you're looking for and I have it—the Angel's Trident!"

"Really!" said Rhino excitedly as he approached the crocodile with Viddi still on his back. "You have it?"

Kineosho looked at Basho who shook his head slightly. Without any hesitation he leapt towards Rhino and Viddi, and whispered something to them. They both nodded.

"Can we see it?" asked Rhino, making a concerted effort not to sound too excited.

"Of course, it's right over there—behind those far bushes. I left it there for safety," said the crocodile, pointing away from the path. "Follow me!" he said a bit more confidently as he began walking away.

Kineosho nodded to Viddi, and she instantly leapt up into a tree and raced ahead in the same direction as the crocodile, passing him. When she spotted a wooden trident sticking out of some bushes, and none of the other crocodiles around, she immediately reached down and grabbed it. She leapt back into the tree and returned to the others. Before the crocodile realised what had happened, he found himself unable to move and was yelping his lungs out. That, incidentally, tends to be quite a common reaction with crocodiles when they have a giant rhino thumping his foot down on their tails.

Viddi handed the trident over to Kineosho. Basho sniffed at it carefully and whispered something into Kineosho's ear.

"Looks like you did have the Angel's Trident after all—sorry we didn't trust you. You can understand, I'm sure . . ." said

Kineosho apologetically. "What is your good name?"

The crocodile mumbled as he shed some huge tears: "Just no faith in goodness in the world these days. It's Al. My name is Honest Al. I can't believe you think I haven't changed after all this time . . ."

Rhino looked at Kineosho, a little confused as to whether or not he should release his foothold. Kineosho shook his head and smiled as he walked towards the crocodile with the wooden trident.

"So then, how does this work?" asked Kineosho. "I just ask the trident, and it will answer all my questions?"

"*Erm*—yes . . ." replied the crocodile hesitantly. "But—it takes time and great skill. I can show you how if you could just get Spike here to ease up a little on the tail."

"Let me give it a try first and see if I can," said Kineosho as he rested the three sharp spokes of the trident on the crocodile's hand. "Okay, my first question is: Oh great Angel's Trident, please could you tell me if you are the real trident?"

After a brief pause, they heard a soft, squeaky, "Yes, I am."

"I didn't hear that—what did you say, dear Angel's Trident?" asked Kineosho, suddenly putting his full weight behind the trident, causing the crocodile to shriek in pain.

"NO!" yelled the crocodile and Kineosho released some of the pressure.

"But you will still help us answer all the questions honestly, right . . . dear Trident?" asked Kineosho as he reapplied his weight to the trident.

"YES!" yelped the crocodile.

"So, where is the real trident?" asked Rhino, taking the opportunity to help Kineosho and in the process flattening the crocodile's tail.

"There is no trident! It's not a thing—it's a place!" shrieked the crocodile. "Please, no more," begged Honest Al. "I'll answer anything you want."

"Okay, tell us about the place then," said Kineosho, signalling to Rhino to raise his foot slightly.

The crocodile sighed and took a deep breath. "If you continue on the path you were on you'll reach a clearing that has three exits—*trident*, get it?"

"Go on," said Kineosho.

"Well, the first exit takes you to the river. There is a banyan tree but you need to be really careful. That path is nasty—it may look peaceful when you first arrive but you will experience the worst of demons. Not all animals return from there, and those who do—well, they come out terrified."

"And the second exit?" asked Rhino.

"That takes you to the bottom of the waterfall—the water is lovely and warm and there's a lot of singing. A lot of animals go there first," replied Honest Al promptly.

"Where does the third one take you?" asked Viddi, quite entertained by the options.

"That takes you to the top of the waterfall—it's a long climb but it is supposed to be really beautiful. There are lots of interesting things to do there, I hear, but I've never been there—on account of my bad knee and all. I swear, that's all I know," said the crocodile.

"Now how about giving back my gold coins?" asked Kineosho sternly, applying pressure on the trident again.

"Please wait! I will!" shrieked the crocodile as he used one hand to rummage in a pouch on his belly. "But I only have two of the coins left! I used one of them to, *erm*—facilitate my way through the talent show."

Kineosho took the coins, raised the wooden trident, and broke it in two. "Let's go," he said, as he headed back towards the path.

"You go on ahead, I'll catch up with you in a while—Honest Al and I have still got some unfinished business to take care of here," said Rhino.

"*Noooo!* Please! Don't leave me alone with him," wailed the terrified crocodile as they left.

Kineosho, Viddi, and Basho heard some loud thuds and shrieks behind them as they rejoined the main path. After a short while, there was silence, followed by what sounded like rather polite conversation. Then, there was a torturous shriek before the rhino finally reappeared from behind the bushes. Rhino shook himself to look a bit tidier.

"There, now I feel much better," said Rhino.

"Obviously you've got some history with Honest Al . . . I'm curious—what did they do to you? There is no way they could have beaten you—not even ten of them together!" said Kineosho.

"Beat me? No! They made me drowsy with some fermented cactus juice and then tried to saw off my horn—for medicinal purposes, they said. If it weren't for my dear elephant friend who saved me I'd have been one hornless rhino!" exclaimed Rhino.

Rhino called Viddi aside and gave her what looked like a large white tooth. "Here you go—a lucky charm for you!" She accepted it happily and put it in the magic sack which had become quite the storage depot for her.

Viddi jumped onto Kineosho's back, thrilled with their victory over the crocodile. She promptly fell asleep as they continued their journey towards the Angel's Trident.

Not long afterwards, they reached a massive clearing. There was no doubt that they had arrived at their destination if what

Honest Al had said were true. Tall trees surrounded the clearing, and the three paths out of it, although not close to each other, were distinct. There were hundreds of animals of different species but the clearing was huge, and it could certainly have accommodated many more.

"Now where do we go from here . . . shall we look around?" Kineosho asked Basho.

"I don't know about you, but Al told me that my elephant friend is in there," interrupted Rhino, pointing his horn at the third exit. "I'll see you all later—I can't wait to meet her again!"

"Hope you find what you're looking for," said Kineosho, as Rhino stormed off towards the edge of the clearing.

Kineosho, Basho, and Viddi wandered around the clearing and spoke to a few animals. It turned out that Honest Al had been surprisingly honest. Those who had been down the second path were keen to explore the third and those from the third, the second. There were only a few animals outside the first path, and those that were there all looked a little shaken.

"I wonder what could be so scary?" Kineosho asked Basho.

"I'm not sure but I think you need to find out," replied Basho. "I have a feeling that exit is the most important one for us. It's late now though, so why don't we rest here and you can check it out tomorrow—it'll probably be safer during the day anyway."

❧ 18 ❧

The first time's a killer

The following morning Kineosho, Basho, and Viddi walked to the entrance of the first path. When they arrived, they found an old black bull kneeling in front of the entrance and they were unable to pass.

"Do we need to give you something to get in?" asked Kineosho.

"No baggage allowed," said the black bull, pointing at the sack Viddi was holding.

"Why don't I go and check it out? You can stay out here and look after Viddi until I get back," said Kineosho to Basho.

Basho agreed a little reluctantly and Kineosho asked the black bull if he could enter.

"Without your jackal? That's very brave, Kineosho," said the black bull.

"How . . . How did you know my name? Do I know you?" asked Kineosho nervously.

"You may enter," replied the black bull, completely ignoring Kineosho's questions. "Remember, no light reveals some dark realities," he added cryptically.

Kineosho cautiously walked through the tunnel of trees behind the black bull, and arrived at an unexpectedly tranquil scene. There was a river flowing gently in the distance, and everything else seemed pleasantly soft, and green. He noticed that there was an old banyan tree on a small hill near the river, and he started walking towards it. There were no other animals in sight. As Kineosho walked, he wondered what all the fuss was about. He did not find the place very scary at all—in fact, he felt very calm and relaxed there.

When he arrived at the banyan tree, he suddenly felt very tired. He yawned and laid his head down near the foot of the tree. As he shut his eyes, the voice of the black bull echoed in his head: "No light reveals some dark realities." He fell asleep.

Kineosho woke up some time later. Half asleep, he stretched and decided to return to the Angel's Trident to call Basho and Viddi. When he looked around, it was clear that night had already fallen. The moon was full and bright and its reflection on the river looked peculiar. He tried to find the exit, but it was confusing as things looked quite different in the moonlight.

Suddenly, Kineosho heard some whispering voices not far behind him. He dashed behind the banyan tree and tried to spot who it was. It was hard to see in the dark though, but the voices drew closer until he could hear what they were saying.

"I can't believe we fell for a roar—when we catch that lion I'm going to skin him alive!" said one voice.

"And then that stupid rabbit and the monkey too!" said another. Then Kineosho heard the sharpening of knives—it was the same sound he had heard in the talent show when the foxes had Lucky tied up on stage.

"But how did they get here?" thought Kineosho anxiously, his heart beating faster.

Then he heard three more voices approaching from another direction. "When I geff def lion, I am gonna kif him," said one of the new voices, sounding as though some of his front teeth had been forcibly extracted by a large rhino.

"Oh no, it's the crocodiles!" thought Kineosho, beginning to panic. He looked around but the forest was black and there was no sign of the exit. He knew that if he stayed there, either the foxes or the crocodiles would find him. Out of options, Kineosho ran as fast as he could towards the river. "I can easily out-swim them all if I can just get to the river," he thought.

By the time he reached the riverbank, the pleasant reflection of the moon in the river had turned into a horrible, wrinkly face glaring at him. As soon as he put one paw into the water, the current became violent and a whirlpool formed instantly around his paw. Kineosho was just able to withdraw his paw from the water in time. The face of the moon in the river now looked positively evil.

In the meantime, both the foxes and the crocodiles had spotted him running and they had begun running towards the river too. Unable to go into the river, Kineosho ran as fast as he could along it, away from the banyan tree. As he ran, the moon faded behind some thick clouds, and it became absolutely black.

Suddenly, he heard a vicious roar coming from the direction he was running in. It was louder than anything he had ever heard. Before he could gather what was happening, he saw a large creature with piercing red eyes appear from the darkness. It started walking straight towards him. As it drew closer, Kineosho saw the form of a ferocious, dark lion become clearer. It roared at him again and Kineosho felt the vibration penetrate his very skeleton.

Shocked, Kineosho scrambled backwards. By then the foxes and crocodiles were right behind him. He was surrounded and could not escape. Loud roars, knife-clanging, and growling overwhelmed his senses. The last thing Kineosho remembered as he helplessly leapt back was the fierce dark lion pouncing towards him as he tripped over a crocodile. He blacked out.

When Kineosho woke, his immediate reaction was to leap back in fear. He found himself slamming against the banyan tree. He was breathing deeply and his heart was pounding so hard that he could hear it. The sun was still out and the scene as peaceful as ever.

"It was just a dream," he told himself aloud. "Just a dream," he sighed and laughed nervously in relief. He paused for a moment to collect himself.

When he stood up, he felt an incredibly sharp pain on his side. It was the side towards which the dark lion was pouncing, before he woke up from his dream. It was the same side that had hit the banyan tree. When he looked, he saw a massive cut and found that entire side of his body smeared with blood. "It was just a dream, Kineosho—you probably got cut when you hit your side against the tree," he said to himself aloud, as he limped towards the exit as quickly as he could.

The black bull ignored him when he came out and Kineosho collapsed outside the entrance. Some of the other animals who were hovering nearby, debating whether to go in, rushed to his aid. They took him aside and tried to revive him. Viddi, who had been entertaining the crowd with some silly antics and stories, quickly arrived at the scene, as did Basho.

Viddi burst into tears when she saw Kineosho's side oozing with blood. She jumped over the crowd and held him around his neck, rubbing his forehead vigorously. But Kineosho did not awake.

"The ladybug with the sewing needle," shouted Basho. "Viddi, find the sewing ladybug from the talent show!"

Viddi wanted to move but found that she just couldn't let go of Kineosho. All the noise around her with animals yelling suggestions scared her even more. Basho didn't know what to do as nobody else seemed to hear him.

"What's going on here?" said a deep voice from above the crowd. All the animals looked up and saw a tall giraffe wearing a collar of bright red leaves.

"It's the lion, he went in there — and was obviously attacked by the demons!" shouted a lively mole from below. She wore an unusual bonnet that was made from dried, blackened leaves. It almost fell off as she leaped manically around Kineosho.

"It looks like he's still bleeding from the attack," said the giraffe, coming in a little closer to examine the body. "Quick, get Sosa!" he commanded the small mole, who almost instantly disappeared into the crowd. A few moments later, a ladybug appeared with her shiny silver needle and the giraffe cleared the crowd, allowing her to patch up the lion's gaping wound. After she had completed her stitching, the mole with the black bonnet placed a dressing of soothing wet leaves on Kineosho's body.

"When will you savages learn, *that* is not the path," said the giraffe, shaking his head in disbelief. "Let them recover and we can check on them later," he said, as he walked towards the second exit of the Angel's Trident. The crowd cheered and a few of them even followed the giraffe, fascinated by his commanding presence.

Kineosho, Viddi, and Basho curled up together tightly and slept, dead to the world.

Much time passed, and the giraffe returned. When he did, Kineosho was awake, albeit a bit groggy. Viddi and Basho were still asleep next to him. The animals had just been telling

Kineosho how a giraffe had commanded his rescue and the story sounded quite fantastic.

"Are you okay?" asked the giraffe in his most medical voice.

Kineosho looked up slowly, and to his surprise he found a most welcome, familiar face. "Twigs?" he replied.

"Kineosho? Viddi! How could I not have recognised you!" said Twigs in disbelief. "How are you feeling?"

"A little weak but yes, alive—and much better, thank you Twigs!" replied Kineosho. The animals around them cheered loudly as though they too had just been resurrected. The noise soon woke up Viddi and Basho.

"Well I must insist you come with me to our home and fully recover there—you'll love it!" said Twigs as he turned around.

The crowd parted for Twigs, and Kineosho, Viddi, Basho, and many of the other animals followed him to the second path out of the Angel's Trident.

☙ 19 ❧

Order of the Black Bonnet

The entrance tunnel of the second path was similar to the one that Kineosho had walked through before. He felt a lot more comfortable that he was not entering alone this time. When he emerged on the other side, he found himself on the edge of an enormous garden that was bursting with colour. It was also a lot busier than the tranquil scene with the banyan tree.

They could hear the force of the waterfall close by and there were many animals walking around. Things appeared to be very organised and all the animals were going about their tasks with some vigour. Unlike the first path, there were well-defined walkways lined with neatly designed, multi-coloured flower beds.

"Welcome to our home," said Twigs cheerfully. "Come, let me show you around."

As they followed Twigs through various picturesque avenues, Viddi could not resist the temptation to pluck a few pretty, pink flowers to braid into her hair. In an instant, a mole with a black bonnet leapt out from Twigs's entourage and slapped Viddi's hand gently. "That's not allowed," he whispered sternly into her ear, before stepping back into the entourage.

Twigs led them to a large open-air auditorium next to a lake. It was elegantly designed and it almost seemed as though the surrounding trees grew in a particular way to accommodate the aesthetics of the area. At one end of the auditorium, on the side closest to the lake, there was a slightly elevated platform. "That's where we have our daily meeting sessions," said Twigs. "We'll meet here again in the evening and I'll tell you more. For now, let me take you to the most wonderful place here!"

He led them to a neat path that went all around that side of the lake — like a promenade. After quite a distance, they reached the bottom of the waterfall.

"The area immediately under the waterfall is reserved for some special events so you can't go there right now," said Twigs, pointing to the two black-bonneted moles zealously guarding a twine barrier. "For now, feel free to relax here and enjoy the water. Have fun and we can meet at the auditorium just before sunset, okay?"

Viddi in particular was fascinated with the place and couldn't wait to leap into the water. Kineosho held her back, dipped one paw cautiously into the water, and withdrew it quickly.

"It's okay, Kineosho, what you see here is what you think it is — there is no reason to be afraid," said Twigs, spotting his hesitation.

"I'll be fine — I think I'm just tired," replied Kineosho.

"Of course you will! See you later then," said Twigs as he walked off with his entourage.

Viddi jumped into the water and splashed around like a mad monkey. Half wet already, Kineosho relaxed. He was relieved that there were no whirlpools or angry faces in the lake glaring back at him.

"Some place, isn't it?" asked Basho.

"Very different from the first path, that's for sure," replied Kineosho.

"So . . . what happened in there? We were all quite scared, you know," asked Basho.

Kineosho paused for a moment and replied: "I'd rather not talk about it if you don't mind—it was too horrible for words. The worst experience I've ever had. I'm never going back there again! Never!"

There was a brief silence, which Viddi swiftly interrupted by waging a water war with some of the other animals playing in the lake. "Why don't you leave the sack here and go help her out. I'll look after it," said Basho, stepping back a few paces to avoid the splashing water.

Bar a few remaining aches and pains, it didn't take long for Kineosho to forget about his recent traumatic experience. He thoroughly enjoyed playing in the water. Viddi had discovered she could use her long and short arms together in an awkward way while she was spinning around to generate enormous splashes. After some intense tidal wave creation, they both came out of the water and rested on the bank, exhausted.

They were soon joined by a small hippo and his little jackal friend—neither of them had had so much fun before.

"I could just fall asleep right here," said Kineosho.

"Oh no," replied the small hippo, "it's not long till sunset and we'll soon have to go to the Great Hall."

"The Great Hall? You mean the auditorium we saw earlier with Twigs?" asked Kineosho.

"Yes," nodded the hippo, "with Elder Twigs."

"So what happens at the Great Hall?" Basho asked the small jackal.

"Oh, it's wonderful!" he replied. "There are songs and chanting and lovely food—"

"—then Elder Twigs talks to us all and reminds us of the rules. Then we go and sleep," continued the hippo.

"And you do this at every sunset?" asked Kineosho.

"Oh yes, we do it three times every day actually. Whenever Elder Twigs rings the bell," said the little hippo.

Viddi, a little bored with the conversation, leant over and tickled the small hippo, making him squeal hysterically. He began rolling around on the bank and soon Kineosho joined in, making him squeal even louder.

"Kilo!" shouted a shrill voice from behind them. It was another mole wearing a black bonnet. She shook her finger and her head in unison and uttered: "Tsk, tsk, tsk . . ."

"*Oooer*, I think you guys had better stop before we get into trouble," said Kilo. "Besides, look, it's almost sunset—we should head towards the Great Hall now . . . If that's okay, ma'am?" Kilo asked the mole.

"Move along then," ordered the black-bonneted mole firmly.

As they walked towards the Great Hall, they heard the loud ring of a bell that startled Viddi. She leapt onto Kineosho's back and they continued.

By the time they reached the auditorium, Viddi was asleep. Kineosho was surprised to see so many animals gathered outside—the amount of chatter was mind-boggling. He heard about a wildebeest's flatulence problem, and a second later, about a gazelle's exterior design challenge.

The animals queued up at the entrance of the auditorium and entered in single file. As they entered, they dipped their feet in some water and one of the cranes standing nearby wrapped their heads in white cloth before allowing them in.

"Ah, there you are, Kineosho!" said another black-bonneted mole. "Elder Twigs sent me to make sure you found your way here all right. I see you've met Kilo already—that's good. Just follow the line and do as the others do."

Kineosho looked at Basho who just shrugged his shoulders. When they reached the entrance, they each dipped their feet in the water trough. As soon as they did, one mole would pour out the dirty water from the trough and another would refill it using a giant coconut shell. Of course, Viddi found this quite amusing. As soon as she dipped her feet, and the mole replaced the water, she happily dipped her feet again, splashing as she did so. Within an instant the water in the trough was replaced and as she was about to do it again they heard a loud, stern voice ordering them to *Move along!*

Kineosho yanked Viddi's arm and they moved through the process. A crane wrapped Kineosho's head in white cloth and pushed him along. Getting the cloth wrapped around Viddi's head proved to be a lot more difficult than the crane had anticipated. It eventually took two cranes to hold her down and another to do the turban wrapping. Finally, they all entered the auditorium in single file. Viddi tried desperately to remove her white head-wrap but found it surprisingly difficult to do so.

The atmosphere inside the auditorium was completely different to outside. Not a single animal said a word, and each had taken its seat with its own kind. A black-bonneted mole rushed up to Kineosho and led them to a demarcated area close to the front of the stage. There they joined a mixture of animals, all of whom looked a little confused about what they were supposed to do.

"They're probably new here too," whispered Basho softly to Kineosho. He nodded in agreement before casting a glare at

Viddi. She was bored and had begun to use her fingers to fidget and make strange noises with her lips.

Once all the animals had entered and were seated, one of the black-bonneted moles walked onto the stage and announced: "Friends of the House of Peace, please rise now to welcome Elder Twigs." All the animals in the auditorium stood up and applauded as Twigs walked onto the stage. His head was wrapped in red cloth and the matching red leaves around his neck seemed even brighter than before.

"Thank you all—please be seated," said Twigs. "Welcome to our new followers seated here in front—I hope you have been made to feel at home over the course of the day. For your benefit, as we do at each meeting, I ask that all our friends present here recite the rules of our path together with me to start off our evening." Twigs looked around the hall briefly. "Meso! Won't you do the honours of leading tonight," continued Twigs, pointing at a chubby young wildebeest in the herd sitting to the left of the stage.

Meso stood up and waddled to the front of the auditorium with a huge smile on his face. He coughed to clear his throat and then began: "Wool number one—Thou shalt attend at the Gweat Hall twee times a day at the wing of the bell." No sooner had he completed the first rule than the entire audience repeated: "Rule number one—Thou shalt attend at the Great Hall three times a day at the ring of the bell."

"Wool number two—Thou shalt not fight or eat each other," said Meso. The audience started repeating the rule before Meso had even finished. "Wool number twee—Thou shalt always obey all orders of he who wears the wed collar." Again, the audience repeated the rule. By the fourth rule, the audience were saying it along with Meso.

"Wool number four — Clawed fwends shall twim their claws at each half cycle of the full moon. Wool number five — Thou shalt maintain silence in the Gweat Hall and never enter without a head covewing. Wool number six — Thou shalt observe the woutine pwescwibed by an Elder. Wool number seven — Thou shalt complete the duties of your wole as assigned without question. Wool number eight — Thou shalt never engage in actions that annoy the Gweat Banyan Twee. Wool number nine — Thou shalt help each other if a fwend has lost his way. Wool number ten — Thou shalt spwead the love and encouwage more fwends to join our path so the fowest will be a happier place. The end!" said Meso with some flair.

"Well done Meso! Let's give him a cheer!" said Twigs. All the animals in the auditorium applauded as Meso walked back to the rest of the wildebeest herd.

"Now our new friends may wonder why we have these wools, I mean rules," said Twigs as the audience laughed. He cleared his throat and continued in the most engaging preacher-like tone: "To lead a happy life, we need consistency and order — a solid foundation. Now that is not to say that everything will remain the same. As you all well know things are always changing. We have the rules to give us some roots to hold on to — to see us through our rough patches. The rules have been passed down from generation to generation to protect us from ourselves and to help us all live in harmony."

"If we deviate from these rules, the Great Banyan Tree from whom all rules originate will be annoyed and it will punish us all — remember the storm in which we lost so many of our friends and family? And when the earth shook? Those of you who have experienced the power of the Banyan Tree first-hand will need no further explanation," said Twigs, looking directly at Kineosho who nodded hesitantly. The animals around him immediately nodded, taking Kineosho's action as validation.

"And now, enough of the serious—let us rejoice and invite our special choir to sing a song of praise in honour of the Great Banyan Tree so that it may bless us with health and happiness," said Twigs as he walked off the stage. After a moment's silence, they heard a clap and a group of fireflies shone their lights above the stage. Much to Viddi's delight, she saw the platypus and the duck choir appear as though by magic. After another clap, a second set of fireflies shone their lights on another part of the stage containing a variety of animals with some weird and wonderful instruments. There were flutes made from bamboo shoots, drums made from hollowed out calabashes and even an intricate-looking harp made from wood and fine twine. The audience applauded.

The unlikely musicians began their composition. Initially the mood was sombre—just the sound of the harp, the flutes, and a soft hum from the choir. The crowd relaxed. Slowly, the music flowed in crescendo and the audience was totally captivated. By the time the conductor introduced the percussion, the tempo had really picked up and many of the animals in the audience were entranced. The choir could not have fit the music better. Some of the animals around Kineosho even began dancing with their eyes closed. "Close your eyes too and nobody will see you," whispered Basho to Kineosho.

It wasn't long before Kineosho too became entranced with the music and found himself dancing with his eyes shut. He enjoyed every beat and note he heard. The words were in some foreign-sounding language, but there was frequent mention of the Great Banyan Tree. Although he didn't understand the words, Kineosho was captivated. It was like nothing he had experienced before.

After some time the tempo wound down and the audience relaxed once more. Many shook their heads positively in acknowledgement and a few uttered some involuntary sounds of appreciation. Viddi was more fidget-free than she had ever been. The experience had taken her aback too. At the end of the performance, the audience cheered and Kineosho let out an enormous roar of appreciation. The platypus turned around and bowed gracefully before taking his leave with the other performers.

One of the black-bonneted moles came onto the stage and announced that the holy dinner would be served outside the auditorium shortly, thanks be to the Great Banyan Tree. She requested everyone to eat well before leaving. The feast that followed outside was delicious. There were many different colours and sizes of cabbits, and the crowd mingled and chatted in melodious cacophony.

Kineosho spotted Twigs and approached him after the meal. "That was the most moving experience," said Kineosho, still feeling light-headed after the performance.

"I'm glad you enjoyed it, Kineosho," replied Twigs with a smile. "Rest well now and I'll send Kilo to fetch you tomorrow morning at sunrise."

✦ 20 ✦

Another day in paradise

Early the next morning, Kilo arrived to find Kineosho and Viddi already awake and talking about the events of the previous evening.

"The sun is almost up, we should head to the Great Hall," said Kilo cheerfully when he heard the giant bell ringing loudly in the distance.

"So what happens in the morning at the Great Hall?" asked Kineosho eagerly as he followed Kilo. "Is there another concert?"

"No, that usually happens only in the evenings," replied Kilo. "In the morning we recite the rules and then do lots of exercise to prepare us for the day ahead. Exercise is one of the most important parts of our daily routine, Elder Twigs always says."

The morning air outside the auditorium smelt fresh and there were as many animals queuing outside to get in as the night before. They dipped their feet in the water and Viddi resisted the temptation to mess with the black-bonneted trough moles again. She was also quite curious as to what was going to happen in the auditorium that morning. Before they went through their ritual head-wrapping routine this time, the cranes gave them each two smaller coconut shells filled with drinking water. Then, they entered the Great Hall, and were quietly escorted to their seats at the front of the auditorium.

The rising sun behind the stage cast a meditative glow over the audience. In a repeat performance of the previous evening, one of the black-bonneted moles walked onto the stage and announced: "Friends of the House of Peace, please rise now to welcome Elder Twigs." All the animals in the auditorium stood up, but this time remained silent as Twigs walked onto the stage.

"Thank you—please be seated," said Twigs. "The morning, as always, is a time for reflection and preparation for the day ahead." Twigs looked around the room and this time called on Kilo to lead the recitation. Kilo cheerfully left the hippo section, and acknowledged Kineosho on his way up to the stage. He promptly rattled off the ten rules of the path and the audience repeated them in similar fashion to the night before.

"Thank you Kilo," said Twigs as Kilo walked back to his seat, pleased with his flawless recital. "And now, let us observe some silence to clear our minds until the sun rises fully."

All the animals maintained pin-drop silence. Kineosho and Viddi looked at each other as they both remembered their morning meditation sessions with Master Wu. They wondered how long it had been since they had broken that routine. Even Basho felt a calmness come over him.

After some time, Kineosho started drifting away in thought and he felt the lightest of taps on his head. He opened his eyes, a little startled. It was Twigs, who simply nodded and signalled him to stay silent and continue. The silence lingered pleasantly for some time until Twigs said softly: "Very slowly now, open your eyes." He remained quiet until all the animals had done so.

"Please take a few deep breaths, enjoy your breakfast outside, take some time for yourselves, and then take a brisk walk to meet me near the waterfall," said Twigs.

When the animals left the auditorium, they found an enormous spread of cabbits and fruit — even bigger than the one they had seen the night before. After the meal, many disappeared into the bushes. Kilo looked a little embarrassed and whispered something into Kineosho's ear. "Oh, really!" replied Kineosho, as Kilo disappeared into the bushes himself.

"Apparently taking some time for yourself over here means taking a potty break!" said Kineosho laughingly to Basho.

A short while later Kineosho, Basho, and Viddi began their long, brisk walk to the base of the waterfall. When everyone from the auditorium had arrived, Elder Twigs called them all to attention. "Now stand an arm's length away from each other in nice straight lines. Today we're going to learn some new yoga stretching exercises."

Kineosho remembered Twigs's neck stretching to an incredible length when they were younger. Twigs did no such thing this time though. He showed the audience what to do from the elevated platform near the waterfall, and they followed as best they could. Some of the animals collapsed with the more difficult exercises. Kineosho was surprised at how out of breath he was, especially given that they were doing the exercises so slowly. With every conscious move Twigs made with his body, he announced whether the audience should be breathing in, breathing out, or holding their breath.

Despite getting tangled a few times with her uneven arms, Viddi thoroughly enjoyed the exercises. When Twigs had completed the routine, he thanked the Great Banyan Tree for teaching them these exercises to help them keep healthy. The audience echoed the thanks, repeating his words verbatim.

"And now, for those of you who don't have duties, Miss Karma will be telling you the story of the day in the shade over there," said Twigs, pointing at a large tree farther up the bank of the lake. Some of the animals, particularly the younger ones, cheered and sprinted off to get a good seat under the tree.

"You should go too, Kineosho," said Twigs, "I think you'll enjoy it—Miss Karma is one of the best storytellers I've met!"

Kineosho, Viddi, and Basho joined the other animals underneath the tree. Some time passed and all the animals continued to stare at the tree. Some of them began to chat.

"*Shhh . . .*" said the tree suddenly, startling many of the animals sitting under it.

"A talking tree?" whispered Kineosho to Basho. Basho shrugged and looked even more intently at the tree.

When all the animals were silent, the tree said: "Are you all ready for today's story?"

"Yes Miss Karma!" shouted the animals in response.

"Very well then," replied the tree. "Yesterday's story was about the importance of keeping your word and all the nasty things that could happen if you don't. Today's story is about how things are often not what they seem." As soon as the calm voice completed its sentence, its source, a large rainbow-coloured chameleon, suddenly morphed into visibility on the tree.

The animals were startled once more and cheered as Miss Karma slowly coloured herself back into a peaceful green. Viddi clapped at the neat magic trick.

"Today's story is about the monkey and the crocodile. Once upon a time, there lived a clever little monkey by a lakeside, not unlike the one you see behind you today. Much farther down the bank, lived a crocodile and his wife. Now in those days animals had not learnt how to farm our delicious cabbits yet. Things were quite different, and crocodiles then, if you didn't know, loved eating monkeys. These two crocodiles were no exception to that rule."

Viddi looked anxiously at Kineosho.

"So one afternoon," continued Miss Karma, "the wife crocodile told her husband that she would really like to have monkey heart for dinner the next day as she was tired of eating fish. The husband crocodile replied that he had tried to catch the monkey many times but he was always smart enough to get away.

"She was not impressed by the excuses and demanded that he use his cunning to trap the monkey somehow. That night the crocodile was pondering how to catch the monkey when suddenly he heard a couple of birds talking in a nearby tree.

"'Oh, this mango from that island in the lake is the best I've ever had!' said one bird.

"'I know — we're lucky that the lake is too deep for the monkeys to swim across and steal our fruit,' replied the other bird with a smile.

"'Hmm . . .' thought the crocodile. 'This could be just the opportunity I've been looking for!' He surprised the two birds by whacking his fishing stick against the branch they were sitting on and grabbed the mango as it fell.

"The next morning, the crocodile woke up early and set off towards the monkey's tree. When he arrived, he called out to the monkey and said, 'Mr Monkey, I've come to apologise for all the times I tried to eat you. I've turned over a new leaf and I hope we can be friends.'

"'Oh?' said the monkey suspiciously. 'And how can I trust that you are not trying to trick me now?'

"'I was visited by a holy llama last week and he showed me the error of my ways. He suggested I repent by doing good deeds to all those I have wronged in the past,' said the crocodile. 'So,' he continued, 'I've brought you this sweet mango from the island in the middle of the lake.'

"The monkey took the mango and after examining it intensely, peeled it, and ate it up. 'Thank you! That was certainly the most delicious mango I've ever eaten!' said the monkey.

"'I'm glad you enjoyed it!' replied the crocodile. 'There are plenty more on the island in the lake—and lots of other tasty fruit too!'

"'Hmm . . . too bad I can't swim. I'll never be able to get across the deep lake,' said the monkey.

"'Well, we're friends now, aren't we?' said the crocodile. 'Why don't you ride on my back and I'll take you across to the island?'

"'You have indeed turned over a new leaf, my friend!' said the monkey gleefully. He hopped onto the crocodile's back as the crocodile walked towards the lake and entered the water. When they were halfway between the lake shore and the island the crocodile slowly started to lower himself into the water.

"'Hey! What are you doing? Why are you going deeper—are you trying to scare me?' yelled the monkey anxiously.

"'Not at all, I'm trying to kill you!' replied the crocodile.

"'But why? I thought we were friends! What have I done?' asked the monkey.

"'Nothing!' said the crocodile. 'My wife wants to eat your heart, so I'm afraid I have no choice but to kill you.'

"The monkey remained silent for a brief moment and thought anxiously to himself: 'I had better think fast and smart otherwise this will really be the end of me!'

"Suddenly, the monkey started clapping his hands and laughing out loud, dancing on the crocodile's back.

"'Stop that you!' shouted the crocodile. 'What's so funny about dying?'

"'Hahaha! Hehehe! Oh dear crocodile, you had a really clever plan but the joke's on you this time, you silly ol' goose!'

"'What do you mean?' asked the crocodile, quite irritated with the monkey's laughter.

"'You may kill me, but you will never get my heart this way,' said the monkey. 'You see, we monkeys are very cautious about whom we give our hearts to. We *always* hide them away in a safe, secret place each morning before we venture out into the jungle. Didn't you know that?'

"'How was I to know?' replied the crocodile angrily, starting to shake his tail.

"'Never mind, turn back,' said the monkey getting even more concerned that he would get thrown off into the deep lake. 'Since you were kind enough to share that delicious mango with me, I will show you where my heart is so you don't get into trouble with your wife. Turn back now — do you see that tall tree on the lake shore near where I live?'

"'Of course I do,' replied the crocodile.

"'Well, I hide it under the second highest branch on that tree. Take me back and I'll give it to you to take to your wife,' said the monkey, sounding a little sad.

"'You will?' asked the crocodile.

"'Definitely,' replied the monkey. 'I understand you were just doing this to avoid upsetting your wife. And after all, we're still friends, aren't we?'

"The crocodile agreed and thought to himself: 'I guess this monkey's not that smart after all! Wait until I tell the wife this story!' He headed back to the lake shore near the monkey's home. No sooner had the crocodile set foot on the ground than the monkey leapt onto the crocodile's head and spring-boarded himself into the tree. He climbed high up into the branches and sighed deeply with relief.

"'*Oy!*' shouted the crocodile to the monkey. 'Where is your heart?'

"'I'd be dead if my heart were in the tree, you silly fool! There's no way you're getting it—or me—ever again!' replied the monkey.

"And so the monkey saved himself. The crocodile turned around, fuming, and cursing the monkey for outwitting him yet again. When he returned home and told his wife what had happened, she grabbed his fishing stick and beat him with it until he was black and blue," said Miss Karma, demonstrating the wife's actions with a broken branch against the tree. Finally, she smiled and took a somewhat dramatic bow in front of her audience.

The animals around the tree clapped joyfully. Viddi grinned as she cheered too, feeling as though she was certainly the hero of that tale.

"I hope you all learnt something from that story," said Miss Karma. "Never forget that brawn is no match for a sharp brain! And now it's almost time for the noon session at the Great Hall—we'll continue with a new story tomorrow." Almost instantly, Miss Karma vanished from the tree.

"That was great!" said Kineosho to Viddi. Basho was still staring intently at the tree trying to figure out where Miss Karma was. Suddenly Basho sprang forwards and looked behind the tree. Kineosho promptly followed and they both sniffed around, trying to see if they could figure out where Miss Karma had disappeared.

"Looking for something?" asked a voice behind them.

"Miss Karma!" said Kineosho as he turned around. "We were just wondering where you disappeared to."

"I find it's generally better to keep a low profile," replied Miss Karma. "Like the story about the donkey in tiger's skin if you know that one. Hmm . . . you really should run along to the Great Hall now—it's not good to break your routine. Why don't we speak a little later?" She quickly ambled off into the bushes without disappearing that time.

The animals chatted for a while about the story until they heard the noon bell ring for the Great Hall. They walked back and repeated their feet-dipping and head-wrapping ceremony before entering the auditorium. Elder Twigs was not there but one of the black-bonneted moles was on the stage, waiting for all the animals to settle down. There were noticeably fewer animals present in the auditorium for the noon session.

Viddi yawned as the mole proceeded to recite the rules in a bland, monotonous tone. After he had completed them, he tamely thanked the Great Banyan Tree for the meal they were about to receive and for keeping them clear of harm's way wherever they were.

Afterwards, Kineosho joined Kilo and some of his friends for a light lunch. "Where is the rest of your family?" he asked Kilo. "I noticed them cheering after you recited the rules this morning, but they are not here now."

"Ah, my father goes to perform his duties as a guard outside an important cave. And my brother and mom are guards too in other parts of the forest. Elder Twigs said that one day I'll be a big, strong guard too. They return in the evening each day in time for the Great Hall."

"I thought all animals had to attend the Great Hall three times a day—it's a rule, isn't it?" asked Basho curiously.

"Oh yes! But Elder Twigs says if we cannot attend because we are too far away, we can take a break wherever we are at that time and recite the rules and thank the Great Banyan Tree and we will still be protected and so it's like attending the Great Hall, even though they're not!" said Kilo, pausing to catch his breath.

After lunch, they headed back to the lake for some fun in the water. Kineosho came onto the shore after a short swim and stretched out next to Basho.

A few moments later, Basho sniffed at the sand. "Can you smell that?" he asked Kineosho.

Before Kineosho could reply, two huge blue eyes popped out of the sand. "Miss Karma!" said Kineosho instantly.

"There's no fooling you, Kineosho!" replied Miss Karma with a giggle as she changed to her familiar green hue.

"I was speaking to Viddi after we heard your story this morning and she learnt something quite different from it — she thought the story meant to tell her that a monkey should never trust a crocodile!"

"Ah, but that's the beauty and often the curse of such stories — every creature takes out of them what they want to, based on their own circumstances and experiences," replied Miss Karma.

"Hmm . . . that's not very consistent though," said Basho.

"No, it's not — but it doesn't need to be consistent. Everything you hear will be different from the way others hear it, because their experiences are different from yours," said Miss Karma. "Come, I'll show you what I mean," as she leapt onto Kineosho's mane and blended herself into it. "Walk over to those two birds sitting in the tree, and ask them what they learnt from the story this morning."

Kineosho walked up to the birds and asked them. "To be discreet, of course! If those birds in the story had not blabbed out loud about the fruit in the first place, they would never have attracted the attention of that horrible crocodile."

"Now, walk up the lake shore, near that marshy area over

there," whispered Miss Karma to Kineosho. "You will find a small alligator there — ask him."

Kineosho found the alligator and asked him the same question. He thought for a while then replied: "Well, I learnt that monkeys are nasty liars but that if you don't want to get beaten by your wife, then you should probably lie too!"

Miss Karma and Kineosho both stifled their laughs, and she told Kineosho to walk farther up the lake shore. There, Basho spotted a female alligator and prompted Kineosho to ask her the same question. "If you want to do a good job, then you have to do it yourself!" she replied before storming off. That time, they were unable to stifle their laughter.

"What's also interesting," said Miss Karma, "is that if you are grappling with a specific challenge, your mind will associate the story you hear with the challenge you face. In fact, that process often gives you the insight you need to actually overcome your problem. Walk back to my story tree now, and I'll show you what I mean."

When they arrived at the tree, Miss Karma said: "Look down and tell me what you see."

"*Erm* . . . the bottom of the tree?" said Kineosho.

"Look closer!" whispered Miss Karma, and Kineosho leant closer to the foot of the tree. There, he saw the peculiar sight of a dancing ant next to a brightly coloured butterfly. The ant was smiling from ear to ear, leaping around from one spot to another in delight, carrying a pretty, green leaf over his head.

"Did you hear the story this morning too?" asked Kineosho.

"Yes!" replied the tiny ant. "And it was like an omen for me — for two weeks I have been trying to climb this tree so I could get the top-most leaf. That is the condition the Queen had set for the hand of my sweetheart, the princess. Hundreds of ants have been trying to reach the top of this tree since she set the challenge and many fell and hurt themselves in the process. I too had fallen many times and then I heard Miss Karma's story this morning. It was like an omen destined for me!"

"What happened?" asked Kineosho.

"Well, the strongest ants had been trying to climb the tree, even beating each other down at times in order to complete the challenge. Now I'm not that strong compared to many of them and I was just about to give up hope. Then I heard the story about the monkey and I thought, what if I could get up there without climbing the tree myself. At that very moment my friend Flaps here appeared," said the ant, pointing at the bright butterfly. "I explained my challenge to him and he was more than happy to carry me on his back to the very top of this tree and—"

"—in the interests of romance!" interrupted the butterfly.

"Here we are, with the leaf from the top of the tree!" said the ant cheerfully. "Thank you Miss Karma, wherever you are! I could not have achieved this without your tale!"

Nobody could see her but Miss Karma smiled quietly to herself. She was still hidden, but no longer in Kineosho's mane.

"Did you know that was going to happen?" whispered Basho curiously into Kineosho's mane. There was no reply.

"Miss Karma?" asked Kineosho, shaking his mane a little. Basho sniffed around but she was nowhere to be found.

Just then, Kilo arrived from the lake, his face all puffed up like an over-fed hamster. His eyes were red and looked as though they were about to burst. Viddi, who had had quite a restful afternoon, was sitting on Kilo's back holding his ears. She pinched them gently and Kilo nodded with some difficulty.

Viddi immediately twisted Kilo's ears and two fountains of water shot out of Kilo's nostrils as he shook his head in all directions. Water sprayed everywhere and all the animals shrieked and rolled on the shore with laughter.

Shortly after, the bell rang and all the animals proceeded to the Great Hall and went through their usual feet-dipping, head-wrapping, rule-reciting ritual. Both Viddi and Kineosho, who had found the whole process a little awkward the day before, were feeling more comfortable and found themselves reciting some of the rules aloud too.

"Now yesterday we spoke about the importance of rules and how the Great Banyan Tree would punish us if we did not follow them with discipline. Today I would like to move from the importance of rules, to the importance of roles," said Elder Twigs, after the bumblebee's buzzing rule recital.

He walked around the stage and paused to adjust his bright red leaf collar. "The roles we play in our community are essential — no matter how trivial they may seem to some. If even the smallest of roles is not followed through properly, it could negatively affect us all. If a bumblebee assigned to collect nectar does not perform his duties, flowers will not get pollinated, and will not be able to create new flowers. And if we don't have flowers to offer the Great Banyan Tree, what will happen?"

"We will all be punished!" replied the audience in unison.

"If a wildebeest assigned to carry logs decides not to perform her duties, then we would not be able to repair our shelters. If we cannot be safe from the elements in our shelters, we will not rest well. As you are smart enough to know, we will be unable to perform our duties properly if we are tired. The knock-on effect would be devastating for us all. If even one of us fails to fulfil our commitment to the Great Banyan Tree, what will happen?"

"We will all be punished!" replied the audience, even louder than before.

"If ever you wondered about your purpose, what the one thing is that you were destined to do — then it must be the role assigned to you. Without you performing that role, we will all be worse off. If you do not fulfil that role, you will have lost your sense of purpose, and that suffering is one of the most terrible things you could ever experience," said Elder Twigs.

Basho coughed and asked out loud a little nervously: "But what if the role does not fulfil you?"

Elder Twigs turned and glared at Basho. "An interesting question but that's not relevant — after all, and I'll ask this to the entire audience: what is more important — one animal, or the whole community? Is it right for one animal to neglect its duty and cause the suffering of everybody because of its selfishness?"

"NO!" shouted the audience, joining Elder Twigs in his glare at Basho. Even Kineosho looked at Basho, somewhat embarrassed to be sitting next to him.

"Know that when the Great Banyan Tree assigns a role it is with all this in mind. Know that you are chosen because you are the best creature for the role and that without your specific and valuable contribution, we — our entire community — would suffer a terrible fate," said Elder Twigs.

"And now, let us invite the choir to help us thank the Great Banyan Tree for providing each of us with a sense of purpose," said Twigs, clapping once as he left the stage. As on the previous night, the fireflies lit up and shone on the choir.

That night the music was different. The percussion started at the very beginning and it was intense. The drummers' rhythm captivated the audience. After the music tapered off, the platypus made an announcement: "Esteemed audience, tonight I would like to welcome a visiting guest artiste from a faraway land—none other than the famous Haathi Oyli Khan with his unique brand of vocal splendour!"

The audience immediately burst into applause. A third set of fireflies then lit up another part of the stage, and the crowd marvelled at the monumentally awe-inspiring elephant seated there.

Haathi cleared his throat and let out a very deep, long, resonating hum. It seemed to last for longer than any animal in the audience could have possibly held its breath. As he neared the end of his deep hum, the percussion started once more and he began to sing.

The audience was engrossed and many of the animals shook their heads elatedly from side to side. Some even involuntarily uttered "*Wah! Wah!*" in appreciation. As the tempo picked up, so did the singing until it seemed that everyone in the auditorium was in a trance. At one point, even Basho began howling, swept up in the moment.

When the performance ended, Kineosho was breathless. "Thanks be to the Great Banyan Tree!" shouted out Haathi Oyli Khan, and the auditorium echoed the words with accompanying applause and whistles.

After dinner that evening, Kineosho said to Viddi and Basho: "This is certainly the most astounding place—I cannot even begin to describe what I experienced today." They both could not agree more.

❧ 21 ❧

Group think

The following morning, there was an air of excitement about as they each wondered what the day ahead held for them. Kineosho, Viddi, and Basho found the silent meditation part of their morning routine especially calming.

When they opened their eyes, even the sun seemed to shine a brighter hue of orange. Kineosho had all but forgotten about his experience on the first path. Their exercises that morning were more strenuous than usual and he felt good about it.

Afterwards, Kineosho asked Twigs: "I remember that your neck stretched to over double its regular length when we were looking for our friends in the forest—how come you don't show that to the others here?"

Twigs smiled and replied: "Well, none of you would be able to do that and the fact that I can do it would be pointless here—in fact, many of the animals may even get discouraged and stop trying altogether. It's better to only provide reasonable stretch goals when you're teaching," he said, winking at Kineosho.

"But don't you care that others won't know what you're capable of?" asked Kineosho curiously.

"When I did my contortionist performance in the talent show many moons ago, I received all the recognition I needed from everyone that mattered to me. I must have extended my neck to three times its regular length and even managed to tie it in a knot after curling it around each of my legs—I think half the audience sprained their necks just watching me while I was doing it!" laughed Twigs. "Since then, *I* knew what I was capable of and it honestly didn't matter to me after that. Anyway, enough about me—did you enjoy Miss Karma's story yesterday?"

"Yes, it was great!" replied Kineosho.

"Well, be sure not to miss it today—I hear it's going to be a good one!" said Twigs.

Kineosho joined the others around the tree and this time Miss Karma climbed down from a branch without any theatrics. "Are you all ready for the story of the day?" she asked with a smile.

The crowd cheered, and Miss Karma began: "Many moons ago, long before cabbits were invented, it was a dangerous time for all animals in the forest. In those times creatures called humans lived here. They used to hunt—not only for food, but also for sport."

"And no creature was safe—from the smallest of mice . . . to the largest of elephants," said Miss Karma, pointing in turn at a mouse and an elephant sitting around her tree. "Fortunately, although they were violent, cruel, and deadly, they weren't the brightest bunch," she continued.

"One day a nasty-looking human hunter set out to catch some birds for his large cage in the village. He tied a huge net between some trees and scattered some delicious fruit and seeds on the ground below it. Then he hid himself in the hollow of a nearby tree and waited patiently for some birds to fall into his trap.

"After quite some time King Akbar, the king of the pigeons, flew past and noticed the feast on the ground. He landed his flock close by, but not too close. 'Hmm . . .' said the king, adjusting his wreath of red leaves around his neck, 'this looks too good to be true—all this food just waiting here for us in the middle of a clearing. Remember the story of the monkey and the crocodile—if it's too good to be true, it could well be a trap! We should be cautious!'

"'Nonsense,' replied another pigeon, Jude, who had always thought the king was too prudent. 'Why should we give up this delicious spread because of some vague fears that the king cannot even prove are real?' Jude kept talking and before long, many of the other pigeons became convinced that King Akbar was just scaring them out of a good meal.

"'Come! I will lead the way,' said Jude. He flew off towards the fruit before the king could stop him. Once he landed he began pecking at the fruit and soon all the others followed him to enjoy the feast. The king thought to himself, 'I know this may not be smart, but I cannot desert my subjects—I'll go along too and keep an eye out.'

"The instant the king landed near the fruit, the hunter released the net and trapped all the birds. 'What a catch!' said the hunter aloud. 'I'll have to find a bigger sack to carry them all home!'

"As the hunter disappeared into the forest, the pigeons turned on Jude for convincing them to throw caution to the wind. 'It's because of your greed that we're all going to die now!' said one anxiously.

"'If only we had listened to our king,' sobbed another. Yet another slapped the rebel pigeon on the side of the head and it looked like a major lynching was about to happen.

"King Akbar glared at them sternly and said: 'Stop quarrelling now! You were all ready to share in the feast, so now be ready to share in the blame too!' The pigeons remained silent and then the king said: 'Now that we've fallen into this trap as the monkey fell into the crocodile's trap, let's think about how we can free ourselves from this mess.'

"The king thought for a while, and then his eyes lit up. 'Quick,' he said, 'each of you spread apart as best you can under the net.' The pigeons did exactly as they were told. Even Jude, the rebel pigeon, asked if he was in the right spot.

"'Yes,' replied the king. 'Now on the count of three I want you all to flap your wings as hard as you can — and do not stop! ONE . . .'

Miss Karma paused and feigned confusion, as she looked encouragingly at the attentive faces below the tree.

"TWO!" yelled her audience, taking their cue.

"—THREE!" shouted out Miss Karma immediately after. "And all the birds began flapping their wings together. Almost instantly the birds lifted off, net and all. The harder they flapped, the higher the net lifted until they were way above the trees.

"The evil hunter heard the commotion and rushed back to find the pigeons and his net flying away into the sky. He yelled and screamed at the top of his voice and beat his head against a nearby tree.

"'Now fly towards the lake shore near the old coconut tree,' said the king. The other pigeons followed his instructions without hesitation.

"Jude however thought to himself, 'Even if we land now we'll never escape this net on top of us. If we're still trapped under it, we will surely die!' As the other pigeons continued to flap, the rebel pigeon suddenly stopped flapping and dived downward and away from the net, setting himself free.

"'Pay no attention to him,' said King Akbar calmly, noticing some panic-stricken faces. 'Just keep flapping towards the lake shore as I said. Trust me, and I will lead us all to safety as I have in the past.' The pigeons continued to fly with the net until they all finally landed near the old coconut tree. When the king recovered his breath, he shouted out as loud as he could: 'Nony!' But there was silence. Then he shouted again: 'Nony!' and still there was nothing. The other pigeons looked anxious. The king calmed them down, and yelled out loudly once more: 'NONY!'

"This time a small head with two big ears appeared from the base of the coconut tree. 'King Akbar?' asked a squeaky voice.

"'Nony! Yes, it's me—we need your help, my dear friend,' said the king.

"A small mouse leapt from the base of the tree, looking quite funny with his tiny head and relatively enormous ears. 'Oh my! You seem to be in quite a fix—I'll gnaw through the netting and free you right away,' said Nony as he rushed towards the part of the net where the king was.

"'No,' said King Akbar. 'First free my subjects for faithfully following my guidance.'

"'Hmm . . . but I am small,' said Nony worriedly, 'and so are my teeth. I may not have enough strength to gnaw you all free. And it is certainly not wise to sacrifice yourself to preserve those who depend on you.'

"'One can lead best by example, and there is no greater nobility than keeping one's word. Besides, I have faith in you, my dear Nony, we'll all be fine—now please—free them first, I insist,' replied the king.

"'Spoken like a true and noble king,' thought the mouse as he gnawed at the net. By sunset, Nony was tired and almost all the pigeons were free. They looked on anxiously and wondered if the little mouse could hold out to free them all.

"Nony was determined to free King Akbar after witnessing his selfless action. That thought alone gave him the strength to continue. Finally, the king was freed and they all celebrated together with song, dance, and delicious food. Well, all except for the evil Jude. He was punished by the Great Banyan Tree, and remained an outcast from the entire forest from that day on . . . and that's the end of today's story," said Miss Karma.

The audience clapped happily.

Later, on the way back to the lake after their lunchtime ritual, Basho asked Kilo, "So are you looking forward to being a guard? When will you have to start?"

Kilo shrugged his shoulders. "I haven't really thought about it much. Elder Twigs said I will start when I am ready for that responsibility — for now, I should just enjoy the stories."

"But aren't you afraid that you might not enjoy it?" asked Basho.

Kilo shrugged again and shouted to the others: "Come on, last one in the water is a stinky Jude!" He dived into the lake with the others, creating an enormous splash.

While Kineosho, Viddi, and the others played in the water, Basho sat on the bank of the lake that afternoon with a number of questions swimming around in his head. When Kineosho finally came to rest on the shore, Basho asked: "How do you suppose the Great Banyan Tree punished Jude?"

Kineosho suddenly had a flashback of his experience on the first path — of the dream he had had under the banyan tree there. He glared at Basho and snarled in reply, "You weren't there — you have no idea what the Great Banyan Tree can do. Will you stop talking about it now and just enjoy yourself like the rest of us!"

Basho had never seen Kineosho react in this way before. He was quite surprised and decided to wander off into the forest.

Later that afternoon when both Viddi and Kineosho were resting on the shore, Twigs paid them a visit. "So how are you enjoying it here, Kineosho?" he asked.

"It's the most amazing place," replied Kineosho. "The music, my new friends, Miss Karma's stories, the beautiful lake, the waterfall . . ." Viddi nodded profusely in agreement.

"Well think of us as your new family," said Twigs with a smile. "You know, tomorrow is a full moon and we have a very special celebration by the waterfall," said Twigs, pointing to the area secured by the black-bonneted moles. "Each full moon we ask the Great Banyan Tree to officially introduce new members into our community — think of it as a welcoming celebration to become part of our family here . . . Kilo and some of your other new friends will be taking part too, and it would be great if you would join us! I really hope you feel welcome here . . ."

"We certainly do," replied Kineosho. Viddi nodded her head again with a huge smile.

"Well good then, I have to prepare for the evening now — I'll see you both a little later," said Twigs as he adjusted his bright red leaf collar and walked off into the forest.

That evening, after the usual rituals had completed, Elder Twigs announced: "Tonight's session will be a little shorter than usual. As many of you are aware, there is a full moon tomorrow, and it is time for us to formally introduce new members into our community. Now, of course, nobody is obliged to take part if they don't want to, but we sincerely welcome those who wish to join our family."

"Many of you will have heard the story of the legendary pigeon King Akbar and learnt that it is important to stay together as a community to help each other. You will also have learnt, as our rules dictate, to follow all orders of the one wearing this red leaf collar—otherwise you too could fall into traps like the pigeon flock. Did you learn that?" Elder Twigs asked the audience.

"Yes!" echoed the auditorium loudly.

"Now what you don't know about that story is that although King Akbar nobly forgave the rebel pigeon Jude, the Great Banyan Tree did not. In fact, it offered him no mercy. He broke not only the rule of obeying his red-collared king's orders, but he also selfishly deserted the others, putting the entire community at risk. After all, if the others had not been strong enough to carry the net without him, the hunter could have cruelly captured them all again. When the Great Banyan Tree saw this, it was very upset. That night it sent some horrible demons to make small cuts all over Jude and used its magic power to place him in a glass bubble filled with salt. The entire forest could hear Jude's screams for days until the bubble eventually floated away with Jude, all alone—suffering inside it—forever. To this day, when it's dark out, you can sometimes still hear Jude's tormented cries—it is a cruel fate I would not wish on any of you." Twigs paused.

The animals looked at Elder Twigs, stunned into silence. Viddi had leapt onto Kineosho's back, wrapping her long arm around his neck and clasping his ear. Even Kineosho felt a little shaken, recalling his dream beneath the banyan tree for the second time that day.

"Of course, it wasn't all bad news. King Akbar guided his flock happily for many years, and the Great Banyan Tree rewarded him with the best of fruit and seeds and everything he ever wanted. His life was filled with purpose, and his role in the forest gave him tremendous joy and satisfaction," continued Twigs as he looked at the somewhat relieved audience. "The pigeon flock too were back to their playful selves soon after and they enjoyed many happy moments with their new friend Nony." The audience cheered in response.

"So think carefully tomorrow evening, our new friends — you will each be asked to make a show of commitment and I wish you all strength to do the right thing. Remember, we will always be here for you when you need us, so keep the faith and trust in our family. Let us go now, eat, and rest before our fun celebration tomorrow!" said Elder Twigs with a humble bow.

The dinner feast that evening was even better than usual. While most animals were quite excited about the next day, there were others, including Basho, who looked more than a bit concerned.

"What's wrong?" Kineosho asked Basho after dinner.

"I'm not sure — something doesn't feel right . . ." replied Basho, shrugging his shoulders. Then he curled up quietly in a corner and tried to fall asleep.

22

The Day of the Jackal

Basho woke up early. He had hoped that he would feel better in the morning, but his uneasiness had not passed.

Kilo arrived as cheerful as always and they all left for the Great Hall. Elder Twigs was not there that morning and one of the chirpier black-bonneted moles supervised the session. At the lake, after breakfast, Kilo introduced Kineosho and Viddi to his father. He was, to their surprise, the backgammon hippo guard outside the talent show cave. Kineosho was quite relieved that Kilo's father hadn't recognised them. The hefty hippo complained about his hard bench at work, and then went on to tell them how he enjoyed the breaks that they all had on full moons. The forest was abuzz with lively chatter that morning.

After a shorter than usual exercise session, they all felt quite relaxed. "I shall leave you all with Miss Karma now for today's story as we continue our preparations for this evening," said Twigs. He called four large wildebeest, a swarm of bees, and Kilo's father aside to help him. The rest of the animals scampered off to get a good seat under Miss Karma's story tree.

"Today's story," began Miss Karma, "is about the importance of whom and what you trust. Now take a deep breath, close your eyes for a moment, and let me transport you back in time — to many moons ago, when Brother Rocco had just invented the cabbits we eat today. There were certainly not as many tasty varieties as there are now, but the invention of the cabbit had changed the forest and animal lifestyles forever."

"A smart lion and his dear friend, the jackal, lived in the forest. Before cabbits, the lion used to hunt and ruthlessly slay his prey — it could have been anything from an old donkey to a young wildebeest that had strayed from the herd," continued Miss Karma, pointing to a grumpy old donkey and a young wildebeest in the crowd. Their ears immediately stood at attention, and they both looked around nervously.

Miss Karma continued: "After the lion had had his fill, the jackal would eat the remaining meat. Now since Brother Rocco had invented cabbits, the entire forest had moved on to them. The jackal still remembered the taste of meat though, and he much preferred it to the strange cabbits.

"Each day after their morning exercise session, the lion would call on the jackal to fetch some cabbits from the nearest cabbit depot. One day, on his pick-up run, the jackal could not help thinking about the tasty meat he used to enjoy before. He decided he had to have it at least once more, but he knew that the lion would never deliberately kill again. Because the jackal was too small to kill an animal himself, he worked out a sneaky plan to trick the lion. That day, the jackal returned to the lion much later than usual.

"When he arrived he said: 'My dear friend, it seems that there was a problem with Brother Rocco's delivery and no cabbits arrived today. We shall have to stay hungry tonight and I will go check again tomorrow.'

"'That's fine,' replied the lion. 'A day of fasting would serve us well.'

"The next day the jackal set off to collect their cabbits and returned late again. This time he said: 'Alas my friend, there were no cabbits for us today either—because of the shortage from yesterday, many families had taken an extra quota and they were all finished by the time I arrived. I shall leave before sunrise tomorrow to ensure I get them!'

"The lion agreed. The next day the jackal set off much earlier and once again returned empty-handed. Once again, he made up an excuse and told the lion: 'It was unbelievable. When I arrived today, I was first in the queue and I waited in the blazing sun until midday. A messenger from Brother Rocco's farm eventually arrived and said that their delivery staff had gone on strike until their employment conditions improved.'

"'It's been three days now, and I'm feeling quite weak,' replied the lion. 'We definitely need to eat something tomorrow otherwise we will not survive. How come you seem to be doing fine?' he asked. The lion did not know that the jackal ate his share of cabbits each day.

"'Oh . . . jackals store food in their bodies for many more days than lions do,' lied the devious jackal, thinking quickly on his feet. 'But leave it to me, my dear friend. You stay here and rest. If there are no cabbits tomorrow I shall be sure to return with a meal for you regardless.'

"The following day, the jackal left early in the morning. On his way, he saw a donkey drinking water. 'Perfect!' thought the jackal. 'Donkey brains for dinner tonight!'

"First, he asked a frog he spotted nearby for the name of the donkey. Then he went to the donkey and asked: 'Pardon me brother, I am a little embarrassed to ask but are you the great donkey they call Brutus?'

"'*Erm* . . . yes,' replied the donkey, a little astonished.

"'I am so glad I finally found you!' said the jackal. 'I have been trawling the forest for weeks, searching for you. I cannot tell you how happy I am!'

"'Oh?' replied the donkey, looking a bit confused.

"'I have travelled from the far end of the forest, great Brutus. Under my care are three plump and lovely she-donkeys that are desperately looking for a mate. They have had many suitors but vehemently refused them all. They insist that they will declare their love to none other than the great Brutus and have undertaken to go on a hunger strike until they meet you . . . I have come to beg you to please grace them with your presence!' said the jackal dramatically.

"'Oh!' replied the donkey, who had become quite excited from the second the jackal had mentioned she-donkeys. 'Did you say she-donkeys?' he asked. 'Why, of course I'll come with you—I am so glad you found me too!'

"The devious jackal led the happy donkey back to a clearing near the lion's cave. 'Wait here for a bit,' said the jackal. 'We can surprise your new companions with your arrival—give me a few moments after I leave, then I want you to shout, "It is me, Brutus, your faithful stallion—here to offer myself to you!" Then just close your eyes, and wait for your life to change!'

"Brutus bounced around the clearing, very excited, and a moment after the jackal left he shouted at the top of his voice 'It is me, Brutus, your faithful stallion, here to offer myself to you!' By this time, the jackal had already told the lion that he had found an animal willing to sacrifice itself for him. The lion entered the clearing and used his last ounce of energy to kill the poor donkey, who was standing there peacefully with his eyes closed and his mouth all puckered up.

"The lion felt awful to have killed an animal for the first time since the forest had moved on to its cabbit diet. Much to the jackal's dismay, the lion decided to offer the donkey's brain as part of a thanksgiving ceremony to the Great Banyan Tree that evening. The lion told the jackal to guard the donkey's body while he bathed before the meal. As soon as the lion left though, the sly jackal smashed the donkey's head open with a rock and ate his brain.

"When the lion returned, he was angry to see that the donkey's brain was missing. The quick thinking jackal immediately replied, 'My dear friend, of course this poor donkey must have been born without a brain—otherwise why would he have come here and offered himself to you?'

"'He's right,' thought the lion. 'Very well then,' he said. 'I'll eat my fill of the donkey and you can have whatever is left.'

"The jackal smiled smugly to himself as the lion ate his leftovers. He felt strangely satisfied that he had fooled both the lion and the poor donkey, to get exactly what he wanted.

"And the moral of that story," concluded Miss Karma slowly, "is that you should be very careful whom you trust." The reaction of the audience that day was quite different from the previous days. Many of the animals, particularly the donkeys and the wildebeest, were rather shaken. Kineosho felt embarrassed. The few jackals in the audience, including Basho, felt the most awkward. All eyes seemed to be on them.

"Come now," said Miss Karma. "It's just a story, you know—it's the moral that's important, not the characters," she continued, sounding somewhat unconvinced herself. "Enjoy the rest of the morning and I will meet you later at the festivities." Miss Karma smiled to herself as she disappeared into a nearby thicket.

"That was a silly story," said Basho to Kineosho. "She's obviously got something against jackals!"

"Yes, you're probably right," mumbled Kineosho, trying hard not to look away as he said it. At that very moment, the bell rang and all the animals began walking towards the Great Hall.

"You know . . . I'm not sure about this place, Kineosho," whispered Basho as they walked back. "Something has been bothering me since we got here and I cannot put my paw on it."

Kineosho just shrugged and did not reply.

After a rather sombre rule recital session and lunch, the mood improved somewhat as the animals headed back to the lakeside for an afternoon of fun. Kilo challenged Kineosho and Viddi to a race into the water and Viddi leapt on Kineosho's back, riding him like a frantic jockey. Kilo was surprisingly fast for his size and won quite easily.

The lake was more crowded than usual as many of the animals who normally went away to perform their duties were also there, enjoying the water with their families.

Basho remained on the shore and continued to ponder what was bothering him. There were many more questions in his mind than answers: What made the Great Banyan Tree so powerful? Why did they have to have the initiation ceremony—couldn't they just continue to live there as they were? Why was the story that day about jackals? He thought it was very unfair that Miss Karma had made jackals out to be such devious creatures.

Some time later, Kineosho and Viddi returned to the shore and lay down. Basho came up to Kineosho and whispered in his ear: "Have you noticed there's something really strange going on with all these rules—it's like all the animals here are just following each other blindly without question. I think we need to be really careful Kineosh—"

"—You're just trying to put doubts in my mind," snarled Kineosho, interrupting Basho. "We're all happy here except for you. Why don't you just leave if you're so concerned!"

"Kineosho, you should really be careful," continued Basho.

"Leave if you don't want to be here!" snarled Kineosho harshly again. Basho looked despondently at Kineosho for a moment and walked away.

"Good riddance," thought Kineosho as he watched Basho leave.

Nearby on the lake shore, two blue eyes popped out from the sand. It was Miss Karma. She shook the sand off her back and walked over to Kineosho. "You know, I think you're very wise—there is little room for doubt here. Without absolute faith, everything falls to pieces," she said reassuringly.

"Tonight is an important night for you. As a lion, you are one of the most important members of our community and you can really help us grow stronger and more united. The question, of course, is whether you are strong, and determined enough to complete the initiation process this evening," said Miss Karma.

"I really feel like I'm part of this family now," replied Kineosho. "So, what will I have to do in the initiation ceremony?"

"Well, you will have to free yourself of all doubts and show complete faith in the Great Banyan Tree and its rules—you have to surrender completely to show your commitment. Only then will you truly be a part of this family," said Miss Karma.

Kineosho nodded and replied, "I won't disappoint you, Miss Karma!"

She smiled and replied, "I know you won't, Kineosho. I'll see you later then." As Miss Karma walked off to help Elder Twigs with last minute preparations, Kineosho joined the other animals watching Viddi's antics. She had found even more innovative ways to generate long-distance water cannons by twisting Kilo's ears in different ways, much to everyone's amusement.

Basho, and some of the other jackals, watched from a distance.

❧ 23 ❧

Initiation

By the time the sun was about to set, the full moon was already visible. It had a gentle radiance about it and even its reflection off the lake was still, and perfect. When the bell rang that evening, it was so loud that even the calm lake water rippled.

"It's time!" shrieked Kilo with a huge, happy smile on his face.

From a distance, they could already hear the faint, rhythmic beating of drums coming from near the waterfall. They all walked towards it. The beat grew louder with each step they took and by the time they were close to the entrance, they found themselves matching their pace to the beat.

When they arrived, they found that Twigs had opened the secured area near the waterfall. A pair of large wildebeest had replaced the black-bonneted moles that normally guarded the area. The water-trough moles and the head-wrapping cranes from the Great Hall were present too.

As the animals entered the waterfall area, they went through their usual feet dipping ritual. Instead of the cranes wrapping their heads this time, they gave them each a lovely, purple flower.

Viddi immediately adjusted the magic sack on her back and neatly braided the flower into the hair behind her right ear.

Kineosho, Viddi, and a few other animals were held back soon after entering. "You're our special guests this evening," said the black-bonneted mole who had been waiting with them. "You'll have the honour of making a grand entrance!"

After all the other animals had entered, the black-bonneted mole escorted them through a narrow tunnel. As they approached a magnificent bamboo bridge, the drums were so loud that they all found themselves involuntarily bopping to the pulsating beat. Kineosho looked in awe at the bridge, which was clearly strong enough to hold the most obese of hippos.

"This bridge is a marvel of engineering," said the black-bonneted mole proudly. "The underground river it spans is not very deep but the rocks it flows over are extremely slippery. Almost all animals that step on them wind up slipping and sliding down into much deeper water and drowning. Brother Archie designed the bridge so that it could be raised and lowered, come, I'll show you," she continued as she led them across the bridge.

When they reached the other side she signalled Kilo's father, who had been waiting there, to raise the bridge. Using all his strength, he turned a wheel that slowly lifted the bridge. As the bridge lifted, Viddi let out a hysterical *Eep!* and gesticulated wildly at the two crocodiles who were sitting behind him.

"What are *they* doing here?" Kineosho asked the black-bonneted mole.

"There is no reason to fear them Kineosho—they are part of our family too. In fact, they are the only creatures here who can walk across this stream without slipping. So after the bridge is raised, they will keep guard here to ensure that no intruders cross the stream to disturb our ceremony—especially since

Kilo's father, who normally stands guard here, will be attending the ceremony today to see his son participate. Now come, let's continue!"

The crocodiles grinned sheepishly as Kineosho and Viddi walked away. The narrow path continued a short while longer before they entered an enormous cavern behind the waterfall. Fireflies lit the sides of the cavern, shining their light through different coloured flower petals for effect. It was beautiful.

The seating arrangement in the cavern appeared to be almost identical to that in the Great Hall. The animals who were already seated clapped and cheered enthusiastically as Kineosho, Viddi, and the others walked past to their special area close to the stage. With the waterfall as a backdrop and the moonlight glistening through it, it felt as though everybody should be gracefully waltzing. Kineosho looked at Viddi and the others, and could not help but smile.

The drum beats died down gradually as the black-bonnetted mole climbed onto the stage. She announced: "My beloved family, please rise and welcome our esteemed leader—Elder Twigs!" The cavern echoed with applause, whistles, and the dramatic drum roll of the percussionists as Elder Twigs took to the stage. Twigs was wearing his customary bright red-leaf collar and that evening he had his head draped in a magnificent saffron cloth.

"Family of the House of Peace—" said Elder Twigs before he paused for another round of applause to die down. "Please be seated. It is the night of a full moon once again. In our presence this evening are a number of friends who will be joining our family tonight—to work with us, help us, and enjoy life with us under the protection of the Greatest of Banyan Trees. Tonight you will witness, once more, our special initiation ceremony—the one in which the young come of age, and our new friends demonstrate their devotion and commitment to their new family, and the Great Banyan Tree." The audience cheered and the drummers took their cue to start beating their drums in slow crescendo.

"First, to symbolise that we are all impure before our initiation, we will do our traditional baptism. Then our new brothers and sisters will demonstrate their faith, and finally they will resurrect themselves, washing off their impurities under the auspices of the full moon behind us," said Elder Twigs, pointing to the gushing waterfall behind the stage. "Please, would you all now prepare yourselves to baptise our new family!"

The drumbeats gradually grew louder and the audience started to sing a lyrical version of the rules. Kineosho had heard many humming the tune since his arrival there. A number of black-bonneted moles walked through the audience dragging large vats filled with a viscous mixture of mud and honey. As they passed, the audience took as much of the gooey mixture as they could hold. Then, still singing the rules song, they marched to the beat towards the animals in the special area. When they arrived, they each smeared the gooey mud and honey mixture all over them.

It didn't take long before every animal in the special area, including Kineosho and Viddi, was covered head to toe with the sticky mud and honey mix. Some of them looked quite uncomfortable while others, like Viddi, seemed to be enjoying the stickiness and were quite happy to help plaster anyone within arm's length with the goo. Kineosho took the magic sack from Viddi and slung it over his shoulder.

By the time all the animals in the cavern had had their turn to baptise them, the drumbeats had reached an incredible volume. The rules song could barely be heard. All the animals there, including Kineosho, found themselves entranced by the beat.

Even the gooey stickiness of the mixture didn't seem to bother anyone any more.

A black-bonneted mole then gave a signal to the drummers to tone down the beat. "And now," said Elder Twigs, "let the demonstration of faith begin!" The drumbeats stopped altogether, and there was absolute silence.

Elder Twigs signalled to the platypus in the audience, and the platypus immediately started a very low hum. Slowly, it began to echo throughout the cavern. The audience, except for those in the special area, joined in and the hum grew louder. Elder Twigs then signalled the drummers, and they began softly beating their drums again and repeatedly chanting, "*OogaJakka! Oogachakka! OogaJakka! Oogachakka!*" The entire audience soon followed until the whole cavern reverberated with the chant.

Elder Twigs gave another signal, and fireflies lit up the darkest part of the cavern right next to the special area in which Kineosho was sitting. It almost seemed like a mirror replica of the special area, except that there were an enormous number of jackals seated there. There were all types — small ones, large ones, fat ones, dark ones. To Viddi's surprise, she spotted Basho there too and twisted Kineosho's ear in joy, pointing to him. Kineosho just looked away when he saw him.

As the chanting continued, a black-bonneted mole took Kilo by the hand and escorted him to the centre of the raised stage. At exactly the same time a black-bonneted mole escorted a small jackal to the centre of the stage from the adjacent, newly lit area. Kineosho recalled that he had seen the small jackal playing with Kilo on the first day that they had met.

"May faith be your guide and give you the strength to rid you of all doubts!" said Elder Twigs loudly above the pulsing chant. Then he handed Kilo an oddly shaped, sharp rock. The chanting and drumming grew louder as Kilo lifted the rock above his head. For a tiny moment he hesitated, as he looked at the small jackal struggling as the moles held him down. Then he brought the rock down onto him as hard as he could. The audience immediately responded with hysterical cheers. Viddi leapt onto Kineosho's back in horror and clasped his ear tightly.

The black-bonneted mole then escorted Kilo to the gushing waterfall and he disappeared into its misty spray for a few moments. The crowd was silent. Then suddenly, Kilo emerged clean with a loud hippo roar and the audience went wild. Kilo's father thumped the ground with his feet in excitement. The entire cavern shook as the others reignited their vociferous chanting: "*OogaJakka! Oogachakka! OogaJakka! Oogachakka!*"

"Remember the story of the jackal and choose your friends wisely!" shouted Elder Twigs above the rumpus as Kineosho suddenly found himself being escorted to the centre of the stage. He could see Basho being led up in perfect synchronisation with him, by an identical black-bonneted mole from the adjacent area. The intoxicating chant grew even louder. Kineosho felt increasingly possessed by the rhythm with every step he took until both he and Basho arrived at the focal point of the cavern.

Kineosho accepted the oddly shaped rock that Elder Twigs had offered him and raised it above his head. He snarled as he looked down at Basho who was desperately trying to free himself. Viddi looked terrified as she clung tightly to Kineosho's back. She whispered anxiously into his ear, "*Don't!*" but Kineosho's senses were clearly elsewhere.

As the chanting and drumming grew louder, Kineosho stared down at Basho with the rock above him, his powerful paws trembling with rage. Suddenly, Viddi sank her teeth into Kineosho's ear as hard as she could and he let out an enormous roar.

The roar was so loud that the chanting stopped for a moment

before continuing. In that very moment, Kineosho had collected his senses and felt shocked to see himself so completely caught up with everything. He quickly whispered something to Viddi before letting out another huge roar. The audience cheered and began chanting even louder. Viddi took the opportunity to disappear off his back.

Then suddenly, Kineosho turned around and threw the odd shaped rock at Elder Twigs's head. Twigs, who was quite taken by surprise, stepped backwards to avoid it and to his even greater surprise found himself tripping over Viddi. Twigs fell to the ground with a thunderous slam and in an instant Viddi snatched his red-leaf collar. She bounced off some animal's head, and climbed as quickly as she could to the highest point she could reach in the cavern. There, she twisted her tail tightly around a sturdy stalactite and grinned down at the confused crowd.

"Quick! Put it on!" roared Kineosho from below. The baffled audience scrambled around in bewilderment as Elder Twigs lay twitching in shock from hitting his head on the ground.

Viddi hung the oversized red-leaf collar around her neck, and shouted at the top of her voice: "*STOP!*"

The animals below looked up and stopped whatever they were doing instantly. Viddi grinned from ear to ear and yelled: "Do as I do!" She clapped her feet together twice. The crowd below looked up at their new leader, a little confused, and tried to clap their feet together. Many of them fell over and Kineosho muffled a laugh.

Then Viddi, in a flash of inspiration, instructed the percussionists to restart their drumming. "Now do as I say!" she yelled. "One! Two! Three! Four! Front left leg to the back, pause, front right leg to the front, pause, jiggle your waist and spin around, jump now—up and down!" She watched gleefully as the animals danced below her. "Again!" she yelled, "and to the beat this time! One! Two! Three! Four! Front left leg to the back, pause, front right leg to the front, pause, jiggle your waist and spin around, jump now—up and down!" The animals followed in perfect sync. Even the black-bonnetted moles who had been holding down Basho released him and obediently participated.

As the animals danced to Viddi's command, Kineosho revived Basho, who had passed out. They sneaked behind Elder Twigs, who was now struggling to get to his feet, and headed for the cavern exit. Viddi in the meantime had added a few more steps to her dance routine and was thoroughly enjoying herself choreographing the show below while hanging from the stalactite.

"Viddi!" shouted Kineosho from the exit. "Get down! We have to go!"

Viddi frowned, a little disappointed to have to leave just when she was getting into it. She looked down like a queen on her subjects and commanded: "Now do this!" She rubbed her stomach with one hand and slapped her head hard with the other. The crowd below immediately copied her and slapped themselves on their heads whilst trying to rub their stomachs. Some of the animals got confused trying to do both things at once and wound up slapping their neighbours instead. Viddi laughed hysterically as a mad brawl broke out below.

In her excitement, her tail slipped from the stalactite and she fell bottom-first into the crowd. Her new oversized red collar went flying off towards the stage. Twigs managed to stretch and twist his neck in an extremely awkward way that just barely allowed him to get to his collar. Viddi in the meantime scrambled over the fighting animals to get to the exit.

"*STOPPP!*" commanded Elder Twigs angrily, having finally managed to wiggle the red-leaf collar around his neck. "Get me up!" he directed the black-bonneted moles. "And get them!" he yelled at the top of his voice, pointing to Kineosho.

"Run!" yelled Kineosho. Viddi and Basho dashed behind him through the tunnel towards the bridge. Fortunately for them, the stampede of animals into the narrow tunnel caused a massive jam behind them. When they reached the raised bridge, they found the two crocodiles there, playing dice with each other.

"Lower the bridge!" snarled Kineosho at the crocodiles.

"Are you kidding—it would take a hundred of us to do it!" laughed the crocodile. "You aren't going anywhere!" Kineosho, Viddi, and Basho tried as best they could to turn the wheel lowering the bridge but it wouldn't budge. Then Basho whispered to Kineosho, "The coins, throw the coins into the water!"

Kineosho reached into his magic sack and felt around desperately for the pair of coins. He pulled his paw out and to his surprise, he found himself holding two of the colourful frogs he had last seen at the pond. "Viddi!" he scolded angrily. Viddi shrugged innocently and smiled a goofy smile as she leapt onto Kineosho's back. Kineosho told the frogs: "Find me the two coins or we're all in big trouble!" as he shoved them back into the sack. He could see some of the smaller animals freeing themselves from the jam and running towards them. "Quick!" he yelled.

He felt something press against his paw and instantly withdrew it from the sack. He showed the two shiny gold coins to the crocodiles. "Look, you like these? They're yours!" said Kineosho as he threw them both into the shallow water. The crocodiles greedily dived in immediately to retrieve them.

"Hold tight!" yelled Kineosho as he grabbed Basho and leapt onto the back of the first crocodile. No sooner had he landed than he leapt onto the head of the other surprised crocodile and bounced over to the other side.

They bolted as quickly as they could towards the exit through the long tunnel. Kineosho could hear Elder Twigs screaming frantically behind them for Kilo's father to lower the bridge. Kineosho had never run so fast and Viddi held on to his back for dear life. The two wildebeest at the entrance had dozed off in boredom and they jumped over them both. Kineosho did not look back. He raced past the Great Hall and through the tunnel of trees leading into the Angel's Trident.

The Angel's Trident was crowded that evening as the only path that seemed to be allowing entry was the first one. Kineosho barged through the crowd, trying to get as far away from the second path as possible.

He shoved through the animals, barely able to see where he was going. They ran deeper and deeper into the crowd until Kineosho rammed into a strange creature that he had never encountered before. It had a long neck, but nowhere near as long as Twigs's—it was like a cross between a goat and a baby giraffe, but with a fluffy brown coat.

"You look like you're in exile," said the animal calmly in a very feminine voice. She seemed to ignore all the gooey mud and honey still stuck to Kineosho and Viddi.

"We need to get out of here. Can you help us please—" begged Kineosho.

"—and what are you?" interrupted Basho curiously.

"I am a llama. And where would you like to go?" replied the fluffy animal calmly to each of the questions.

"Home," whispered Kineosho and Viddi together.

"That would be through that first path over there," replied the llama just as softly. "But I imagine you will not go there again just yet. Am I correct?"

"I can't—never again!" replied Kineosho.

"Ah . . . *Never*," replied the llama with a gentle smile. "Well, it is pointless leaving the Angel's Trident, for you will be as lost as when you entered. So you leave yourself little choice but to go in there," said the llama, still maintaining her calm tone. She pointed to the third path out of the clearing.

"What's in there—" asked Kineosho nervously.

"—and do they have anything against jackals?" asked Basho, interrupting once more.

The llama smiled again and said: "No—they welcome jackals there and it is quite different from where you've just com—"

"—*Eeep!*" shrieked Viddi suddenly right into Kineosho's ear while pointing frantically at the entrance to the second path.

"It's Twigs! Quick, run now before they catch us!" said Kineosho, panicking.

Before he could bolt, the llama put her hoof onto Kineosho's paw, looked directly into his eyes and said: "Stop—nothing will happen to you." Kineosho froze. It was as though time had slowed down to a standstill.

Viddi looked at Basho who just shrugged his shoulders.

The last time Kineosho had experienced anything like that was in the training session with Master Wu and the levitating tree. He could do no more than breathe deeply and look at the llama.

"Very soon, a storm will be here," said the llama, looking up at the sky which had started clouding over. "When it starts, follow me closely—do you understand?" asked the llama calmly.

Kineosho looked anxiously at Basho who nodded. Within seconds, there was an intense bolt of lightning. It struck a tree near the entrance of the first path causing it to burst into flames, startling all the animals in the clearing. The llama appeared indifferent to it. Then a massive downpour began. The llama turned around and began walking. Kineosho, Viddi, and Basho followed her closely. The rain was falling so hard that they could barely see where they were going. After quite some time the llama stopped, turned to Kineosho and said: "Rest here, the storm will pass soon."

"Are we on the third path?" asked Kineosho anxiously.

"No," replied the llama.

"Where are we? What am I supposed to do?" asked Kineosho, sounding increasingly distressed.

"You're somewhere safe and you're supposed to do whatever you want to do, of course," said the llama as calmly as ever.

"Please *stop* with the *riddle speak!* I really need something here—can't you at least give me some help, some guidance—please!" pleaded Kineosho.

The llama looked at Kineosho and thought for a moment. Then she said: "I know it didn't end well for you on the last path you chose but be sure to remember what you've learnt."

"You mean the rules?" asked Kineosho.

"The rules are far less important than the principles behind why they are there," replied the llama in her soothing voice. "But right now, you should close your eyes and rest."

Kineosho, Viddi, and Basho closed their eyes for what could have been no longer than a blink and the llama had disappeared into the pouring rain. When they closed their eyes again, they fell into a deep sleep.

Part III

❧ 24 ❧

Finders seekers

The next morning, Kineosho awoke to the nervous chatter of some animals behind the bushes. He looked around to try to establish where he was. "We're obviously no longer in the Angel's Trident," he thought as he woke up Basho and Viddi.

"Do you know where we are?" Kineosho whispered to Basho as the chattering behind the bushes continued.

"Gita?" asked Viddi.

"Gita what? *Ow!*" replied Kineosho, a little louder than expected as he tugged out a bit of leftover sticky mud stuck in his mane. Suddenly the nervous chatter behind the bushes stopped.

Viddi poked her head through the bushes and yelled "Gita!"

"Wax on!" replied a happy voice behind the bushes. "*Aaaargh!* It's that monster! Keep it away!" replied another, panic-stricken voice. "It's you!" replied yet another with excitement.

Kineosho looked at Basho, a little confused. Viddi immediately leaped through the bushes and gave the turtle there a big hug. "Gita!" she said as she bounced around happily. Memories of her cabbit-waxing days with the turtles gushed back.

"No—keep it away! Keep—keep it away!" stuttered the eagle who was with Gita. He shook his head, and backed away apprehensively from Viddi.

"Thank the Baobab we found someone we know!" said the excited armadillo. "We've been walking around lost for days now!"

Kineosho looked at the peculiar trio and then at Viddi. "Viddi?" he asked. "Friends of yours, I take it?"

"No—Keep—keep it away!" screeched the eagle again, backing himself against a tree.

"Wax on," replied the turtle. "Wax off!" she shouted right after.

"Wait—just calm down all of you," said Kineosho. "Who are you?" he asked the armadillo.

The armadillo took a deep breath, and replied: "Milo. Well, obviously you don't remember me but if you'll recall many moons ago when you first arrived on this side of the river, you ran into some crocodiles?"

"Yes, and I was quite badly beaten up . . ." replied Kineosho.

"Exactly, well your friend here," he said, pointing at Viddi, "called on me for help when I was passing by—see, I've still got the gift she gave me!" He dug out a gold coin from his pouch and showed it to Viddi who had a huge smile on her face. "This jingling any bells yet?"

Kineosho nodded as he recalled the dressing of leaves and the strange turmeric-like smell when he first woke up after his thrashing. "I don't think I was conscious enough to thank you then, but I really did appreciate your help," replied Kineosho gratefully.

"Well, since then my healing powers have been fading. None of my special herbs and druid mixtures seem to be of any use against this new range of afflictions," said the armadillo sadly. "First I met this turtle, over here," he continued, pointing at Gita who was still making little circular motions with both her flippers. "I've tried just about every druid potion I can imagine but she just cannot seem to stop what she's doing."

"Wax on," said the distressed-looking turtle to Viddi, continuing to make little circles with each flipper in turn.

"When I was young, my father always mentioned the Third Path as somewhere with help for many with such seemingly incurable diseases. We asked dozens of animals along the way but nobody had heard of it so we kept searching. Then, I met this eagle walking on the ground," said Milo, pointing to the eagle, which oddly looked like he was trying to climb up the tree backwards to create even more distance between himself and Viddi. "As eagles soar above the forest, I was sure he would have come across the Third Path at some point but when I asked him, he told me he didn't know and he refused to fly!"

"Refused to fly?" asked Kineosho. "What do you mean, he refused to fly?"

"Exactly that—he said he had been walking around and hopping on the ground for many moons now. He kept having horrible nightmares about a cruel beast that threw things at him every time he tried to fly. So, he decided to walk and hop around instead. When I tried to heal his wings and even his head, yet again none of my mixtures worked. I think—I think I've lost my *mojo!*" said the armadillo, quite distraught.

"The Third Path—what about the third exit out of the Angel's Trident? Do you think—" whispered Basho to Kineosho.

"Do you know where it is?" interrupted Milo desperately. "The Third Path, I mean!"

"Well, I'm not sure, but I have a hunch," replied Kineosho.

"Wax on!" said the turtle excitedly.

"Wax on!" repeated Milo, not quite knowing what else to say.

"Let's figure out where we are first and then we can go," said Kineosho. "Viddi, can you climb that tree and see if you can spot

201

the Angel's Trident from there?" asked Kineosho, pointing at the tallest tree he could find.

Viddi dashed up the tree and back down again almost instantly. She pointed past the thick bush where they had woken up: "It's over there, through past those bushes!" she said excitedly.

"Wax off!" said Gita loudly.

After a few minor detours, they wound up back on the main path towards the Angel's Trident. As they walked, Kineosho recounted some of their bizarre adventures. The eagle hobbled and hopped behind them trying to keep up.

"Look, there it is!" said Kineosho, pointing at the third exit out of the clearing. The previous night's storm had left large puddles all over — not that it made any difference to Kineosho and Viddi, as a lot of the gooey mud and honey mixture had not properly washed off yet. As they walked, Basho looked around nervously to make sure there was no sign of Twigs or his henchmoles.

When they arrived at the third exit, Viddi was the first to notice a small, well-maintained pond close to the entrance. The pond was surrounded by rocks in front and a small forest of bonsai trees behind it. Viddi leaned over the rocks and curiously looked to see if she could spot any fish. When she noticed something move, she plunged her long left arm into the water and felt around. The deeper she reached into the water, the more she stuck her tongue out until finally she lifted her hand out and yelled to the others, "Look what I found!"

When Milo saw the small, strange, lizard-like creature that Viddi held in her open hand, his eyes immediately opened wide. He joined his hands together and raised them as high as he could, and said: "*Axolotl!*"

"I think you had better put him down, Viddi," whispered

Kineosho. Viddi placed the odd-looking creature carefully onto the wet rocks in front of the pond.

"Axolotl!" said Milo again. "This must be the entrance to the Third Path!" he whispered excitedly at Kineosho.

"Hello," said the axolotl as he looked at Milo and slowly smiled a very awkward smile.

"Hello," replied Milo, practically in shock that the creature had spoken to him.

"Heal well. I'm going back into the water now," said the axolotl.

Milo nodded as the axolotl slipped backwards into the water.

"What was that?" asked Basho curiously.

Milo took a deep breath and said: "*That* is one of the most legendary healers of all time. Actually I really thought he was a legend. But obviously he's not. He was real. I had only heard about him in stories. You know you could just cut off one of his legs and the entire leg would just grow back on its own! But I always thought the axolotl was only mythical. But he was real. Right there—I'm babbling."

"Yes, you are!" said Kineosho, laughing.

"We're here—we've arrived!" said Milo, turning around to face Gita and the eagle who had finally caught up with them. "We've reached the Third Path!"

"Wax on!" said Gita happily, moving her flippers in circular motions even faster than she had been doing.

"Wax on!" said Kineosho and Viddi together.

The turtle's excitement about reaching her destination made Kineosho feel a little more at ease about entering the third path. If that wasn't enough, the voice they heard coming from just inside the third entrance certainly tipped the scales.

"Kineosho?" asked the voice.

"Uma!" blurted Kineosho with glee, as her familiar but much larger face appeared out of the entrance.

"Great Banyan Tree! How long has it been?" asked Uma as Kineosho just shook his head and shrugged in disbelief. "I see you're still playing in the mud—am I going to have to rescue you again?" she laughed. By this time, Viddi had stopped madly bouncing around with joy and leapt to give Uma's trunk a hug. "Come, come! Don't wait outside, my dears!" said Uma as she ushered them all onto the third path.

As they walked in, a small wildebeest smiled cheerfully and said, "Mind your step—it's a steep path in places!"

"Thank you," replied Milo, still a little overwhelmed from meeting the axolotl.

"I can't believe it—you must be the dear elephant friend that Rhino rushed off to meet when we first arrived here—I should have known!" said Kineosho, equally overwhelmed with the reunion.

"Ah yes, Rhino! We met many moons ago and I was so happy to see him again—we will meet him later. Come, let's get you home and cleaned up first," replied Uma.

Kineosho marvelled at the lovely path—the sunbeams shone through the tall trees as they walked along. While the path was well defined, things appeared a lot more natural and less organised than the second path. Viddi hesitantly looked at the flowers and resisted the temptation to pick them for her hair.

"Go ahead, take it!" said the small wildebeest cheerfully to Viddi. "I can see that you want to!" Viddi looked sheepishly at Uma who just smiled and pointed her trunk at a pretty daffodil nearby.

As they continued upwards, Kineosho felt a strange sense of calmness come over him. Everything appeared to be much more relaxed than on the second path. "So what happens here?" asked Kineosho as they continued walking.

"Well, I will give you the full tour later, but for now let's just say there is something here for everybody. You will meet a variety of creatures, healers, artists, and mystics — all here to help themselves better understand who they are," replied Uma.

"And no jackal-sacrifice rituals, right?" asked Basho again nervously.

"Definitely none!" laughed Uma. "And you are all free to leave any time you'd like, although as you'll find, most choose never to leave once they arrive here."

After quite a climb, they reached the top of the path — there was a large clearing surrounded by magnificent trees. There were many paths out of it and at the very far end, there were some rapids leading to the top of the waterfall. The sound of the water gushing down through the rapids was both awe-inspiring and soothing at the same time. "Every time I think I cannot find something more beautiful, I'm always proven wrong," thought Kineosho to himself.

Uma led them to a quieter part of the clearing and they caught up. Kineosho told the story of how Uma had helped save him during the terrible storm when they were younger, and the animals that had gathered around them cheered with joy. Milo explained how he felt he had lost his *mojo*. He was curious to know if there were other druids nearby who could help him heal his two patients.

"All in good time!" replied Uma as they heard the sound of a bell in the distance. Kineosho and Viddi both looked at Uma as though expecting her to lead them to a Great Hall equivalent.

"Right now it's time for a light lunch!" said Uma as four small wildebeest brought them a spread of chopped cabbits and some fruit. As they continued chatting over a relaxed lunch, Rhino appeared from one of the paths, making Viddi choke with surprise. She rushed over to give him a big hug. Rhino appeared to be much calmer than before and greeted them all in the happiest of voices.

After lunch, Uma said: "Rhino and I have a little recruitment work to complete this afternoon but before we go, we're going to take you all to get a little cleaned up, and a lot more relaxed."

Kineosho and his unusual companions followed Uma and Rhino as they left the clearing along one of the many paths. As they walked, Uma explained: "Every creature in the forest is different and we found that having rules forcing them all to behave the same, led to much inner conflict. Each path out of this clearing—and there are many paths—leads to a different experience. You will find some interesting, others peculiar, and others healing beyond your wildest dreams."

"Is there singing?" asked Viddi curiously.

"Singing?" replied Uma with a laugh. "Yes, there could be singing in some! For now though, we definitely need to get all of you cleaned up before you explore any further!"

❧ 25 ❧

Rejuvenation

They continued walking into the forest until they reached a slightly misty area. As they went a little deeper into the mist, they all heard a strange gurgling sound. Moments later, they arrived at a large clearing with dozens of small pools of bubbling water.

"Rhino and I are off for a short while, but we'll leave you in the capable hands of Rose here," said Uma, pointing to an elegant flamingo. "We'll meet you after you've finished your therapy for the afternoon!"

"Therapy?" asked Kineosho.

"We call it *Exfoliatory Aromatherapy*," said Rose with a welcoming smile as Uma and Rhino walked away into the mist. "I'll explain in just a moment, but first let me assign your individual masseurs—I think you'll find this most enjoyable, and cleansing, if nothing more!" she laughed softly. She pointed at a few animals seated high on some nearby trees, summoning them to come down.

When she arrived, YaYeh, Kineosho's odd-looking masseur, took his sack and placed it on the side of the pool, much to

Viddi's concern. "It's okay, it'll be safe right here," said YaYeh, reassuring her. Viddi and Basho looked at each other, terrified of the bubbling water in the pools, and refused to leave Kineosho's side. With some difficulty, Rose and YaYeh managed to convince them to enter one of the larger pools together. It didn't take long before all of them were enjoying the warm bubbly water.

The eagle was a much tougher sell but eventually his masseur convinced him to submerge his feet, at least, at the edge of his pool. Neither Gita nor Milo needed any convincing at all, as they both dived into their individual pools and quite happily splashed around until Rose told them to calm down.

"Today we'll focus on getting you cleaned up and relaxed, all right?" asked Rose. They all nodded. "Now I want you all to close your eyes and rest your heads at the edge of your pool. Take a deep breath — in — and out, — in — and out . . . In — and out . . .

" . . . In — and out," she continued in a slow, soothing tone.

Rose nodded to the masseurs and they each dropped a handful of sweet scented flower petals into the water. The warm bubbling water seemed to react with the flowers to create a sweetish fragrance. "Keep your eyes closed, and just continue to breathe deeply. Enjoy the beautiful, relaxing scent of the flowers. Clear your mind of all thoughts, and relax your shoulders."

Rose's voice was calming and as she continued her simple instructions, Kineosho and the others started to feel more relaxed. After some time Rose signalled the masseurs to start their work. As they scrubbed the remnants of the mud and honey out, Rose continued to keep them all focused on their breathing and the sweet scent. She gradually moved on to repeating some calm, reaffirming statements: "You are in a warm, safe environment. Your worries are being washed away by the healing waters of this volcanic spring. As you close your eyes and breathe in, take in all the positive energy of the universe. Hold your breath for a moment, and feel that energy becoming a part of your body. Now, breathe out slowly and expel all the stress and negative energy from deep inside you."

Kineosho and the others soon found themselves practically dozing off to Rose's hypnotic tone. The fragrance in each pool had penetrated their pores and their breathing subconsciously followed the rhythm of Rose's voice. When she stopped, with the exception of Gita who had fallen asleep, they all opened their eyes, feeling completely refreshed. Rose told Gita's masseur to lift her gently out of her pool and to allow her to rest for some time.

"What are you?" Basho asked YaYeh curiously, as he looked at her long fingers.

"*Shhh* . . ." whispered Rose softly, and told them all to rest silently outside the pool for a while.

When Kineosho finally reopened his eyes, he could not determine how long they had been there. But everything was as he remembered it—his sack was next to him, and Viddi, Basho, and the others were waking up slowly too. The masseurs brought some large coconut shells filled with cold water and offered them to Kineosho and the others to drink.

"How do you feel now?" he heard Uma's voice ask softly.

"Incredible!" replied Kineosho, Viddi, and Basho in sync and Uma and Rose laughed. Even the eagle, who had been hesitant about the bubbly water experience, seemed to be in a better mood.

A few moments later, they heard a bell ring in the distance and Uma gently awoke Gita. "Come my dears, let's have some dinner," said Uma, and she led them back to the clearing near the top of the waterfall.

They caught up a bit more over a light dinner and they all felt very relaxed. Even Gita, although still unable to say more than

Wax-on and *Wax-off*, found herself moving her flippers in little circles much less. That night, they all slept well.

When they woke the following morning, they chatted awhile before Basho said: "Hmm . . . I feel like we should be doing something right now."

"I've been thinking about that too," replied Kineosho. "And about what the llama said — the routine and morning exercises really did us a world of good, and we should continue that."

Viddi nodded in agreement, thinking back to their regular morning sessions with Master Wu and how much she had enjoyed watching the League of Domino Mice. They went off to a secluded spot to complete their meditation and exercise routines and felt quite happy with themselves.

❦ 26 ❦

The therapy stork

"Today we'll take you on a grand tour so you can find your way around," said Uma at breakfast. "There's a lot to experience here and some of it may seem strange at first so keep an open mind. First, let's take a few moments for ourselves and we'll meet here again in a bit to start the tour."

"The routine may not be too difficult to stick to here after all!" thought Kineosho to himself, noting the similarity to Twigs's path.

A short while later, Uma led the tour down one of the larger paths out of the clearing. "Many seasons ago, there were just a few ways in which we could embark on a journey of self-discovery. Now some of those original techniques, although very simple, are effective, and are still practised by many animals — and those of you who visited the second path out of the Angel's Trident would have certainly experienced some of them," said Uma in her tour-guide voice.

"Since then," she continued, "an increasing number of animals wanted to become involved—particularly after cabbits were invented, and animals had more time to focus on themselves and their higher-level needs. So, as seasons passed, the original techniques were modified and specialised to cater to the large variety of animals who live in the forest. In fact, the demand for new techniques has grown so great that we've had to develop our very own *Specialist Therapy Creation Centre*. That is the first stop on our tour this morning." Uma paused for a moment and pointed with her trunk to a large hole in a thicket.

Kineosho and the others peered through the hole. If any of them had known what a Wall Street trading floor looked like, they would have sworn that they had just seen a replica of it. There was a giant bear standing on a platform in the centre of a large clearing. He was surrounded by dozens of different animals shouting out things at him, each trying to be louder than his neighbour.

"What's happening in there?" asked Milo, fascinated by the chaos.

"Well each day, the bear receives a list of new therapy names—like the one he just mentioned now—*Kinaesthetic Huna Massage*. The bidders then shout out their best explanation for the therapy and the most interesting one gets to use the name and develop a full service offering around it," replied Uma.

"And then they go out and practise it?" asked Milo, with a look of concern on his face.

"Well, they have to have completed at least one full course on their own and demonstrated significant good intention to help others in order to become a bidder. I know the quality control aspect does not sound perfect, but it's largely self-regulating and it's worked well for us so far," replied Uma.

"Hmm . . . it all sounds rather complex," said Milo.

"Things kind of just evolved that way. The basic principles of each therapy, you'll find, are quite similar and very simple — they address each creature holistically. They teach about acceptance, the ability to distinguish what's important from what's not, the steps to maintain a healthy and positive lifestyle — and so on," said Uma.

"So why the strange names and the complicated explanations if the underlying basics are so simple?" asked Milo.

"The *strange names* as you put it, give the animals tailoring the content a sense of purpose and ownership. The complicated explanations, believe it or not, are more for their clientele. Simplicity is often perceived negatively and as lacking in both value and credibility by most animals," said Uma. "Goodness, you sound just like an axolotl — you aren't related, are you?" asked Uma with a laugh.

"Well — *erm* . . . no," replied Milo hesitantly. "I did want to ask you though, why is Axolotl outside the Third Path — surely the greatest healer would be practising and teaching the most popular therapy here?"

Rhino coughed uncomfortably and Uma paused before replying. "The axolotl did not appreciate how things were work-ing in harmony here. He insisted on over-simplifying everything to the point where many of the animals began losing their sense of purpose. In fact, he caused quite a stir by barging in on a few of the lectures, explaining the basic underlying principles, and leaving the teachers looking foolish. The students left, feeling that their teachers had completely duped them. We all tried to explain to the axolotl the need for this way of working, but he would not listen to reason — so we had no choice but to banish him from the Third Path."

". . . banish him from the Third Path . . ." whispered Milo, shaking his head, shocked at what he had just heard.

"We should move along now, there's quite a bit more to see—and I know just the thing to help cure our turtle friend over here," said Uma, patting Gita gently on the head with her trunk.

"*Wax on!*" said Gita excitedly and everybody laughed.

Uma then led the others around a number of paths out of the clearing, showing them some shortcuts and explaining the different therapies on offer. They ranged from different types of meditation to exotic healing therapies and other more fun-sounding activities like group humming.

"So you can see, there is something here for everyone," said Uma, as she continued walking down one of the paths. "And for you, my turtle friend, there is something very special," she said, pointing to a group of eight turtles waiting outside an exit.

To Gita's surprise, all the turtles there shared her affliction. Their flippers moved around in little circles and they only seemed to be able to say *Wax on!* or *Wax off!*. Gita recognised one of the turtles, but she had never seen the others before.

Even Milo, who had slowed down his pace to that of the hopping eagle, was surprised at the curious sight.

"What's wrong with them?" asked Kineosho.

"It's hard to say exactly, but I think it's likely a case of severe burnout from their daily duties—you know, repeating the same thing over and over until their minds cannot process anything else. It can affect any animal, but for some reason turtles seem to be more susceptible to it," said Uma.

"Can you heal them?" asked Milo.

"I deal with a different kind of affliction, but Toby certainly can. Many moons ago, he designed a revolutionary treatment called *Neuro-Linguistic Crystal Therapy*. He has since adapted it, specifically to help turtles with this condition—" replied Uma.

"—in fact, you can *all* try it out. The basic principles behind NLC are extremely useful for most newcomers on this path," interrupted a deep, charismatic American-sounding voice from behind them.

"Dears . . . meet Toby!" said Uma, turning around to face a rather cocky red-breasted rooster.

Toby gave them a short bow and said, "Go on, give it a go—you'll love it!"

"*Wax on!*" shouted Gita enthusiastically, which Kineosho repeated cheerfully in chorus with the other turtles.

Milo hesitated, torn between what he had been thinking about doing, and witnessing this revolutionary cure. He whispered something in Viddi's ear and she nodded in reply. "We're going to sit this one out for now, if that's okay?" he asked Uma politely.

"There's no time like the present—don't put off till tomorrow the good you can do today," said Toby, looking a little disgruntled with the armadillo's request.

"We're just feeling tired today—we'll probably get much more out of it when we're well rested," replied Milo diplomatically.

Toby shrugged and let out a deep sigh. "Suit yer'self buddy—no time like the present is all I'm sayin' . . ." He turned around and escorted Gita, Kineosho, the eagle, and the other turtles through the exit off the path.

Uma and Rhino agreed to meet them all later at the clearing. Milo and Viddi waved goodbye and quickly scurried off to one of the shortcuts that Uma had shown them earlier.

☙ 27 ☙

Turtle let go

"How is everybody feeling today?" asked Toby loudly as soon as everyone had settled in.

His question was met with ambivalent responses. There were a couple of low muttered, unconvincing *Okay*s and many more *Wax off*s.

"I can't hear *youuuu*—" said Toby again, putting a rooster foot to his ear in a rather uncomfortable-looking pose.

"*Wax off!*" yelled the turtles, looking more anxious.

"That's better! Well now, for those of you who don't know me, I am Toby," said Toby proudly displaying his big red chest. "I'm here to help you to help yourselves—so that you can be the best *YOU* that *you* can be. Today, I need you to leave your baggage outside—and that's not the baggage I'm talkin' about, you," he said, pointing to Kineosho who was removing his magic sack from around his neck.

"What I'm talking about is your mental baggage—all the things that are holding you back from being all that you can be. We're going to talk about goals and targets, and how you're going to go about achieving them. And for the turtles amongst you, we're going to snap you out of this awful mess you seem to have gotten yourselves into. We're going to get you back on the *roooooad* to recovery!" declared Toby confidently.

The turtles were clearly pumped up and raring to go. They moved their flippers in little circles even faster than before.

"So what is this *Neuro-Linguistic Crystal Therapy*, I heard many of you ask each other outside," continued Toby, sounding even more enthusiastic. "Well, I can tell you that I've spent the better part of my life studying and understanding the mind, body, and spirit of forest creatures. And with my experience I have arrived at a winning formula."

The turtles listened eagerly as Toby paused. He turned around to his assistant kangaroos and signalled them to go out into the audience. "Every one of you is unique—and special. My assistants are now going to run some complex diagnostic tests on each of you so that we can match you with your most appropriate crystal. By the time they retrieve your individual crystal, we will have completed our morning task of determining your goals—your target—your destination. Then, we will use the spiritual crystals together to redefine the way you see things and to put you on the path to achieving your goals."

The assistant kangaroos rushed into the audience and began their diagnostic tests. These related to reflex responses and more generic diagnostics like pulse rate, head size, and body mass. When they had completed their tests, the kangaroos left the therapy clearing and Toby continued his monologue.

"Many of us in our daily lives lose track of what is important to our overall wellbeing. When we veer off course too much, our bodies and minds react negatively—we may fall ill physically—or become unable to do the things we would normally do," said Toby, looking at the eagle. "Or otherwise, we seem to lose total control over everything—even the most basic of activities—like many of you turtles will know. For others, the lack of a clear goal leaves them feeling out of place and disoriented—feeling as though they are not living up to their true potential."

"Today we're going to fix all that," continued Toby. "We're going to work with each of you to define your goals. Then we're going to use your individual crystals in the afternoon to ensure that your energy is channelled in the right direction to achieve the goals you have defined for yourselves."

"Why does he keep repeating himself?" Basho asked Kineosho.

Kineosho shrugged and whispered back, "Perhaps the turtles are a little slow?"

Toby and the few remaining kangaroos mingled with the audience and started their goal discovery process. To Kineosho's surprise, Toby came to him personally and asked: "So tell me, what is your goal?"

"I don't know—well, I haven't really thought about it," replied Kineosho, looking a little nervously at Basho.

"Don't look around at your friends, this is about *you*—not them," said Toby calmly. He paused, then asked: "What would you say your strengths are?"

Kineosho thought for a moment, and replied: "I'm strong, smart, a good friend, I have a powerful roar, should I go on?"

"Actually yes, please do," replied Toby with a smile.

"*Erm* . . . well, I am good at lots of things," said Kineosho.

"Such as—?" asked Toby calmly.

"Well—I can chop cabbits, I'm agile, I can think on my feet, I'm . . . *erm*," said Kineosho hesitantly before stopping.

"Excellent, that's very good," said Toby in a reaffirming voice. "Now, tell me, how would you say you define success?"

"What do you mean?" asked Kineosho.

"What would make you feel, the best that you could possibly feel, if you achieved it?" asked Toby.

Kineosho looked at Toby, and shrugged.

"Being the best cabbit chopper in the world, perhaps? Or the most agile lion?" asked Toby.

"No, I mean it would feel good but . . . I don't think it would be the *best* I could feel," replied Kineosho.

"What then? The fastest thinker on his feet, or the strongest, perhaps?" probed Tony.

"No, I don't think so," replied Kineosho.

"Hmm . . . let's think about it a little differently. If you could be like somebody else, who would you like that somebody to be? Who do you *aspire* to be like?" asked Toby patiently.

Images of Griffon, Master Wu, Curie, Twigs, Uma, even Viddi, and many others raced through Kineosho's mind. "Master Wu?" thought Kineosho aloud as the image of him levitating and moving the giant tree flashed before him. "Or my father?" as he thought about Griffon's victorious return from his battle. "Or mom?" as he thought of Curie patiently teaching him about surviving in the jungle. As the images raced through his mind, he did not even notice Toby repeating his probing question. Amidst the chaotic stream of thoughts, Kineosho's mind was for a brief moment transported to a calm place, far away.

Suddenly, Toby clicked his left claw near Kineosho's ear and asked: "What do you *really* want?"

"I would be happy if I could just –" muttered Kineosho.

"—just what, Kineosho?" interrupted Toby.

"If I could just be *home*," blurted Kineosho.

"Home?" asked Toby slowly with a smile. "That's interesting," said Toby, pausing for a moment. "Tell me about your home."

"It's across the river, and I want to get back there. I tried—" said Kineosho, interrupted by a look of utter disgust from Toby. "—What?" asked Kineosho.

"*Tried! Tried! Tried!*" said Toby in dismay as he shook his head. "Well at least you know what you want now. We can *try* to get you there with your crystal this afternoon," said Toby sarcastically as he strutted off to attend to some of the other participants.

Kineosho looked at Basho and shrugged, a little confused at what had just happened. Moments later, he reflected on what he had said and thought to himself: "I want to be home. Yes, I definitely want to be home." Suddenly, he felt quite different—as though something inside him had magically clicked into place.

Toby's assistants had a much easier time with the turtles. They asked each of them to say *Wax On!* if what would make them happiest would be returning to their normal behaviour. Each of the turtles immediately replied with a convincing *Wax on!*.

"I want to fly!" screamed the eagle suddenly, startling everyone including Toby.

"I think we've done well this morning—I know it's often difficult to articulate your goals but it's a critical step for *Neuro-Linguistic Crystal Therapy* to be effective. We will take a short break for lunch now—thank you, and please give yourselves a round of applause for a task excellently completed," said Toby, leading the way.

When the animals returned after their lunch break, they found the layout of the therapy clearing slightly different. The kangaroo assistants got each of the creatures comfortable in their own separate areas. They laid them all belly down with their heads resting on the softest of genetically modified memory sponge. Then the kangaroos strapped them all down snugly so there was little room to move.

When all the animals were comfortable, Toby said: "After many moons of intensive research I have discovered the profound Secret. The greatest artists the world has ever known—yes indeed, even the greatest minds that the world has ever known, have followed what I am about to teach you today. That is the reason they achieved their greatness, and so shall you achieve your greatness after you learn this Secret."

"No doubt you have all heard the expression *seeing is believing*. Well, my dear friends, in-depth study has led me to the certain conclusion that this expression has been mistranslated for generations—the true wisdom that was meant to be communicated was not *seeing is believing* but rather *SAYING is believing!*" Toby paused, and then repeated: "—*Saying is believing*."

"What we say to ourselves in our minds and through our mouths influences not only our attitudes and behaviours, but also the outcomes of our actions. We constantly use phrases like *try my best*, *attempt to do* or I *hope to finish*—haven't you all found yourselves using such terms? Yes, you have—I know you have otherwise you would not be here!

"It is the mere potential of a negative outcome that exists within such phrases that so very often leads us to failure. With the discovery of this Secret, the concept of *Neuro-Linguistic Crystal Therapy* was born—and that my friends, is the wonder you are about to experience now," said Toby with dramatic panache. The turtles looked at Toby as though they were about to burst with excitement. Even Kineosho could barely contain his anticipation.

Toby clicked his claw authoritatively and commanded: "Crystals!"

The kangaroos then entered the therapy clearing with some pomp, each pair carrying a magnificent large crystal proudly above their heads. The crystals varied in size, shape, and colour but each looked astoundingly beautiful.

"These are your specially selected and cleansed individual crystals based on your extensive diagnostic tests this morning. My assistants will take some time now to tune them to your body energy before we continue," said Toby. Each pair of assistants took their cue and hummed softly as they slowly moved the crystal they were holding over the entire body of the patient beneath them.

While the kangaroos tuned the crystals, Toby continued with his lecture. "What we say in our minds and out loud is what we put out into the universe. The universe reciprocates and returns to you what you ask for—you may hear many others refer to this phenomenon as the Law of Attraction. Your individual crystal has a special power to re-condition the way you say things—the way you put things out to the universe. You want one hundred percent positivity to achieve the goal you defined for yourself this morning—there should be no room for doubt, or the possibility of failure!"

The humming gradually decreased in volume, and the assistants slowly moved the crystals in small circles as high as they could above the patients' heads.

"Now, close your eyes and feel the energy of your crystal circulating above your heads. Absorb its power with every breath you take in," said Toby in a tranquil tone. "When you're ready, I want each of you to say out loud *how* you're going to achieve your goal—in as much detail as possible. Do not be afraid, the special power of your healing crystal will guide you away from any negative energy that may prevent you from achieving your goal . . ."

The clearing remained peacefully silent for a few moments. Toby walked up to Kineosho and the eagle, both of whom were strapped in at the front of the therapy clearing. He whispered to them that it would be best to wait until the turtles were healed before articulating their own plans as the turtles' process often became quite loud and distracting.

A short while later, it so happened that Gita was the first of the turtles who decided to state how she was going to achieve her goal. Of the many phrases that were going through Gita's mind about her happy future life *Wax on!* was certainly not one of them. "*Wax on!*", however, was the exact phrase that came out when she opened her mouth. No sooner had she said it than the two assistant kangaroos thumped down the large crystal onto her head. They energetically yelled: "*Turtle let go!*" as they raised the crystal back up.

"*WAX OFF!*" shrieked Gita, startled at what had just happened and irritated that she was unable to move because of the straps. This promptly resulted in Gita getting another hard bonk on the head with her special therapy crystal.

At about the same time, another turtle said: "*Wax on!*" and he received an equivalent crystal treatment administered by his two kangaroos. Not long after, there was a cacophony of "*Wax on!*", "*Wax off!*", thuds and "*Turtle let go!*" yells that filled the clearing. It would wane for a short time and then the volume would pick up again. At one point, the racket got so loud that Kineosho found himself thinking about designing a revolutionary pair of noise-cancelling headphones rather than planning how he was going to get home.

This went on for quite a while until one of the turtles suddenly yelled "STOP!" just after being whacked a solid one on his head for saying his umpteenth *Wax on!*. The clearing found itself in a deafening silence.

"I'm okay!" shouted the turtle excitedly, smiling at the assistant kangaroos. "*I'm okay!*"

"*Wax on!*" shouted a couple of other turtles in reply, promptly earning themselves another dose of *Neuro-Linguistic Crystal Therapy*. That restarted the cacophony but it wasn't long before another turtle, Gita this time, yelled: "Wait!" This time the other turtles didn't quieten down much. They were all encouraged by the first turtle's miraculous recovery and were determined to say something else too.

The healing seemed to be as infectious as viral hepatitis and soon after, the last of the badly bruised turtles breathed a sigh of relief. The turtles cheered, and Toby happily joined in their celebration before escorting them out.

"You see, it works!" he said to Kineosho and the eagle with a wink. "Now, relax for a moment, clear your mind, and talk about how you're going to achieve your goal when you're ready."

"Well, I think it would be good to try to spea—" started Kineosho before he was rudely interrupted by a thump on the head with the large amethyst that had been hovering above him. "*Ow!*" he screamed in pain.

"What's better than *trying*?" asked Toby firmly. Kineosho paused.

"It would be good to ask others about going home," said Kineosho.

"Very good—find out more about your challenge," said Toby.

"Then, I'll return to the first path and tr—*erm* . . . not sleep," said Kineosho hesitantly before he was whacked on the head with his crystal again by the assistant kangaroos. "*Ow!* What now? I didn't say *try!*" he yelled immediately, earning yet another bonk on the head.

"Not sleep? Didn't say try?" asked Toby sarcastically. "You're speaking so negatively—come on, be positive!"

"Okay, I will enter the first path and stay awake. I will then cross the river. And then—" said Kineosho.

"—how will you cross the river?" interrupted Toby. "Details!"

Kineosho thought for a moment, and said nervously: "Swimming . . . I'll cross the river by swimming?" Once again, the crystal came plummeting down onto his head.

"*FUDGE!* That hurt!" cried Kineosho.

"Why do you doubt yourself? Be confident in your positivity—remember any negative thoughts you put out there will doom you to failure!" said Toby sternly.

"I'll swim across the river and then I'll be at home—goal achieved!" said Kineosho as quickly and confidently as he could.

"There you go—see, that wasn't so difficult, was it? Excellent Kineosho!" said Toby. "And what about you—you've been very quiet," he said to the eagle.

The eagle smiled smugly at Kineosho, and without hesitation said: "I will walk to the edge of a cliff, flap my wings as hard as I can and fly first thing tomorrow!" Within an instant, the eagle's crystal came hammering down on his head.

"What the—?! That was perfect!" cried the eagle.

"Tomorrow? *Tomorrow?* Procrastination is just another form of negativity with respect to your goals!" said Toby. Kineosho put out his tongue and rasped at the eagle.

"I will fly as soon as I get out of here!" said the eagle, irritated that he could not even shake his head in irritation.

"Another creature healed with crystal power!" said Toby, wiping his brow with his wing. "I love this job! Remove the crystals and clean up the room for tomorrow!" he instructed the remaining assistants as he escorted Kineosho and the eagle out.

❧ 28 ❧

Axolotl

Dinner that evening was merry. The turtles were chatting away with each other, carefully avoiding any topics to do with work or wax. Some of them looked more weathered than others, although all of them had lumpy black and blue bulges on their heads. Even Kineosho had a couple of nasty bruises following the crystal therapy.

"They look pretty happy now," said Uma to Milo.

"Definitely! It's a pity I missed the therapy session—it would have been a great healing technique to learn," replied Milo. He appeared to be much more cheerful than when he had left Uma that morning.

"Well, it didn't help me much—I still can't fly," sneered the eagle.

"Neuro-linguistic therapies don't work well with all animals," replied Uma. "If the issues are embedded very deep in the mind, a more intensive healing procedure is needed. Why don't you join my *Tepla* session tomorrow? Quite frequently, in order to address a current issue you need to dig deep into the past to get to the root cause of the problem — I have a feeling it may be just what you need," said Uma.

"Sure," said the eagle reluctantly, "just so long as there isn't any head-bashing involved!"

"No, no head-bashing!" laughed Uma. "I'm off for now, but you two may find it quite an interesting experience too — you should come," she said, pointing at Kineosho and Milo before she left.

"Why are you staring at him like that?" Kineosho asked Viddi, who had been staring at Milo with a strange expression on her face. Viddi replied with a shrug and a big grin.

"*Erm* . . . let's go somewhere quieter where we can talk," whispered Milo to Kineosho. Viddi and Basho followed them to a secluded spot behind some bushes at the edge of the clearing.

"What's going on — the two of you have been acting weirdly all evening," prompted Kineosho.

"*Eep!*" squealed Viddi, madly pointing under the armadillo.

Milo looked around cautiously and gently reached into his pouch. He slowly drew out his little hand, revealing the axolotl. The axolotl looked around curiously but said nothing.

"I thought he was banished from here —" whispered Kineosho.

" — and that's why we have to be very quiet about this, right?" said Milo, casting a stern look at Viddi. She nodded. "After what the elephant said I could not leave Axolotl outside — this is where he belongs — and there is so much we need to learn from him . . . I can just feel it!" said Milo.

The axolotl looked at Kineosho and smiled innocently.

"So what happened at the therapy today — did it do anything for you?" asked Milo, as he laid the axolotl down gently near a puddle.

"It did wonders for Gita and the other turtles but I don't think it's given me more than a solid headache," said Kineosho, rubbing one of the bumps on his head. "The morning session was very helpful though—I think I've figured out what I really want more than anything . . . to go home!"

"Defining your goal is important," said the axolotl. Everybody paused and stared at him, as though in shock because he spoke.

"The whole Neuro-Linguistic Crystal thing was crazy—I eventually wound up saying everything positively, but I'm pretty sure I did it so I wouldn't get whacked on the head again—certainly not because I believed what I was saying," said Kineosho.

"Given enough time and repetition, you can fool yourself into believing anything," said the axolotl.

"But you're still fooling yourself—right?" asked Kineosho with a grin.

The axolotl smiled.

"There are so many alternative healing and spiritual courses being churned out daily here. Each sounds more complex and fantastic than the next. Worse yet, many of them seem to be contradicting each other! I thought the Third Path was about a simple, holistic approach—am I wrong?" Milo asked the axolotl.

"No," replied the axolotl.

The others stared silently at the axolotl. "I don't understand," said Milo.

The axolotl paused for a few moments, looked at Viddi and said: "Shall I tell you a story?"

"Yes!" replied Viddi immediately, clapping her wonky hands.

"*Shhh* . . . quietly!" whispered Milo to Viddi. They all looked at the axolotl. He paused and looked back at them. Then, he slowly began his story.

"Once upon a time, there were six blind mice who were lost in a jungle. As luck would have it, one of them accidentally bumped into a kind little warthog who offered to help.

"'Where would you like to go?' asked the warthog.

"'We're looking for an elephant named Panacea,' replied one of the blind mice.

"'Do you know where Panacea is?' asked the warthog.

"'No,' replied another mouse. 'And we're blind so we can't even tell you what Panacea looks like,' it said sadly.

"'I have not met Panacea, but I'm sure if we ask around in the jungle we'll find someone who will be able to help us,' said the warthog.

"The warthog walked slowly through the jungle and the mice followed, each holding another's tail. Whenever he met an animal, he asked it about Panacea. It seemed that many animals had heard of Panacea, but they didn't know where to find her. They walked around for many days searching in different directions but with no luck.

"Then one day, the warthog had an idea. He asked a small sparrow if it could tell them where the nearest elephant was. The sparrow happily obliged, flew around the area, and returned with directions. The warthog and the chain of mice behind him headed off to speak to the elephant, who fortunately was not far away.

"When they found the elephant, the warthog asked: 'Do you know where we could find an elephant named Panacea?'

"'Of course, Panacea is a dear aunt of mine. If you walk down that path and follow the river downstream until you reach a large banyan tree, you will be sure to find her.'

"'Thank you!' replied one of the blind mice and they continued on their journey. Some time later, they arrived at the large banyan tree and the warthog was quite excited to see a large elephant sleeping nearby.

"'Is that Panacea?' the warthog asked a crocodile on the riverbank.

"'It is,' replied the crocodile. 'But I wouldn't wake her right now else she'll be really grumpy.'

"'We really just want to know what Panacea is like,' said one of the blind mice. 'Could you lead us to her?'

"The warthog led the six blind mice to where Panacea was sleeping. He placed each of them in a different spot around her and then left to get a drink from the river.

"By the time the warthog returned, the six blind mice had touched the part of the elephant they were closest to and examined it thoroughly. Afterwards, the warthog led the mice to the river and asked: 'So, did you get a good idea of what Panacea is like?'

"'Yes!' replied one of the blind mice. 'Panacea is nowhere near as large as I expected—in fact she felt like a short, soft leathery whip.'

"'What!' said another mouse. 'Panacea is enormous—she stretched farther than my hands could reach—and solid as a rock!'

"'If I didn't know better I'd say you were both blind! Panacea is like a smooth horn with a very sharp end,' said another mouse.

"'Ha, I'm not sure what planet you were on! Panacea is like an enormous, thin leaf that flaps when you blow at it,' said another of the blind mice.

"By then the mice had begun quarrelling loudly with each other. One of the remaining two mice shouted that Panacea was actually like a massive tree trunk, and the other insisted that she was like a scary fat snake, adding even more fuel to the fire.

Finally, the warthog shouted: 'Wait! You're all correct—let me explain!'

"'Panacea is a very large creature. You each only felt a small part of her and believed it to be what she was like as a whole. So you're all correct, but only partially right—Panacea is the sum total of everything you described, and more!'

"The six blind mice were very pleased and thanked the warthog for his kindness," smiled the axolotl as he completed the story.

Viddi could not resist clapping again, and both Milo and Kineosho looked in awe at the axolotl.

"Thank you," whispered Milo, almost with tears in his eyes.

"May I ask a question?" asked Kineosho.

The axolotl smiled innocently again.

"In the crystal therapy session, one of the steps in my plan to get home was to find out more about the first path out of the Angel's Trident. The large banyan tree in your story reminded me of the one I had seen there—please could you tell me what you know about the first path?" asked Kineosho.

The axolotl paused for a moment. "You are already on the first path," he replied. "Everything you experience is either preparing you, or hindering you."

"But when I was on the first path I experienced some terrible dreams when I fell asleep under the banyan tree. It was so real that I woke up badly wounded—almost killed," said Kineosho.

"Everything in your mind is real," said the axolotl. "You can only cross the river with an empty mind."

"But I thought if I don't . . . *erm* . . . if I stayed awake I would not experience the dreams," said Kineosho, rubbing one of the bumps on his head.

"Whether you face whatever is in your mind right here, or immediately before you cross the river, or in a dream—it doesn't matter. But you will certainly have to face it, otherwise it will be impossible for you to go home," said the axolotl.

"Can I go home too?" Viddi asked the axolotl, feeling a little left out of the conversation.

The axolotl smiled. "Of course, it surely wouldn't be home without you," he replied.

For a while, none of the animals said anything. They looked at the axolotl with mixed emotions: Milo still with awe; Kineosho with concern; Viddi with glee; and Basho with intrigue. The axolotl looked around and seemed fascinated by a pile of leaves near a puddle, but said nothing.

❧ 29 ❧

Roots

"So Uma, what exactly is *Tepla*, and how did you learn about it?" asked Basho curiously, as they made their way down a new path the following morning.

"It's short for *Transcendental Early and Past Life Acupuncture*," replied Uma as they continued walking. "I stumbled onto it by accident many seasons ago.

"One morning, I was in deep meditation near the river—a very peaceful place. Some naughty porcupine youth decided to play a prank and shoot their sharp quills at me. Most of them just bounced off but as luck would have it, three of the quills they shot at my ears struck some very special pressure points. The stimulation of those points whilst I was in deep meditation transported my mind back to what seemed like another world.

"It was as though I were another creature altogether, living in a different time. I felt my much smaller incarnation in that world—a bear! I was working with another bear, healing animals with sharpened twigs—helping them to see things in their past. Often what they saw gave them clarity on some of their current dilemmas and a better understanding of why they react to things the way they do.

"When I awoke from that meditation, I knew that I had found my calling and I have not looked back since. I worked with a group of porcupines to perfect the technique and it has helped many animals to come to terms with their earlier life experiences," continued Uma.

"We're almost there," said Rhino as he heard the chattering of animals in the distance. Soon after, they arrived to find a sizeable prickle of porcupines, and many other animals waiting near an exit off the path.

Rhino escorted the crowd off the path into a large clearing and told the animals to stand at least one arm's length apart in every direction. Uma asked the newer members to stand in front of the stage so it would be easier for her to coach them when necessary. She waited patiently for the crowd to settle and welcomed them.

The prickle stood in a straight line in front of Uma on the stage, facing the audience. All but a rather nervous-looking one among them seemed quite excited to begin the session. "Now, let's start with some simple breathing exercises to ease us into the meditation this morning," said Uma, sitting down facing the enthusiastic crowd.

Kineosho and Viddi immediately recognised the breathing exercises—they were almost identical to the ones Master Wu had taught them both so many moons ago. The familiarity was pleasing.

Slowly, Uma led the group from the breathing exercises into deep meditation. As she calmly instructed the audience about what to focus on, the prickle inhaled and exhaled loudly to maintain a constant rhythm for the animals to follow. The animals gradually started breathing in harmony with each other and were looking quite relaxed.

"Now I want you all to take your minds back to the earliest memory you have of yourself," said Uma in a gentle voice. "Don't worry if you find your mind wandering. When it does, simply bring it back to focus on the earliest memory you have each time." Uma signalled the prickle to disperse into the audience to start their work.

"You may feel a few tiny quill pricks on your ears but focus only on your memories. Just experience the brief physical sensation and continue with what you were thinking about," said Uma. The porcupines extracted some of their quills and proceeded to perform their unusual form of acupuncture on some of the animals' ears. Each time they completed the procedure on an animal they went to the next one and looked to Uma for a signal. If Uma felt the animal was ready, she nodded and the porcupine would measure the ear with its little fingers and start the quill pricking and turning process.

Kineosho's mind had wandered back to when he first met Uma. He remembered mistaking her for a large rock and the scolding he had received after he had yanked her tail. The memory was clear and familiar. Kineosho was startled when he felt the first little prick on his ear. His mind immediately drifted off to the first silent meditation session he had experienced with Twigs. He recalled how he had felt when his head was touched during that meditation. Then, he consciously brought himself back to his earlier memory of Uma.

He barely felt the second prick on his left ear, but when the third quill was deployed, Kineosho found his mind drifting back to an even earlier memory. He saw Master Wu levitating in front of him with the large tree hovering directly above him. The memory was so vivid that Kineosho could even smell the earth where the tree had been uprooted.

The porcupine then turned the first quill gently and Kineosho found his mind wandering off to a completely different scene. He was sitting near the riverbank and saw a bright light across the river. Moments later his mind flashed on the blurry image of the female leopard he had seen. He recalled how determined and curious he was to discover what was on the other side after that experience.

No sooner did he try to focus his mind to see the blurry image more clearly, than the porcupine gently turned the second quill. Once again, he found his mind transported to another peculiar memory. This time, he was back in the talent show walking towards the elegant female leopard. He recalled approaching her, and their conversation that followed — it was as though she were right there in front of him. Then, Kineosho felt something he was almost certain he did not feel in the talent show. When the leopard showed him the mark behind her ear and said, "I'm waiting for someone", he remembered experiencing a brief and unusual sadness.

At that very second the porcupine twirled the third quill, and Kineosho found his mind suddenly propelled back into the present. He breathed heavily as he tried to make sense of everything he had just seen. He remembered everything he saw, but the thing that persisted was the feeling of peculiar sadness he was certain he had not experienced earlier.

"Close your eyes and focus on your breathing again," whispered Uma in Kineosho's ear before returning to the stage. Kineosho shook his head to clear his mind and returned his focus to his breathing. Still, remnants of that odd feeling lingered on.

Kineosho had experienced his quill pricks much sooner than

most of the other animals. Many of those that had experienced the acupuncture, seemed to behave quite differently afterwards. Some were withdrawn, others more excited and still others looked relieved.

When the porcupine standing next to the eagle got his nod from Uma, he struggled a little to find the eagle's ears. He carefully measured three spots around them and clinically poked his quills in. The porcupine paused for a moment as the eagle adjusted his head, then he proceeded to turn each of the quills gently. As soon as he turned the first quill, the eagle jerked his head in surprise. "*Shhh . . .*" whispered the porcupine softly, "keep your eyes closed and continue to focus on your breathing."

The eagle's head felt woozy after the second quill was turned and he found some unfamiliar thoughts wandering rapidly in and out of his head. Suddenly he jerked his left claw violently and Uma came down from the stage to stand next to him. The eagle began to breathe deeply as a vision of a cabbit being lodged in his claw flashed behind his eyes. With his eyes still shut, he desperately looked at the scene trying to understand what was going on. He remembered that he had been flying relatively low that day. The eagle shrieked and shook as though he were having fits when he first saw an image of Viddi swirling around a tree branch at high speed. Uma immediately whispered to the eagle: "Don't be afraid — nothing will hurt you here, just focus on what you are seeing, and keep breathing."

A vision of a large cabbit hurtling towards Viddi's feet flashed behind his shut eyes. And then as though it all happened in slow motion, the eagle saw the very moment Viddi's feet made contact with the cabbit and sent it hurtling upward towards him. He remembered trying to avoid it, but it all happened too fast. The cabbit had firmly lodged itself between his claws. No matter what he tried, he could not free himself. The eagle saw himself flying higher and higher, not even paying attention to his direction. The harder he tried to dislodge the cabbit, the farther and higher he flew. He recalled the terror he felt, when he believed that he would never be free of that cabbit. Then suddenly, he flashed on himself being somewhere on the ground on the other side of the river. The cabbit had dislodged from his talons. He recalled the relief he felt, and the fear to flap his wings ever again.

The eagle's head grew even woozier as the porcupine twirled the third quill to complete the procedure. When he opened his eyes, he breathed heavily as he immediately looked around to find Viddi. When he saw Viddi, he glared at her. "This is entirely *your* fault!" he muttered angrily. "It all makes perfect sense now—Why I could not bring myself to fly—why I felt so terrified when we first met!"

"*Eep?*" asked Viddi, quite confused and concerned about the eagle's menacing glare, which was getting closer as the eagle had started to hop angrily towards her. Before the eagle could say or do anything further, Uma thumped the eagle's head gently with her trunk, startling him.

"I think you may want to try flapping your wings now," said Uma calmly. The eagle did, and nothing happened.

"Don't try . . . just fly," whispered Kineosho to him, remembering what the eagle had said the day before. The eagle shut his eyes and flapped his wings again. This time, to his surprise, he lifted a little off the ground. He flapped a little harder, and found himself practically suspended in mid-air.

"Fly!" yelled one of the porcupines below. The eagle flapped his wings harder and found himself being elevated even higher. He could not believe it as he lifted himself above all the animals in the clearing. Kineosho and Viddi both looked up in awe, feeling like they had witnessed a miracle.

By the end of the day, not all the animals had experienced the quills. Uma told many of them to return the next day for further exploration. When Kineosho and the others left the therapy clearing, he asked a rather nervous-looking Milo whether he had seen anything interesting.

"I saw Axolotl!" whispered Milo excitedly in reply.

"You mean he got out of your pouch!" asked Kineosho.

"No, I mean I saw Axolotl during my meditation—I think I had seen him before, many moons ago with my father. They were talking about the need for a destination for healing. A place where the Council could gather and share their knowledge," said Milo.

"Kind of like this place?" asked Kineosho.

Milo paused. "Well . . . yes—but different," he replied. "Everything was simple and there were so many armadillos . . . I have to ask Axolotl about it after dinner."

On the way back to the main clearing, both Viddi and Basho noticed the porcupine who had not been as enthusiastic as the others, quietly crying off the path. Viddi went up to her and thought about giving the porcupine her usual head-rubbing remedy for all ailments, but decided against it when she saw her sharp spines. "Why are you crying?" asked Basho as the others joined them.

The distraught porcupine looked up at them, turned her back slightly, and replied in her most damsel-in-distress voice: "Look! Look what's happening to me!" They all looked at the large quill-less patches on the porcupine's back.

"I'm so ugly! Why is this happening to me?" asked the panic-stricken porcupine.

"What's your name?" asked Milo softly, and slowly.

"Vanita," replied the porcupine, losing focus on her angst for a second.

Milo examined the quill-less patches briefly. "Hmm . . . I've seen this before," he said calmly, despite really feeling quite ecstatic that he had recognised the condition. "It looks like an acute form of porcupine alopecia—"

"Acute? Acute?" asked the porcupine in disbelief. "It's A-ugly if anything," she blubbered aloud, before she began to bawl.

"*Shhh* . . . take a deep breath, and calm down. Have you experienced any major loss or stressful life event recently?" asked Milo.

Vanita sniffed. "Yes, my partner left me for a younger porcupine a few weeks before it started and it has just been getting worse since! That horrible slimy slu . . . I hate her!"

"Hmm . . . That trauma is likely what caused it then—but don't worry, I can definitely treat it!" said Milo, a little more cheerfully than he had hoped it would come out.

"Really?" asked the porcupine, widening her eyes at Milo. "You can fix me?"

"Yes, certainly. Stop crying now and come join us for dinner. I'll ask Uma where we can find the herbs that are required and we'll have you back to your beautiful self in no time," replied Milo.

When they returned to the main clearing that evening, Milo was looking and feeling much more positive. Uma and the prickle joined them for dinner, and were happy to offer coaching and interpretations for animals who were confused about what they had experienced during their *Tepla* session that day.

Milo didn't mention a word about the memory he had recollected. Instead, he told Uma about Vanita's alopecia and asked where he could find a couple of exotic sounding herbs.

Uma paused for a moment, and said: "I don't know personally but I know just who you should be speaking to. I'll introduce you to the Council of Druids tomorrow morn—"

"Did . . . did you say the Council?" interrupted Milo feverishly. "When the porcupine was doing its acupuncture—today—in the session, I saw something. It was Axo—*erm* . . . my father—he spoke of a Council gathering—lots of armadillos," said a very flustered Milo, looking like he was about to hyperventilate.

Uma smiled and replied: "Many moons ago, before I had arrived here in fact, legend has it that an axolotl and an armadillo apparently created the Council of Druids—a place where many medicinal herbs were studied, classified, and distributed for treatments. Nobody ever found out what happened to the original axolotl and armadillo but the Council still remains—and yes, there are many armadillos in it!"

Milo looked at Uma, speechless.

"I'll introduce you to the Council tomorrow," repeated Uma slowly. Milo nodded manically in response.

"As for Vanita," continued Uma, "the herbs you mentioned will remedy her condition, but I would suggest that she also attend tomorrow's *Tepla* session to make sure that we address the root cause of the problem too. Would that be okay?"

Milo nodded again as he tried to spot Vanita, who had been hiding herself in a nearby bush.

"What about you? How did you find the session today, Kineosho?" asked Uma.

"It was interesting and the memories were vivid," replied Kineosho, "although I'm not sure I understand how the scenes that came to mind are connected. In fact, a couple of them left me feeling a little strange . . . what I felt today was quite different from how I remembered feeling on the actual day."

"Sometimes you need a couple of *Tepla* sessions to join the dots so everything makes sense. Your mind stores different aspects of an event without you realising it. These aspects often swim around in your subconscious and surface with certain triggers," said Uma.

"Looks like you've got this leopard doing the butterfly stroke in your subconscious at the moment," whispered Basho to Kineosho with a nudge.

"That's why we normally run these sessions over a few days," said Uma. "It gives enough time for most creatures to make sense of the different aspects that come up, and tie them together in what's often a completely different perspective of the same event."

"I wonder where the eagle is?" asked Viddi quite randomly.

"Probably out flying as high as he can, and scared silly to land anywhere in case it's all just a dream!" laughed Uma in reply. "It's not uncommon after a miraculous realisation of that sort actually—we call it *going podie!*"

"Podie?" asked Kineosho.

"*Podie* . . . short for Post-Discovery Euphoria, mate—geez, I could tell you a story or two about that," replied a nearby echidna in a funny Australian accent. He simply sounded funny, so they all laughed.

Shortly after, Uma excused herself, and many of the others also took their leave. Milo, who had remained conspicuously quiet since his conversation with Uma, was quick to disappear into the bushes too.

Kineosho, Basho, and Viddi returned to the quiet spot they had found the day before and discussed what Kineosho had seen during his meditation. Viddi happily reminisced about Master Wu. Basho recalled Chocolate Moose, and some of the more amusing acts they had seen in the talent show. They all wondered what had happened to Lucky the rabbit, and laughed remembering his comical escape from the foxes. The remnants of Kineosho's uneasiness from earlier that day disappeared.

Basho heard some rustling in a nearby bush and thought it was Milo, but nobody appeared. They waited a short while for Milo to return but he was nowhere to be seen.

❦ 30 ❧

The best medicine

Kineosho woke up earlier than usual. To his annoyance, the first thought that came to his mind was the uneasy sadness he had experienced during the *Tepla* session. He dug into his magic sack and looked for the rock he had picked up in the talent show, hoping it would refresh his memory. When he found it, he stared at the rock, but no revelations materialised. Soon after, Viddi and Basho woke up, and he felt a little better.

After completing their morning routine, they arrived at the main clearing for breakfast, surprised to find Milo already there. "Where did you disappear to last night?" asked Kineosho.

"Sorry about that — I had a lot to take care of," replied Milo. "It took me ages to find Vanita — the bush she had been hiding in was some kind of weird poison ivy for porcupines. I eventually found her bawling and itching away near the entrance of the Third Path — not a pleasant sight, I assure you! Anyway, I told her that she should attend the second *Tepla* session with Uma this morning and that I would get the herbs she needed in the meantime."

Viddi looked curiously at Milo and tried to peer under him. Milo smiled. "Axolotl has gone, Viddi," he said.

"Why? What happened?" asked Kineosho.

"After I left Vanita, Axolotl and I had a long chat about what I had seen, and what Uma had told me. He explained what had happened to my father and told me how the Council of Druids was formed—it's far too much to explain but I feel like I finally know what my role is here. I had lots of unanswered questions and it all finally makes sense now," said Milo, looking quite content.

"Where did Axolotl go?" asked Viddi, a little upset.

"Home . . . I guess," said Milo a little sadly. "I think Axolotl had just been waiting here for me."

Viddi leapt over and rubbed Milo's head affectionately in small circles. Milo smiled and the others laughed. Uma and Rhino arrived shortly after to join them.

As Uma polished off her last cabbit, she said, "It seems the Council of Druids will only be convening again four seasons from now."

"Four seasons!" said Milo anxiously, his eyes widening as though he was about to burst into tears. Rhino nodded solemnly to him in confirmation.

Uma was silent for what seemed to be an eternity to Milo. "Nah, we're just playing with you," said Uma with a wink. Rhino guffawed and the others followed suit. "Actually, we're going to leave a little early to introduce our friend to the Council before we start today's session," said Uma, smiling at Milo. "I'll see you all later at the *Tepla* clearing."

"Ah! You!" said Milo, exhaling deeply in relief. He looked as though he was going to burst into tears regardless. Rhino nudged him playfully with his head and they went on their way.

Viddi leapt onto Kineosho's back and together with Basho, they made their way along the path leading to the *Tepla* session. About a quarter of the way there, they heard a voice whispering at them from the bushes.

"*Pssst* . . . Hey, come over here for a second, won't you?" said the voice in a posh English accent.

Basho, recognising the voice, immediately looked back at Kineosho and shook his head. "Just keep walking," whispered Basho. "Don't look back!"

"*Pssst* . . .!" said the voice again from behind the bushes. "You're looking so down today—very low energy, and I know just the thing that will help you, ol' chap!"

Basho looked back again at Kineosho and shook his head in warning. They continued walking.

"*Pssst* . . .!" said the voice again. "I'm just trying to help you ol' chap—I heard you're looking for the leopard!"

This time Kineosho turned around immediately. "Be careful," whispered Basho anxiously but Kineosho did not hear him.

"The leopard?" he asked the bush. "Who told you I was looking for a leopard? Come out from behind there!"

A crocodile wearing a black bowler hat peered out from behind the bush.

"Crocodile!" snarled Kineosho as he turned to continue.

"Wait!" said the crocodile. "Don't judge me based on my fellow crocodiles. I've been reformed for many seasons now—sincerely! I just want to make amends now that I'm on this path, see ol' chap—you know, balance the karma?"

Kineosho looked back and said, "Oh, so where's the leopard then?"

"*Erm* . . . Don't I get a charitable donation for my efforts first?" asked the crocodile with a sly grin.

"Don't trust him," whispered Basho again, but Kineosho did

not listen. He stuck his paw inside the magic sack and pulled out one of the frogs who croaked happily until it saw the crocodile. It then quickly leapt back into the sack. Kineosho rummaged a little more until he found the last remaining gold coin.

"I assume this will do?" asked Kineosho, as he tossed the coin at the crocodile.

"Come, follow me," said the crocodile, smiling as he caught the coin, "I know a shortcut." Kineosho followed as did Basho behind him, shaking his head in disbelief. The crocodile led them through a short stretch of dense bush and on to another well-defined path. "So you have to follow this path down for quite a while. At the end of the path there is a large—" said the crocodile before Kineosho smacked him on the head with his paw.

"Lead the way!" snarled Kineosho.

"Wha'? Woh? You don't trust me? It's jus' 'cos I'm a crocodile innit?" asked the crocodile, accidentally replacing his posh English accent with a crude cockney one. He shook his head and began walking down the path.

"No I don't, and yes it is," replied Kineosho. "If this is a trick, you're going to be sorry!"

The crocodile shook his head again and said melodramatically in his recovered posh accent: "Can't a creature of the Great Banyan Tree repent and change? When you prick me, do I not bleed? When I—"

"—Lead!" interrupted Kineosho with a growl.

They walked for quite some time before they arrived at a large crowd of animals waiting to enter a cave of some sort.

"The madam leopard is in there," said the crocodile, pointing to the cave. "See, I told you that you could trust me . . . but you just wouldn't believe me! May I take your leave now? I have so many more of my wrong-doings to make up for."

Kineosho looked at Basho who just shrugged in response. "Are you sure she's in there?" asked Kineosho, glaring at the crocodile.

"Oh yes, certainly ol' chap!" replied the crocodile confidently in his poshest English accent. "Just call for me if you don't find her—and I'll even return your treasure. That's how very certain I am." In the split second that Kineosho looked into the huge crowd, the crocodile let out a snigger as he quickly scurried off the path into the closest bush.

"You know she's not going to be here, don't you?" Basho asked Kineosho.

"You don't know that for sure," replied Kineosho, still looking into the crowd for any sign of the elegant female leopard. "Besides, she could be inside already."

They waited for quite some time outside the cave before there was some movement. The small bloat of hippos standing guard suddenly shuffled their positions and allowed the crowd to enter in single file.

"What's with the security?" Kineosho asked one of the hippos, as he was about to enter the cave.

"Just move along," replied the hippo in an unfriendly tone.

"This is one of the most popular therapies during this season—" said a mongoose in front of Kineosho. "—There are visiting teachers from all over the world," interrupted another. "—Yes—it's amazing! I can't believe this is only your first time," chirped yet another excited mongoose from the troop.

"Really?" replied Viddi, equally excited after the mongooses' enthusiasm.

When they entered the cave, they found the layout to be like an indoor version of the Great Hall. It was enormous, and the stage was just as large as the one there. In fact, Kineosho half-expected Twigs to suddenly appear.

Suddenly, Viddi tugged at Kineosho's ear and used her long arm to point to an unusual-looking monkey already seated in the audience. "There!" said Viddi excitedly, and urged Kineosho to walk in that direction. When they were closer, to their surprise, the strange little monkey looked freakishly similar to Viddi.

"*Eep?*" asked the monkey, looking at Viddi.

Viddi, for the first time, looked incredibly shy and fluttered her long eyelashes.

"Oh, this is too weird," whispered Kineosho to Basho. "Do you mind if we join you here?" Kineosho asked the monkey.

"Abu!" replied the monkey with a huge grin, as he extended his long right arm to welcome them. Even more to their surprise, the little monkey's right arm was disproportionately longer than his left—in fact, his arms almost looked like a mirror image of Viddi's arms.

"Viddi!" replied Viddi with an equally huge grin. She extended her long left arm in reciprocation. If little monkeys could blush, that would have been a very pink moment indeed. Kineosho looked at Basho and they both struggled to stifle a chuckle as they took their seats.

A flamboyant drum roll interrupted Viddi and Abu's cutely awkward moment. The entire audience stood up and cheered. The mongooses that had entered before Kineosho were seated nearby and they went completely berserk. They each took out well-camouflaged objects that looked like mini-vuvuzelas and began blustering into them, making irritatingly shrill whistling sounds. The noise blared throughout the cave, causing the crowd to cheer even louder.

Two hippo guards rushed into the crowd towards the mongooses and angrily snatched the mini-vuvuzela whistles. The mongooses shrugged at each other and began putting their fingers in their mouths to continue their performance.

When the drum roll stopped, the audience quietened down and a deep charismatic voice echoed through the cave: "Friends, Rabbits, Cockroaches . . . I —" and the crowd burst into applause. "Thank you! I — would now like to welcome on stage the most famous energy healer, and the sexiest camel this side of the river . . . King Ibrik!"

The mongooses whistled loudly and the crowd cheered as a truly magnificently groomed camel strutted onto the stage. He was escorted by a bright spotlight, courtesy of a group of fireflies. "Thank you! *Shukhran!* Thank you *habibi!*" said King Ibrik in a strong Arabic accent as he bowed his head dramatically. King Ibrik paused as he waited for the audience to quieten down.

"So, how many of you are Briki virgins here . . . first-timers I mean?" King Ibrik asked the audience. About a quarter of the audience raised their paws and claws, at which the mongooses punched their hands in the air and yelled "Woo woo woo woooo Briki virgins!" causing the rest of the crowd to burst into laughter.

"— bugger, I see they let you lot in again too," said King Ibrik, shaking his head. "Just no quality control in the spiritual world these days, is there?" The crowd roared again. Even Kineosho and Basho found themselves laughing at the bizarre scene.

"Well I suppose there are quite a few first-timers so I should probably give you an introduction about how this works before we get the healing going on," said King Ibrik. "As you've probably gathered by my exotic accent, I'm not from these parts. In fact, I'm more moons away from here than many of you can count — especially you lot," said King Ibrik, pointing to the mongooses. They promptly broke out into another round of "Wooo woo!"

"Now, seriously for a moment . . . let me give you a brief history of Briki Energy Healing—it really is a very effective technique perfected over hundreds of seasons by Master Healers from all over the world," said King Ibrik in his thick Arabic accent.

"It all started one summer afternoon when a giant panda named Yinyang was deep in meditation under a banyan tree in a forest many moons away. Yinyang was an odd-looking panda in that the left half of his body was entirely black, and the right half completely white. He had been meditating for quite a while when a colourful butterfly began to flutter around him. Soon, the butterfly decided to sit on the very tip of the panda's nose.

"Before long, Yinyang began to twitch his nose trying to get rid of that itchy feeling you get when a butterfly is sitting on your nose. The more he twitched his nose, the more the butterfly flapped its wings to maintain its balance, irritating the panda's nose even more. Soon, Yinyang could not bear the itchy feeling and he inhaled deeply before letting out an enormous sneeze.

"When he opened his eyes after the sneeze, Yinyang had a moment of clarity. On his left black paw, he felt wonderful, given that the sneeze had healed his itchy nose. On his right white paw, however, he felt sad for the gooey fate of the colourful butterfly, which his sneeze had propelled backwards into a tree at rocket-speed. It was at that very moment that the panda realised the dual nature of energy, and in fact—the universe.

"Now many before him had believed that any creature could channel universal energy to heal. But Yinyang realised then why so many clinical trials for this sort of healing had proved inconclusive at best. He realised that creatures may well have been channelling what they thought was positive energy for healing, when, in fact, that may not have been the case. When he tried to communicate his incredible discovery to other energy healers of the time, they simply scorned him and continued with exactly what they had been doing.

"So Yinyang travelled the world, trying to find a source of irrefutable positive energy to use for healing. He met and discussed his ideas with many healers, but with no luck.

"Finally one day, when he was about to give up on his quest, he came upon a group of camels in a desert. As he approached them to ask for some water, one of them had just finished telling an incredibly funny story about a female camel he was pursuing. They all laughed hysterically and even Yinyang found his damp spirits being lifted immediately. At that moment, Yinyang realised that he had found exactly what he had been looking for.

"He discussed his ideas with the camels, who were already well aware of the positive healing energy of laughter. Over many moons, and much research later, they perfected a technique to capture and dispense this positive energy using a specially designed object called a briki," said King Ibrik.

He held up a metal kettle-like container by its wooden handle. It was the size of a large coffee mug. "A briki, friends!" he said proudly.

The crowd immediately responded with applause and started chanting: "Briki! Briki! Briki! Briki!"

"So now, join me in welcoming our latest international Briki Grand Masters — Bin-Nas, Bin-Sharm, and Slaps to begin generating some of that positive vibe and get the healing going on!" said King Ibrik. The crowd cheered at the top of their voices as an echidna, an aardvark, and an overweight orang-utan rolled onto the stage.

"Hey he's that funny animal from dinner yesterday!" said Kineosho to Basho, pointing at the echidna.

The crowd continued chanting "Briki! Briki!" as a few young female camels dispersed into the audience. They each carried a briki and did some stretching exercises when they arrived at their designated spots.

Bin-Sharm, the aardvark, did a few stretching exercises of his own and ended by extending his incredibly long tongue in the air and waving it at the crowd. Bin-Nas, the echidna, who basically looked like a spiny version of the aardvark, raised and dropped his spines making a strange hissing noise. He punched his long claws into the air to get himself psyched up.

Slaps made himself comfortable in the middle of the stage, and did no stretching whatsoever. Instead, the orang-utan slowly looked around at the crowd from left to right, making an exaggerated chewing action with his mouth. Then suddenly, he looked straight ahead and slapped himself really hard on each cheek and yelled "*WooHaa!*", much to the delight of the audience.

"All right, quieten down, you sexy Sheilas at the back," said Bin-Nas the echidna, in his Australian accent.

"Our lovely assistants out there will capture the positive energy you generate with your laughter into their brikis. Remember, the more you laugh the better. And if you laugh at yourselves, even better—that's the strongest kind of good vibe you can generate! Oh yes, and before I forget, our legal representation has warned that any assistant camel butt-pinching will be rewarded with a swift kick in the head," said Bin-Sharm, the aardvark as he whipped out his long tongue and slapped himself on the head with it.

Then the firefly spotlight moved onto Slaps in the middle of the stage. He was still looking forward a little blankly and chewing away. The audience quietened down. "Oh my, it is me already *lah*," said Slaps in a Malaysian accent, and the audience burst into laughter.

"What you all laughing at *lah*, you tink it is funny I just sitting here super-fat like dis," he said with a straight face. "Well, I tell you — it is not funny. In my youth, I was a handsome and beautiful orang-utan. I had girls from all species chasing me *lah* . . . it was so great.

"Then I started my spiritual journey. I travelled . . . all over . . . until I came across this famous course called *Tepla* — you all heard of it yah? Transcendental Early and Past Life something," said Slaps.

"Acupuncture!" shouted an ostrich in the audience.

"Yah! Acupuncture, that's it!" continued Slaps. "Well, let me tell you, if you ever do that therapy don't ever do it sitting next to a wildebeest *lah!* Apparently, as I discovered, the acupuncture point for past life regression in wildebeest is very close to the pressure point that makes them . . . well," said Slaps. "Fart!" as he put one hand under his armpit and quickly lowered his arm to make a disgusting sound.

"Ugh!" shouted the audience, and the mongooses started trying to make the same sound with their armpits as well.

"No, seriously," continued Slaps. "Just one wrong prick, and *pooh*! You were wishing you had paid more attention to holding your breath in that free-diving course you did last summer!" said Slaps as he waved his hands frantically in front of his nose. The audience burst out laughing, and the assistant female camels walked around moving their brikis about, to capture the positive energy.

"Anyway, that was just the beginning *lah*. When the lady wildebeest next to me had her second quill turned she suddenly had a vivid vision from her past. Of all things, she saw herself as a cuddly koala bear graced with the healing power of hugs. Really wonderful for her, except she woke up suddenly and started randomly trying to hug everyone. Can you see it, huge ten ton wildebeest thinking she's a koala going berserk hugging everything around her?" The audience rolled on the floor with laughter.

"You're laughing?" asked Slaps with a serious look on his face. "The mad cow crushed every bone in my feet when she hugged me! I couldn't walk for weeks *lah!* And the amount of weight I put on because of that . . ." said the orang-utan, slapping his face in disbelief.

"*Aww* . . ." chirped the aardvark, preparing himself to put on an exaggerated Indian village accent. "And here we were thinking you were just big-boned," he said, shaking his head from side to side, bringing on another roar of laughter from the crowd. The firefly spotlight shifted onto Bin-Sharm, who extended his tongue way above his head and waved it at the crowd.

"So," continued Bin-Sharm in his strong Indian accent, "seriously, that is no laughing matter. And speaking of sad things, that is reminding me of the time when grandmother passed on many moons ago—the Great Banyan Tree rest her snout. I just was a young aardvark then—so innocent and sweet—"

"—What happened to you since yesterday!" heckled one of the mongooses.

"I met your mother!" replied Bin-Sharm coolly, causing the other mongooses to break out into a loud "Wooo woo!" chant.

"Actually seriously dude, I think she probably was your mother—short, fat, rather amorous—sound familiar? Anyway, she had developed this revolutionary new process called *Accelerated Grief Relief*. So you know, I figured I had better try it out," continued Bin-Sharm, with his Indian accent totally flowing like the Ganges now.

"After all, you may not know this but grief, sadness, loss—that kind of thing *really* goes down well with female aardvarks . . . they're very sensitive, you know. Anyway, my shrink at the time told me it's a good idea to get in touch and feel up a feminine side, or something like that . . ." said Bin-Sharm. "So I thought, why the funky skunk not?" he continued, shaking his head and wiggling his eyebrows at the same time.

By this time, the audience was in stitches and the young female camels were zipping about the crowd collecting the positive energy into their brikis. Kineosho had long forgotten about looking for the leopard and was thoroughly enjoying the show.

"So, I went to the session and sat next to this cutie pie—oh, I can still remember her sexy snout—so long, so elegant, so very beautiful, so delicate, so intricate, so soft, so smooth, so divinely divine, so—" said the aardvark, before Slaps gave him a solid slap across the head.

"Family show *lah* . . . Focus!" yelled Slaps.

"*Ow!* Okay!" yelped Bin-Sharm. "Suffice it to say, she was well *humna humna humna humna*—you know what I am meaning right?" he asked the crowd while moving his elbows up and down, giving them a huge wink.

"Anyway, so the *Accelerated Grief Relief* process began with a quiet meditation session in absolute darkness. The mongoose, I admit, was very good—everyone felt very calm and relaxed. We were all told to focus on a good memory of nana . . . then suddenly, the mongoose ran around the room biting, headbutting, and scratching everyone. It was total chaos! Everyone was screaming and yelping, trying to figure out what was going on. Even the cutie pie I thought I was doing quite well with whacked me across the head with her snout. Okay, okay, I admit I did try to get in a small nibble when all the biting was going on—but I was only trying to help the healing process!

"Anyway, soon after, the mongoose opened the door and all the mourners bolted out—well, as best we could given the painful injuries we had all sustained . . . more like limped and straggled out. When we were all outside, the mongoose asked how many of us were still experiencing any grief about nana. To be honest, we were all so concerned about our own very real physical pain that we had all but forgotten about nana. So the mongoose jumped around with joy, claiming huge success for her revolutionary technique. Needless to say, it wasn't a very popular technique once animals heard exactly how it worked, but I believe there is still a strong following in certain masochistic sloth communities," said Bin-Sharm.

"What was really most sad was that I never got to see that cutie pie again," continued Bin-Sharm adding an extra dose of melodrama to the Indian accent. "In fact, I pined and pined for so many days thereafter—first for my bite wounds . . . mostly because I thought I was going to get rabies and die—but then also for my heart," said Bin-Sharm in a sad voice with both hands holding on to his chest.

"*Awww . . .*" sympathised the audience in response.

"Yeah, blast that heart-breaking, neurotic mongoose! Or is it psychotic . . . I can never remember the difference between those two—" said Bin-Sharm.

"—*Eeeeaasy lah!*" interrupted Slaps. "When a *neurotic* adds one and one, she gets two and has a panic attack about it. When

257

a *psychotic* adds one and one, she gets three and is quite simply very happy with that!" The crowd burst out once more.

"Actually I hear you Bin-Sharm—it's all gotten so complicated. Everyone is making up these terms pretending they've come up with something fresh and original," said Slaps in a sombre voice. "Half the time I don't even understand what animals here are going on about *lah*—I mean, what's this about *immersing yourself in the fields of pure potentiality?*"

"Oh, that just means you should aspire to be the best you can be," replied Bin-Sharm without hesitation. Slaps looked at him with a wide-eyed, enlightened look on his face.

"Wow . . . how did you . . ." asked Slaps as he slapped his own head, bringing about another round of laughter.

"I had a single-celled amoeba as a life-coach—next best thing to an axolotl if you want to keep things simple!" replied Bin-Sharm with a smile.

"So, how about the *Secret Law of Attraction* then?" asked Slaps.

"You only find what you're looking for!" replied Bin-Sharm.

"Universal language of mystical omens—" asked Slaps.

"—trust your gut!" retorted Bin-Sharm.

"Cultivate intuitive empathy without absorbing people's negativity—" chirped a tit from the audience.

"—you don't have to inhale the poo, just know it's there!" chirped Bin-Sharm right back.

"Open to the magic of synchronicities and déjà vu—" challenged Bin-Nas.

"—cool stuff happens at the strangest of times!" replied Bin-Sharm immediately.

"Restoration of karmic harmony—" dared Slaps immediately after.

"—it all balances out in the end—hey, I could go on all day!" replied Bin-Sharm in his Indian accent, and the audience responded with a loud round of applause.

"Speaking of restoring karmic balance, and getting back to my story, what pain the universe giveth, it also taketh away. Actually, things got real bad for me after that therapy. The awful heartbreak, and possibly an infection from the mongoose bite, took its toll and left me a rather sorry half-blind, asthmatic aardvark looking for love in all the wrong places. But *faartunately*, my long lost brother heard my desperate cry for help in a dream, and magically arrived at my humble hole-in-the-ground from over the seas—" said Bin-Sharm, with a huge smile returning to his face.

"—yeah, *magically* my spiny ass. I had to bribe this stork with some dirty favours—don't even want to talk about it now. And what a total mess he was when I arrived," said Bin-Nas in his Australian accent that just seemed to breed chuckles regardless of what he said. "—they should call 'em aardvark tears instead of crocodile ones.

"I mean seriously mate, where I come from, we always say the best way to get over one Sheila, is to get right under ano—". Before he could finish, he was interrupted by a whack on the head from Slaps, who immediately yelped in pain himself. He had clearly forgotten that slapping a spiny echidna isn't the smartest way to reprimand one of them.

"*Erm* . . . yeah—I'd like to apologise in advance to the more sensitive members of the audience," said Bin-Nas before clearing his throat. "Anyway, as luck would have it, the next best thing had just arrived in our neck of the woods—*Strip Yoga Therapy*. It's not really a participation activity—more like an armchair therapy. I had seen it work for tons of my mates back home, so

I took Bin-Sharm and signed us both up for a session—it was great!"

"Oh *yessss*, it very much was," confirmed Bin-Sharm in his Indian accent and kept on shaking his head.

"So we enter this underground cavern yeah, and there was this contortionist Sheila there—as far as snakes go, she was certainly one of the most flexible I've *ever* seen. And the music was superb—I can still hear the wolves whistling away in my mind—totally awesome!" said Bin-Nas. "Then she danced and stretched her body in ways that made my snout get into knots just trying to imitate her. Mmm . . . Mmm . . . Mmm . . . At the end of the therapy Ruby shed her skin in a contorted grand finale—I swear it must've taken an hour to get all of Bin-Sharm's tongue fully back into his mouth!"

"But you know these things are not for everybody," said Bin-Sharm. "Remember that turtle couple who came to that session?"

"Oh yeah! He had heard about a *Hot* Yoga session and thought it was some kind of Vikram Yoga—you know, the one you do in the extreme heat of a volcanic sauna? Anyway, the poor bugger took his turtle Sheila there and couldn't peel his eyes off Ruby—his girlfriend came out beating him over the head with a barstool yelling *"Turtle let go! Turtle let go!"* Funniest thing I've ever seen!" said Bin-Nas.

"Funny it may have been *lah*, but Bin-Sharm makes a good point. Not everything is for everybody in this spiritual world," said Slaps as the firefly spotlight focused on him once more. "The Banyan Tree alone knows how many snails we've lost doing Tai Chi—they were just moving so . . . extremely . . . slowly . . . that the instructors kept burying them thinking that they had passed on.

"Oh, then there were those silly tsetse flies who kept forgetting what came after inhale in their yoga postures so they just kept inhaling until they bloated and popped themselves—may the Great Banyan Tree let them sleep in peace.

"You know, the more I think about it, the more I feel we need a creature-specific guide to the journey of self-discovery—at least a warning guide that tells a sparrow it's probably a bad idea to get toe massage reflexology done by an elephant. You know, something that tells a jackass not to pay too much attention to underwater breathing therapy, and a spineless jellyfish to avoid chiropractic chakra massage—it would make life here so much safer!" said Slaps with a profoundly straight face.

"Yeah, speaking about chiropractic chakra massage," chirped Bin-Nas, "did you hear about a giraffe named Loaf who went for that recently?"

"No, what happened?" asked Bin-Sharm.

"Apparently they were performing the chiropractic massage on Loaf and discovered that he had a couple of extra chakras in his long neck—mate, they surgically removed half his neck trying to make him fit into their chakra model!" said Bin-Nas.

"No way *lah!*" said Slaps.

"Yeah, now they call him Half-Loaf—poor bugger," said Bin-Nas sadly.

"You know, I'm sad to say that there have been a couple of really suspect therapies coming out of the *Specialist Therapy Creation Centre* recently. Someone told me that some devious crocodiles were rigging the lists, adding some of their own therapies each day . . . seriously, I mean: *Crocodile Love You Long Time* therapy?" asked Bin-Sharm in his cutest Thai accent. The audience went wild. Even Kineosho found himself involuntarily smacking his feet on the ground. His cheeks were aching.

"Yeah, and don't even ask about the *Crocodile Ganja* ther-apy—that stuff is some majorly stinky funk!" added Bin-Nas.

"*Ganjaaa!* Woo woooo!" yelled one of the mongooses, bring-ing on another bout of hysterical guffaws in the audience.

"Oh yes, we love medicinal herbs *lah!*" said Slaps, chewing and scratching his head and stomach at the same time. "I remember this one time a group of delinquent marmoset monkeys con-vinced a newbie armadillo in the Council of Druids that they needed those cocaine—coca leaves to chew on . . . they claimed that the trees in their area were growing very high recently and they needed the coca to help with their altitude sickness!"

Abu laughed so hard that he snorted. Viddi found this most amusing and was quite happy to try it herself. It wasn't long before Abu and Viddi had their own laugh and snort show going on. Pretty soon, the mongooses joined in and there was a real ruckus in the audience around them.

"Geez maties, why don't you two get a room already!" said Bin-Nas, to which Viddi and Abu both fluttered their eyelashes and looked away, rather embarrassed.

"Clearly you mongooses don't need any type of Inner Child therapies either," said Slaps. "You'd be like little foetuses wad-dling around," continued Slaps, comically attempting to waddle in a small circle himself on the stage.

"*Hypnotic Inner Child Therapy!*" said Bin-Sharm, back in his Indian accent. "That was one of the first therapies I went on—it was amazing . . . it was also the first time I witnessed an animal totally *going podie!*"

Bin-Sharm turned and paused for a second to prepare himself for his most pretentious English accent. "*Going podie*—that's short for experiencing Post-Discovery Euphoria, for the uneducated riff-raff among you. Quite like that hug-frenzy lady wildebeest that ol' Slaps told you about earlier," he said, sticking his long snout in the air.

A fresh wave of laughter swept across the audience, and even the assistant camels giggled as they continued capturing the abundantly positive vibe into their brikis.

"So, in my group, there was this quirky female ostrich named Sparrow—strange name I know, but don't ask—I think her father had some weird thing going on there. Anyway, the ostrich unfortunately had serious obsessive-compulsive disorder issues and had tried lots of different therapies. Nothing worked—kept burying her head in the sand any time somebody touched her . . . quite funny playing tag with her actually—the game would just like—stop.

"Anyway, this owl with the largest eyes looks into Sparrow's eyes and starts rolling his own eyeballs back and forth in a half-moon. Pretty soon, the ostrich is hypnotised and the owl starts suggesting stuff to her about letting go, releasing fear and getting in touch with her inner child. Spoke to her for quite a while actually. Finally, the owl told Sparrow that when she woke up she would no longer bury her head in the sand, and that she would live freely through the eyes of her inner child.

"The owl snapped his beak, and the ostrich awoke from the hypnosis. It really was quite miraculous—I even touched her myself with my snout and Sparrow just looked at me and smiled. No nervous tics, head burying—nothing!" said Bin-Sharm.

"It always amazes me, that no matter how serious the situation might seem, things can always get better by simply viewing the challenge from a different perspective," added Bin-Nas.

"Yep—it appeared as though she were completely healed. She was. In fact, everything was fine during the owl's celebratory speech, and then Sparrow went totally *podie*. Her eyes widened like saucers and she had this mischievous grin on her beak. During the closing meditation, she somehow managed to tie four of the other animals' legs together, including mine! Tripping me was fine, but I still remember poor Half-Loaf whacking his head on that dizzy mole—it was mad!

"Sparrow dashed out of the session screaming '*Whee! Whee! Free! Free!*' and flapping her wings like a psychotic ostrich," said Bin-Sharm, flapping his little elbows and leaping around the stage. The audience roared once more. By this time, Kineosho's sides were aching. Viddi and Abu seemed to have perfectly synchronised their odd laugh and snort combination. Even Bin-Nas, Bin-Sharm, and Slaps found themselves chuckling on stage.

"Yeah, we never saw her again after she went *podie*—crazy ostrich!" said Bin-Nas, as a huge drum-roll filled the cave. The mongooses whistled at the top of their voices and the crowd went wild.

The firefly spotlight shifted onto King Ibrik as he returned to the stage. "Friends, please give a round of applause to thank our Briki Grand Masters: Wellington Bin-Nas; Tamsic Bin-Sharm; and Bornanew Slaps . . ." announced King Ibrik. The audience gave them an energetic encore of applause.

"To conclude the day's healing, our lovely assistants have handed me their collection of positive energy in their brikis. The Grand Masters and I will be standing at the exit to channel the concentrated healing power to each of you. I wish you all much light . . . and health!" said King Ibrik. The fireflies lit up the cave as King Ibrik, Bin-Nas, Bin-Sharm, and Slaps headed towards the exit with the full brikis.

As each of the animals exited the cave, one of the Grand Masters moved their briki in a symbolic triangle above its head. He then tapped the briki lightly on its head saying: "Have fun and be happy!" Some of the reactions as the animals left were quite comical—especially the mongooses, who all made a peculiar blubbering noise with their lips whilst shaking their heads vigorously. Most other animals seemed to experience a warm, tingling sensation from head to toe. Kineosho was no exception.

A smitten Abu accompanied them on their way back to the main clearing. Following some coyness, Viddi and Abu held each other's longer hands as they walked along the path. After they managed to trip a few creatures who tried to walk over their arms, a pair of flamingo victims urged them to use their shorter arms instead, for public safety reasons.

Dinner that evening was light-hearted and fun. Viddi joined the others in exchanging funny stories and Kineosho felt happy. Thoughts of the leopard and trying to understand what had happened with her at the talent show had completely slipped his mind.

Not long after, the porcupine with alopecia returned to the clearing with Uma and Rhino. As soon as she spotted Viddi, she ran up to her and manically began apologising. "I had this vision in today's *Tepla* session and you were in it—you know, when you were very young, I saw you and made some horrible comments about how freakishly ugly you were, do you remember?" asked Vanita anxiously.

Viddi looked at Vanita a little confused and shrugged, not remembering it at all.

"Well, I did. And I think this is the universe just restoring karmic harmony! Please can you forgive me?" begged Vanita apologetically.

Viddi looked at Abu, and shrugged again. "Sure!" she replied happily.

"Oh, thank you!" replied Vanita, looking relieved.

Milo soon arrived at the clearing, having spent the day with the Council of Druids. He looked positively happy. "I found my *mojo* . . . it was the most incredible experience being with the Council!" he said glowingly to Kineosho and Uma. "And I found the herbs you need too!" he chirped to Vanita.

That night there was a calm, sweet fragrance in the air. The animals exchanged random banter for a while longer and drifted off into a peaceful slumber.

❦ 31 ❦

Murder on the dance floor

The following morning, the pleasant atmosphere of the evening before still permeated the air. Abu joined Viddi, Kineosho, and Basho for their early morning routine before they all headed for breakfast.

Uma asked what had happened the day before, as she missed Kineosho at her *Tepla* session. Kineosho told her about the crocodile, and how he had led them to the Briki Energy Healing cave.

"We've been trying to catch that shifty crocodile for a few moons now," said Uma. "He eavesdrops on conversations after *Tepla* sessions and uses the information to trick animals into giving him 'donations'! He must have spotted the opportunity yesterday since we weren't around."

"I told you not to trust that scaly handbag with feet," whispered Basho to Kineosho.

"Still," said Abu, raising his long right arm to the sky, "Abu wouldn't have met this fine creature had he not tricked them — I am the most grateful animal in this jungle!" He looked with adoration at Viddi, who batted her long eyelashes in shy reply.

"In fact," continued Abu coyly, "if it's okay with you, Kineosho, I would like to steal Viddi away for a few moons?"

Basho immediately looked at Kineosho with a concerned expression on his face but said nothing. Kineosho looked at Uma who just smiled and shrugged.

"Why not?" replied Kineosho, smiling as he saw the excitement light up Viddi's face. Viddi and Abu both immediately leaped onto Kineosho and each clasped an ear as they hugged him tightly. They left soon after, romantically walking off hand in hand into the sunrise.

"The next *Tepla* session is not for a few days, any ideas about what you'd like to try in the meantime?" asked Uma.

"I was thinking I would just have a wander around and relax," replied Kineosho.

"Probably a good idea," said Uma, "you've had an intense time since you arrived on the Third Path. Anyway Rhino, my porcupine friends here, and I are off to do some recruiting in the Angel's Trident today—you're welcome to join us later if you'd like."

As Uma left the main clearing, Milo polished off the last of his cabbit and left with Vanita to collect the alopecia herbs from the Council of Druids. Soon after, the other animals left on their various paths until only Kineosho and Basho remained.

"It feels a little strange without Viddi, and the others," said Kineosho after some silence.

Basho nodded in reply.

"That Briki healing yesterday was something else, wasn't it?" asked Kineosho.

"Great fun!" replied Basho with a smile.

"Shall we have a wander and explore around?" asked Kineosho.

"Sure," replied Basho. He waited for Kineosho to stand up, which seemed to take a long time.

They picked a random exit from the clearing and started walking down the path.

"You know, we never really looked around properly in the Briki cave—I mean, the leopard could well have been there and we would never have known," said Kineosho.

"True," replied Basho, stopping to scratch his ear.

They continued walking down the path for some time and saw nothing exciting. The path was a peculiar one, as it seemed to extend endlessly. By the time late afternoon had arrived, they had still not found any exit from, or end to it. Kineosho was tired and they decided to rest for a while before returning to the clearing. As soon as he laid his head on the ground, he fell into a deep sleep.

When Kineosho woke up, to his surprise he found himself back at his regular sleeping place. He heard the familiar bell ring in the distance and looked at Basho who was still asleep. Viddi was not there. "How bizarre—that path yesterday . . . was that just a dream?" he thought to himself. Then he looked around and for a brief moment, an awkward sensation came over him. Everything around him seemed familiar, yet unfamiliar. The feeling passed quickly though, so Kineosho did not think much of it. He woke Basho and they completed their morning exercises before heading for breakfast.

Uma, Rhino, and the porcupines were already there. Just before finishing, Uma said: "There were a huge number of animals at the Angel's Trident yesterday—apparently many rushed out from the Second Path after one of the moles there went *podie* during their silent meditation session. She started throwing stones at the other animals to bless them so lots of them bolted!

Anyway, we're going to be away for a few days on a recruitment drive—you're welcome to join us if you'd like?"

"I'm feeling a little tired—I think I might stay and relax a bit longer," replied Kineosho. "Do you think I could speak to you before you leave though? Something strange happened yesterday and it's left me feeling uneasy."

Kineosho took a walk with Uma to a quiet spot and described what had happened the day before.

"Is there really an endless path like that, or did I just dream the whole thing?" asked Kineosho, curious to understand what happened.

"I think you've experienced an overwhelming amount in a short time. And Viddi leaving yesterday has probably not helped the situation," replied Uma.

"Viddi?" asked Kineosho. "What does she have to do with that path?"

"Well, think of it like this: sometimes when a part of you is focused on something other than your goal, it's quite difficult to take steps towards achieving it," replied Uma. "Remember the storm when you were hanging off the muddy mountainside? You only managed to climb out when you fully focused your mind, and everything was working together on the task."

"So . . . what do I do if it happens again? Focus?" asked Kineosho.

"Yes—bring your focus back to your goal as best you can. That's all any of us can ever do when we find ourselves straying," replied Uma.

"The other thing is that when I woke up this morning, I had an uneasy feeling of being isolated . . . you know, a little out of place. Do you think that's because of Viddi leaving too?" asked Kineosho.

"Perhaps, but Kineosho, there is something I should tell you that I don't think you've realised yet. There may be many animals around you here but this path is a very individual one. Particularly, for the goal you've chosen—to go home, I mean. Regardless of your interactions, friendships, and close bonds it can still be an extremely lonely path. If you find yourself in that place, you will have to learn to deal with it effectively. I've seen many animals collapse into a downward spiral because of it, and many of them never recover," said Uma in a concerned tone.

"That sounds dire!" laughed Kineosho, who had been hoping that the feeling was the result of a dodgy cabbit he had eaten. "How do *you* deal with it though, just in case?" he asked curiously.

"How you deal with any strong emotions and feelings—by expressing them in some way that prevents you from drowning in them," replied Uma. "There are plenty of courses you can take here to help with that, if you need them."

Kineosho nodded in reply as they walked back to the main clearing. By that time, most of the other animals had already left for their therapy sessions. Uma, Rhino, and the porcupines left soon after on their recruitment drive and Kineosho and Basho were alone in the clearing once more. Kineosho felt much better after the chat with Uma, although he still felt a little tired.

Basho agreed that a nap would be a good idea for them both and they dozed off under a shady tree. Kineosho woke up a short while later with what felt like a bad dream, although he could not recall what it was about. When Basho woke, they decided to explore a different path.

Kineosho was relieved that the path they chose was visibly different from the one they had picked the day before. After walking a long distance though, they both noticed that this path seemed to have no exits or end either. A creepy sense of déjà vu overtook them both. They both turned around and ran back as fast as they could. The path, however, now seemed to extend endlessly in both directions. Eventually they tired, and had no choice but to stop running. When they did, Kineosho thought back to his conversation with Uma that morning.

"Focus on the goal," he thought sternly to himself. He reflected on the one he had articulated to Toby and thought about crossing the river to go home. "We need to focus on the goal," said Kineosho to Basho.

"To get back to the clearing?" asked Basho.

Kineosho looked back at him, confused.

"Or to find the leopard?" asked Basho. "Or Viddi? Or home? Which goal?" he asked again anxiously.

A myriad of tangled thoughts suddenly raced through Kineosho's mind. They were so fast that he could not grasp a single one. Soon, a sense of panic clawed itself in — one that he had never experienced before. He laid his head on the ground and shut his eyes, hoping that the feeling would pass. It didn't. The turmoil continued until everything in his mind became a distant blur, and his thoughts faded into blackness.

The next morning, Kineosho awoke to find Basho sharpening his claws next to him. He took a deep breath before he looked around, hoping to find himself in a more sensible place. He closed his eyes in disappointment when he realised that they were back at their usual sleeping spot.

Kineosho did not say a word as he completed his morning exercises with Basho. Breakfast was quiet without Uma and Viddi. Even Milo was not there. Despite the fact that there were many animals around, Kineosho felt alone and quite depressed that morning. He finished breakfast quickly, and decided on a different path to explore with Basho.

Eerily, his experience on that path turned out to be almost identical to the one the day before. This time though, the panic Kineosho felt was worse. He could feel his heart racing and his breathing becoming increasingly shorter and more difficult. Even when Kineosho shut his eyes tightly, images of home, Viddi, and others continued to gush through his mind. No matter how hard he tried to stop it, it just would not stop.

He collapsed with anxiety, and could not remember what happened next.

The next morning when Kineosho awoke and found himself in his usual sleeping spot, he practically froze with angst. As he headed with Basho for their morning routine, he said to him: "Something bad is happening, Basho. We don't seem to be going anywhere — and I don't think we're dreaming any of this either!"

"I'm not sure, but it *is* a bit strange," replied Basho. "Perhaps it will be different today though?"

During breakfast, Kineosho felt even more isolated and depressed than he had felt the day before. Once again, the same distressful sequence of events repeated itself.

The next day, and the day after that, almost exactly the same thing happened. It seemed that regardless of the path Kineosho or Basho chose, the road always led nowhere. Worse yet, the feelings of loneliness and despair that Kineosho felt each morning were creeping into his very being. They affected everything. His appetite gradually shrank, and he became increasingly irritable. Soon, Kineosho struggled to even wake each morning, let alone start his daily routine.

Kineosho was certain he was not trapped in some kind of spiritual Groundhog Day—he noticed each day how the moon was waning, and then how it started growing again. He noticed how there were different animals at breakfast each morning. Still, the sequence of déjà vu events continued and the feeling of isolation became overwhelming. Even Basho had become much quieter than usual.

Finally, one morning when Kineosho awoke, he could not bear that soul-destroying feeling of hopelessness. That morning, he did not wake Basho. He did not complete his exercise routine either. Instead, he went straight to the main clearing for breakfast. He was unable to eat and the other animals looked at him quite strangely.

Kineosho knew that regardless of the path he chose, the outcome would be the same. He did not know why, but he was certain it would be. So that morning he decided to stay in the clearing. When most of the animals had left, Kineosho walked to the far end of the clearing near the rapids. The bank of the rapids was slippery and steep, so not many animals ventured there.

As he watched the raging rapids from the bank, his mind wandered to the harsh storm in which Viddi had rescued him. Suddenly, the feeling of isolation turned into one of intense anger. He snarled as he dug his claws deeper into the muddy ground. He hated being there, alone.

The more thoughts raced through his mind, the more resentful he became. He growled angrily and swiped his claws through the air as an image of Abu and Viddi appeared in his mind. And it was not just them that made him angry—it was everyone: Uma; Griffon; Master Wu; and even the elegant leopard. He felt that they had all left him stranded in his time of need.

As his resentment boiled, he could feel it becoming more

difficult to breathe. It was as though an enormous boulder had been squashed down against his chest. He gasped helplessly as he looked at the rapids. At that moment, he wondered if he were better off just leaping into the raging water, and letting nature take its violent course.

Then, as though to taunt him even further, the opposite bank cast the very same blurry image of the leopard he had first seen at home. In total frustration, and not knowing what else to do, Kineosho angrily raised his front claws in the air and roared at the leopard as loudly as he could. He roared again with all his might.

Kineosho could feel his heart thumping, and his throat burning with rage. He roared again as the echo of his own roar saturated the air, and once more as he crouched low — preparing to leap to a final, meaningless end.

"Excuse me. Would you mind keeping it down?" asked an annoyed little voice.

Kineosho looked ahead from his crouched position, startled.

"If that's okay with you," said another little voice coming from an identical creature next to it. They were short, pear-shaped, furry creatures that Kineosho had never encountered before.

"Sensitive ears," said another little voice from yet another identical creature. When Kineosho turned his head to look along the bank, he saw that there were dozens of them. They appeared to be walking in single file along the bank of the rapids, doing a peculiarly synchronised dance-walk.

"S — s — sorry," stuttered Kineosho, still a little dumb-founded. "Where are you going?"

"Home, of course," replied the next creature that waddled past before him.

"Home?" asked Kineosho in a hopeful voice. "You mean across the river?"

"I suppose you could say that," replied the next creature in line.

"H . . . How?" asked Kineosho.

"How we've been taught to," replied another, sounding a little irritated at having to answer questions whilst doing his jig.

"Thank the Great Banyan Tree," whispered Kineosho after a brief, breathless pause. He shut his eyes for a moment. The creature's reply had ignited a spark of hope in his mind.

"I've been on an endless road to nowhere — for so long, you have no idea — I'd do anything to get out of here! Can you teach me how — please?" asked Kineosho.

"Well, you'd have to learn our super-special power-walk — but why not!" said the next furry creature cheerfully as it danced past him. "And I know what you mean — I feel like I've been on this path forever too!"

Kineosho squeezed in behind the twenty or so furry animals that had already passed him along the bank. At first, he stumbled clumsily as he tried to copy their dance-walk. It was a lot more difficult than it looked.

"What are you anyway?" asked Kineosho curiously, trying not to trip with his new strut.

"Us? We're lemmings!" replied the animal behind Kineosho jovially.

"Well, nice to meet you all, and thank you," replied Kineosho. "Your timing could honestly not have been better! I was just about to — oh . . . never mind."

Kineosho soon mastered the lemmings' rhythmic dance-walk and was doing it in perfect sync with them. They slowed down a little as they passed through a very dark, narrow path away from the rapids. Not long after that, Kineosho could hear the powerful force of the waterfall nearby. The long narrow path was curvy, and eventually widened onto a rocky cliff adjacent to the top of the waterfall.

They paused for a moment on the narrow path when the first lemming in line set foot on the widened area leading to the cliff. The lemming gleamed with happiness as she took a deep breath and yelled, "Onward home!" Each of the lemmings behind her yelled the same, one after another just like a Mexican wave, but with words. Kineosho was no exception. As soon as he yelled it, a sense of freedom overcame him. He felt relieved that he would not have to repeat that déjà vu experience ever again, and glad that he could finally leave that place.

While the lemmings yelled out "Onward home!" in domino style, the first lemming had energetically restarted her peculiar dance-walk. They all followed, excited. Kineosho could not see her, but the lemming went all the way to the edge of the cliff and smiled gleefully as she leaped off it. The second lemming followed closely and she did exactly the same. So did the third lemming, and then the fourth.

When Kineosho finally danced his right foot onto the widened area, he slowed down his dance-walk quite a bit, a little confused at what was going on. The lemmings behind him were beginning to get annoyed, and started to push and prod him forward. Hesitantly, he obliged, but his earlier sense of relief quickly turned into panic with each step forward.

By the time the third lemming ahead of Kineosho had leapt off the cliff, he had practically stopped his march altogether. His pause caused the lemmings to bunch up behind him. The more they did, the harder they began to push.

Kineosho looked at the edge of the cliff in fright and desperately dug his claws into the rocks as best he could. The lemmings behind him were relentless, and becoming increasingly annoyed. Kineosho used every ounce of strength that he had to push back, but the force of the lemmings was too strong.

"ONWARD HOME!" yelled the lemmings with a powerful final heave, and pushed Kineosho off the cliff.

Kineosho struggled to hold on to the edge of the cliff with his front paws. He desperately clutched and tried to pull himself up but it was hard to get a grip on the loose rocks. To aggravate matters, the momentum of the lemmings that had been pushing him propelled them forwards, and many wound up leaping off Kineosho's head instead of the cliff edge.

Memories flashed before his eyes as Kineosho held on for dear life. Scenes with Curie, Griffon, Master Wu, Viddi, and of home flooded through his mind. For a moment, he even saw Basho looking down at him from the edge. But he could not hold on. When his left paw slipped from the edge, he knew that the inevitable was near. Kineosho closed his eyes as he felt the rocks under his right paw shifting and his final memories faded into blackness. He fell.

After all the lemmings had leapt off the cliff, there was an eerie silence. Basho peered over the cliff edge, unable to move. Time passed, and darkness slowly encroached on the forest.

❦ 32 ❦

The Art of Living

It was a relatively peaceful evening. There was just the chirpy sound of crickets against the ambient gush of the waterfall. The moon was almost full, and it filled the forest with a warm glow. Bar the occasional creak or crack of a twig as an irritated ferret stepped on it, there really wasn't much else going on.

"Something's missing, in the depth of my mind, ta ta tah ti da tah . . . life's so unkind, it keeps remind, wish I could rewind—*Argh!*" snarled the ferret as he kicked some dead leaves on the ground. "That's just rubbish!"

"You've been trying to start with that line for days now—why don't you try a new intro," said the second ferret, holding what looked like a miniature red bass guitar.

The first ferret did not reply and kicked the ground again in frustration, sending a few more dead leaves and pebbles flying off.

"Mofo, don't move!" whispered the second ferret suddenly, grabbing the other by the arm. He had noticed that one of the pebbles had bounced off a large creature lying on its side on the ledge. They both stood still and waited for a reaction but there was none.

"It's probably dead," whispered the second ferret, "and will you take it easy with the tantrums before you get us both killed!" The ferrets continued on their way, squeezing behind the creature on the ledge.

"Hey, wait Rosco," said the first ferret as he passed behind the creature. "Check out that massive bruise . . . dude, it's the roaring kitty from the talent show, remember—I think he's dead!"

"That's wonderful. Leave him alone, Mofo!" whispered Rosco in reply, pushing him to move on.

"Wait, check this out!" replied Mofo with a grin as he leapt across the lion's body. He grabbed the lion's mouth and used his fingers to open and close it as he said: "Don't be scared Wosco. I won't hurt you. I just want to be your fwend!" Mofo burst out laughing at himself.

"I'm not scared, you idiot!" snapped Rosco. "We have enough things to worry about, and it doesn't help that you're not focusing on them."

"*Awww* . . . Meow! Meow!" continued Mofo stretching the lion's mouth to make a funny face.

"Great—that's hilarious Mofo. Let's go already!" said Rosco, shaking his head.

"Spoilsport," muttered Mofo as he climbed over the lion's body. As he did, the lion let out a low grunt.

"Hey, did you hear that?" whispered Mofo. He leapt back over the lion and used his fingers to open one of the lion's eyes. Then much to Rosco's shock, he slapped the lion's face twice. "Kitty! Are you okay kitty?" asked Mofo with genuine concern.

The lion let out another groggy grunt as he slowly opened his eyes.

"Quick, get some water!" shouted Mofo to Rosco, who replied with a look of disbelief.

"From where?" asked Rosco sarcastically. "Down there?" he asked, pointing to the huge drop from the ledge to the bottom of the waterfall. "Or shall I just make a bucket out of this rock and get it from the waterfall?"

"Break a branch and wet it," replied Mofo calmly.

A few moments later Mofo splashed the wet branch onto the lion's face. "What's your name, do you remember your name?" asked Mofo.

The lion wiped some of the water droplets off his face. "K . . . Kineosho," said the lion eventually.

"What kind of name is that?" asked Mofo with a disgusted look. "How about we call you . . . Keo."

Kineosho shook his head trying to clear his mind and recall what had happened. "Am I dead?" he asked after a few moments.

"Yes, I'm afraid so—" replied Mofo in a sombre voice.

Rosco promptly interrupted him, delivering a sharp nudge in the ribs: "—No, you're not dead. What happened to you?"

Kineosho slowly recovered his senses, and told the ferrets what had happened at the cliff with the lemmings. He described what had happened to him before that too. Kineosho also told them about the awful feeling of isolation he had experienced. The ferrets listened attentively.

"Well lucky for you the cliff is not too high above this ledge—it's a *looooong* way down from here to the bottom!" said Rosco.

"Yes Keo—I don't get why you didn't just express it all though—you know, get it out there. Everyone is plagued by their own pain—expression helps you confront the turmoil instead of getting lost in it. You probably could have avoided this drama altogether," said Mofo.

Kineosho immediately thought back to what Uma had told him before she left. He tried to shrug his shoulders but it was too painful. "How?" asked Kineosho.

"Well, we do it with music—" replied Rosco.

"—Well we *used to* do it with music," interrupted Mofo sadly.

"Yeah, things haven't been the same since the talent show," continued Rosco.

"I recognise you two now!" said Kineosho. "I saw your performance there—you were amazing! Weren't there three of you in the show?"

"Yeah," replied Mofo, a little bitterly.

"Gigalo took off with a pair of polecat groupies after the show and we haven't seen him since. We haven't produced anything after he left either—things have just not been the same without him," said Rosco sadly.

"Can you sing, Keo?" asked Mofo.

"I don't think so," replied Kineosho.

"Well give it a try—you've got quite a story to share with what just happened. Come on, we'll even give you a beat," said Rosco as he picked up his red bass guitar and started strumming. Mofo was quick to add some vocal percussion and they soon developed quite a groove. "Go on, just try it!" said Rosco enthusiastically.

Kineosho coughed, and then started to sing to the beat.

I was confused
The paths were endless
Driving me mad, sad
So many options I had

Meeting the lemmings
Happy at first, I almost burst
Reached a cliff, to jump off stiff—

"—*Whoa* kitty! That's . . . pretty . . . well, bad," interrupted Mofo. "I don't mean good bad, I mean just *bad* bad!" he continued, shaking his head.

Kineosho looked at Rosco hoping for redemption, but he only received an embarrassed nod in acknowledgement.

"You've got a story, kitty—you've got to say it with some soul!" said Mofo passionately. "Try like this . . ." he continued, as he waved his arm to Rosco to start him strumming again.

In the darkest
recesses of my mind
something's missing
I know not what.

Mofo paused his deep-voiced narration and nodded to Rosco. Moments later, Rosco added some light vocal percussion in the same beat as they had given Kineosho earlier. Mofo tapped his feet for a few counts and then started his rap.

No rhythm, no rhyme
No sense of time
fare you well
my monkey mate
for you it's great
please wait—too late
'fore I know it
I see your gait

how cruel is fate
to clean my slate
and leave me now
at this lonely gate
Trying hard to think
and to reflect
time to cash 'n' collect
my reality check

All is not well
in my state of mind
First one river to cross,
'n' now there are nine!
All is not well
in this state of mine
no wine, no lime,
just nothing is fine . . .

Rosco looked at Mofo and smiled in encouragement, signalling him to keep going. After a short Rosco solo, Mofo took a deep breath and continued.

sinking into madness
down my path o' sadness
for everywhere I tread
has me running scared
every single road
adding to my load
look left, look right
no end in sight
how long can I run
how long can I run

All is not well
in my state of mind
my sanity now
I just cannot find
All is not well
in this state of mine
No ties that bind
Just axes to grind . . .

So suicide I say
is the only way
To escape this mess
I must impress
This bodily heap
to take a leap
Now here I am
a sacrificial lamb
about to be free
from insanity
And what do I see
but a vision of me
Singing this song
that's saying it's wrong!

All is not well
'cos life's unkind
All I want now
is peace of mind
All is not well
in this state of mine
All I want now
is peace of mind . . .

"Yeah!" shouted Rosco emotionally as he strummed off with a flourish. Mofo grinned in reply, punching his fist into the air.

"That was amazing," whispered a voice in Kineosho's ear. Kineosho turned his neck and felt an overwhelming sense of relief as he saw Basho sitting next to him.

"Now *that's* expressing!" said Mofo to Kineosho with another animated punch in the air.

"I feel better just hearing it all out loud," replied Kineosho.

"Yeah . . . when you express, things become real. When all this abstract stuff takes a real form it's easier for your head to deal with it," said Rosco, putting his hands to his temples. "Sometimes you can find something that captures what you're feeling and other times you can't—that's why it's better to learn to express yourself—you know, create your own outlet instead of relying on others for it . . . hey, you can't always find a couple of sharp rappers when you need 'em, right!" said Rosco with a wink.

When Kineosho looked at Mofo again, Mofo was almost in tears. "I thought we had lost it for good, dude," said Mofo to Rosco.

"I guess you just needed something to focus on—you know, a goal—even if it was just a little one," said Kineosho. The ferrets looked at him a little confused, and Kineosho told them about his experience with Toby. Kineosho was still sore and tired, and soon passed out after that. Rosco and Mofo chatted a while longer before they fell asleep on the ledge too. That night, everyone slept well, and much calmer than when they had arrived there.

The following morning Kineosho awoke in pain, but was most relieved not to find himself back in his usual sleeping spot. When the ferrets finally woke up, they helped Kineosho walk as Basho led them back to the main clearing.

When they arrived, Kineosho told Uma, Rhino, and Milo

about his adventures on the endless path. He also told them about the lemmings, and the ferrets' song as Milo examined his badly bruised side and numerous gashes.

"Some arnica extract should help bring down the bruising and I'll put a wet leaf dressing on those cuts. We'll have to strap your chest for a while until that hairline rib fracture mends too," said Milo confidently. He was clearly in his element.

"Here is your sack, by the way," said Rhino, handing it to Kineosho. "I was wondering where you had gone without it."

"Well, it certainly sounds like you've had an eventful time," said Uma with a smile. "I have to take our new recruits on their tour—why don't you rest a while and recover?"

After breakfast, Kineosho and Basho went off with Milo, and the two ferrets decided to join Uma on her tour. Except for a few excruciating moments during Milo's treatment, Kineosho felt much better. Then, he rested.

One morning after he fully recovered, Uma led Kineosho, Basho, and the ferrets down a new path. They walked for quite a while and Kineosho started getting a little nervous.

"Don't worry," laughed Uma. "This path definitely has an end, and quite a few exits at that!"

Soon, they arrived at the end of the path and Uma was right—there appeared to be dozens of tiny paths leading out of the clearing.

"You go down that one," said Uma to the ferrets, pointing to one of the broader paths. "It's not quite rap, but the group humming course may give you an idea of how to structure your own course."

Mofo and Rosco both thanked Uma and waved their good-byes. "Take it easy kitty, and rest that singing voice—seriously . . . please do!" said Mofo with a wink.

"And thanks for the tip about goals, Keo — the timing could not have been better," said Rosco. "Have fun and don't go leaping off any cliffs now!"

As Mofo and Rosco went on their way, Uma suggested that Kineosho wander through the different courses and try some that looked interesting. "It sometimes takes a while to find your niche but there's always at least one you'll find yourself comfortable with — just be patient with yourself until you do!"

That morning was a busy one for Kineosho and Basho. The first exit they chose led to an Indian mynah bird named Javed who was teaching a course on expression through poetry. Javed recited an exquisite piece of his own as an example and the class was captivated. Poetry, however, reminded Kineosho of his short but disastrous extempo experience with the ferrets, so they decided to move on to audit the next class.

The next exit they took led to an unusual knitting course being taught by a pretty, purple spider named Aneeta. She explained how knitting was both creative and relaxing at the same time. Basho was intrigued and even Kineosho was fascinated by the rhythmic clicking of the needles. He found it difficult to hold them with his large paws though, so once again they decided to move on.

The day progressed and they audited a number of classes ranging from marmosets teaching origami and architect lemurs designing tree houses, to a host of different animals teaching the most bizarre-looking musical instruments. They met Jenyne, an elegant flamingo teaching synchronised pole dancing, and even a pair of crocodiles demonstrating the calming art of bonsai gardening. There was something for everybody.

The variety of options for self-expression was quite

overwhelming. Kineosho was about to try a fun-sounding course on the art of burglary by a small raccoon, when Basho nudged him to check out an adjacent clearing.

The clearing was a somewhat noisy and animated one, and there were many different animals there. When they peered into the entrance, a lanky heron with some colourful paint marks on her feathers approached them.

"Ciao!" she said with a smile. "Welcome to the *Art of Living!* I am one of the instructors here and my name is Agliaolio'alia—but you can call me Alia for short," she continued with an enthusiastic Italian accent. "Come in, please, come in! Let me show you, what we do here."

Basho listened with fascination as Alia explained the concept behind the *Art of Living* and showed them the variety of canvasses and gorgeously hued paints that they used.

Kineosho's attention, however, was distracted by a tiny, but focused artist. The dormouse was skilfully using his fingers to create a bright, abstract painting. To Kineosho, the scene seemed to portray some young animals playing in colourful sand. His mind immediately wandered back to Curie. He fondly recalled the time she had taught him about sand art and *pawcollages*, and smiled at the memory.

Before Alia had finished her flamboyant pitch, both Basho and Kineosho knew that this was the self-expression course for them.

Over the moons that followed, Kineosho learnt the basic techniques through much practice. Alia was a passionate and demanding teacher. Once Kineosho became familiar with the techniques, he worked hard to master them by copying some magnificent artwork created by instructors and past students.

Kineosho and Basho both maintained their strict daily routine in terms of diet, meditation, and exercise. They thoroughly enjoyed the *Art of Living* course and while memories of home and Viddi, and thoughts of the elegant leopard did sneak into Kineosho's mind, his focus on the course kept him sane.

One morning, when they arrived at their art therapy studio, Alia took Kineosho and Basho aside. "You have learnt a lot about technique and some of the items you have reproduced are *mwah!* Fantastic!" said Alia, making an odd smacking sound with her beak. Basho looked at her in surprise, sure that she should not have been able to make that sound.

"Now though, the time has come for you to develop your own unique style — your true art and expression — the kind that comes from deep inside you. No copying!" said Alia enthusiastically as she led them to the area where Kineosho had first seen the dormouse painting his masterpiece.

Kineosho stared at the blank canvas for some time, at a loss for a subject. He tried to think logically about the options. He could draw Griffon, Curie, Master Wu, or any of the other animals he had met. He could draw one of the interesting scenes from his memory like the Great Rat Race in the talent show, or the animals huddled around the tree listening to the delightful stories of Miss Karma. There were plenty of options.

When Alia appeared again after some time, Kineosho had still not begun. She told Kineosho to pick any option because he could always change it, or do another, if he found it wasn't working. "Just start now!" she said. Kineosho dipped his paws into the paint and began. He continued for a long time before he stepped back to look at his creation. When he did, he was dismayed at the mess of colours on the canvas. "This is even worse than my attempt at singing," he thought. "I can't do this!" he muttered.

Alia, who had been watching from behind, walked up and stood beside him. "Of course you can, Kineosho! This is only your first time—even the greatest artists and musicians like Haathi Oyli Khan took a while to create something beautiful of their own. You certainly have some talent—it's only a question of developing your style and confidence!" said Alia in her passionate Italian accent.

Over the days that followed, Kineosho tried painting many of the options he had identified, but none of them came out to his satisfaction. In fact, he felt that he was getting worse rather than better. He became more dismayed and disillusioned, despite many sincere, positive comments he received about his work from others.

One evening, after a particularly bad day, Kineosho joined Uma, Alia, and the ferret musicians for dinner. He explained what was going on, and how he felt that his paintings were getting worse. "Perhaps art is just not my thing," he said in conclusion. "Perhaps I should try something else I might be better at," continued Kineosho in a disappointed tone.

"*Ha!*" said Alia followed by some horrendously vulgar Italian expletives. "Art is your thing—you *keepa* drawing from the wrong part of yourself, I *keepa* telling you," she continued angrily. "You cannot think and draw," said Alia, slapping Kineosho's head hard with her right wing.

"She's right," said Uma calmly, trying to diffuse the situation. "I've seen some of your work—a lot of it is good but you're not happy with it because you know your own potential and you're not living up to it. The best artists experience emotion fully, and express it with an uncluttered mind," said Uma.

"—Yeah! Don't think about it, dude. Just close your eyes, feel it, and create!" said Mofo punching his fist into the air.

"Remember what you felt before the cliff—the confusion. Not knowing where to go, or what to do . . . running around in circles without end, the unexplained leopard, the conflicting goals . . ." said Rosco. Basho shook his head frantically at Rosco, worried that Kineosho could wind up back in that horrible state of mind if he continued to remind him of it. "Well, that's what you need to focus on and express—*that feeling*—not just the nice picture of you lying on a ledge afterwards," continued Rosco.

That night Kineosho did not sleep well. Even Basho was awake, concerned that Rosco's revival of unpleasant memories could take them both to a bad place again.

The following morning, Kineosho and Basho completed their morning routine and had breakfast a little earlier than usual. As they headed to the art therapy studio, Kineosho's mind raced with thoughts like the ones he had experienced when he was hanging off the cliff. Suddenly, thoughts of the green-eyed leopard and the talent show entered his mind again and Kineosho was spooked. Even Basho could sense that something was not right and he stepped up his pace towards the studio. Kineosho followed him blindly until they arrived.

They were there early and none of the other animals had arrived yet. Kineosho removed his sack and threw it next to the canvas, still flustered from the flurry of thoughts. "Focus, Kineosho!" he said aloud, startling Basho who was standing next to him. "Don't think about it. Just close your eyes, feel it, and create!" muttered Kineosho irritatedly, repeating Mofo's words from dinner the previous night.

Kineosho closed his eyes and for a moment, his mind peeked into a peaceful darkness. As soon as he opened them again, thoughts flooded back into his mind. He let out a low growl as his frustration grew.

Suddenly, Basho called out to Kineosho, pointing at the psychedelic croaking frog sitting on his magic sack. When Kineosho saw it, he realised that the sack must have opened when he had thrown it down earlier. The frog leapt away into the bushes, happy to be finally out of the sack with no crocodile nearby. He didn't think twice about the frog he had left behind in the sack.

Kineosho went to make sure that nothing else had fallen out. When he came closer to the sack, he noticed that the black bandana that Master Wu had given him was hanging out of it. Kineosho took the bandana out and closed the sack.

"I had forgotten all about this!" said Kineosho to Basho, wrapping the bandana around his paw. He told Basho what Master Wu had told him when he had given him the gift. "If ever I needed to clear my mind of clutter, it would be now," said Kineosho, going back to the canvas.

Kineosho took a deep breath and closed his eyes, the bandana wrapped tightly around his paw. His mind quietened down once more and Kineosho felt optimistic. He opened his eyes again to start painting and to his dismay the rush of confusion and mixed emotions returned. He removed the bandana from his paw and threw it down in disappointment.

"You looked so calm when your eyes were closed—maybe you should paint like that!" said Basho jokingly.

Kineosho immediately looked at the bandana, and again at Basho with an embarrassed grin. He picked up the bandana and shook his head. "Of course," he said, taking a good look around him. He stood in front of the canvas and wrapped the black bandana around his head, covering his eyes. Kineosho waited a few moments for his mind to quieten down, and it did.

Then he slowly focused and took his mind back to the first source of his recent confusion—the scene he had experienced during the *Tepla* session with Uma. Soon, he felt as though he were still in the talent show, with the elegant leopard right beside him. The same feeling of sadness he had experienced during the session with Uma returned to him. This time there were no porcupines twirling needles and no distractions.

Kineosho felt around for the paint and Basho helped his paw find its destination. Then he felt the dimensions of the canvas and he began to paint. Alia had arrived in the meantime and was watching from a distance. She signalled the other animals entering to be quiet and to watch Kineosho.

It was as though Kineosho were possessed. He could not hear or sense anything around him. Behind the blackness of the bandana, he could already clearly see the final work of art he was producing. At that point, he knew that even the bandana did not matter. He was painting without distraction. He removed the bandana and continued without pause, oblivious to everybody watching him.

The image of a deep green leopard's eye with an unusual reflection of Kineosho in it gradually became visible on the canvas. The colours were dark, but vivid. The peculiar sadness he had experienced spoke from every inch of the canvas.

As Kineosho etched the final touches with his claws, he wondered if anybody else would see what he saw. When he completed it though, he knew he did not care if they did.

After a pause, Kineosho stepped back and looked at the canvas. He knew it was truly a work of art and his painting immediately brought him to tears.

Suddenly, he heard the claps and cheers of Alia, Uma, and a group of animals behind him. He looked around and even Mofo was there doing his signature punch in the air. Not all the animals there liked the painting and as Kineosho had expected, it really did not matter to him.

Kineosho returned to the main clearing that evening feeling like something inside him had changed. It had.

As he settled to have his dinner, he felt something leap on his back and try to strangle his neck. Kineosho immediately stood up and tried to shake it off.

The more he shook his head, the more the creature tightened its hold around his neck. Then Kineosho felt something clutching his ear, which was followed by an excruciatingly loud *EEP!* He stopped shaking his head immediately.

"Viddi?" he asked excitedly, leaping around trying hard to look at the back of his neck. He looked like a clown doing so, much to the amusement of everybody there.

Viddi climbed down and grinned happily at Kineosho.

"We all missed you," said Uma cheerfully.

"How are you? What happened to Abu?" asked Kineosho, noticing that he was not around.

Viddi explained sadly that Abu had left to cross the river with a dear friend, and that she was not able to go with them. Kineosho gave her a big hug and said that whatever had happened, he was truly glad to see her again.

The remainder of that evening was like the evening after the Briki therapy session — it felt like they were all floating in a light and bouncy cloud of laughter. The warm and fuzzy *pick up just where you left off* feeling was the cherry on top of Kineosho's day.

❧ 33 ❧

Cry baby, cry

The following morning, Viddi was unusually quiet through their exercise and meditation routine. When they arrived at the main clearing for breakfast, she suddenly burst into tears. Kineosho tried to console her, but she would stop crying for a moment and start bawling again the next.

Uma and Rhino were not there that morning as they had left for the first day of a new *Tepla* session. Vanita, who was on medical leave, was quick to spot Viddi in distress and hurried over to her.

"What's wrong?" asked Vanita, joining Kineosho in trying to console her.

"I—m—mi—miss Abu," sniffed Viddi sadly.

"I understand," said Vanita in a comforting voice. "You know, when animals experience severe heartbreaks or emotional trauma like a painful loss of some kind, many find solace through *Aura of Life Ventilation*. After I started Milo's treatment, my alopecia started healing but I was still very upset about losing my partner to that skanky wh— . . . Anyway, I went for *Ventilation* and it really helped me—in fact, I made many new friends there!

"Perhaps you should try it—it's very popular and there are sessions starting daily. I can take you there after breakfast if you'd like?" asked Vanita, pleased that she could finally do something nice for Viddi.

Viddi looked at Kineosho and Basho, who both nodded in agreement. Viddi could not eat much that morning as she kept bursting into tears. They all left soon after and Vanita led them to a large, tree-lined auditorium that was very far away. By the time they arrived there, Viddi had stopped crying.

Kineosho was surprised to see a crowd almost as large as the one for the Briki session. Strangely though, the audience did not appear as diverse. There were at least ten times as many sheep there as any other creature. After a while, the crowd settled and an old bearded goat took to the stage.

The goat looked calmly at the audience and cleared his throat. The sheep immediately responded quite comically with a domino effect of *Shhhs*.

Then a deep, charismatic voice echoed over the auditorium: "Welcome all, to *Aura of Life Ventilation*. For the new brothers and sisters of our family, I would like to introduce you to our founder—the goat, who at the tender age of three days, started developing this miraculous cure . . . Brothers and Sisters—*Momo!*"

The sheep clapped and cheered wildly as the goat took a humble bow on the stage. Momo waited patiently for the audience to quieten down.

"Thank the Great Banyan Tree, for blessing me with this knowledge that I will share with you today. Through a combination of dreams, intuition, and much research, I created this process and perfected it over many seasons. Today brothers and sisters, I will teach you first to expel your loneliness and insecurities, then to breathe the very energy that drives your life force, and finally, to see the true and beautiful aura around you. Are you ready?" asked Momo loudly.

"Yes!" replied the sheep passionately.

"Momo can't hear you!" said the deep voice, loudly echoing over the auditorium.

"*Yes!* We're ready!" yelled the sheep manically in unison.

When the crowd quietened down, Momo continued. "It's true that I started developing this therapy when I was just a wee goat. When we're very young, we don't realise what we're doing when we cry. We have a need and have to satisfy it. We often cannot do it ourselves so we scream and wail for someone to help us — we need that attention to survive."

"When we grow up, we lose much of the benefit of that cathartic wailing and screaming. We still need that attention from others at times but instead of being empowered to ask for it, we are conditioned not to ask. This causes us to bottle up our unsatisfied need for attention — this is where the feeling of loneliness you experience comes from," continued Momo.

The audience *Ooh*ed and *Ahh*ed in acknowledgement of Momo's logic and their new-found realisation.

"Today I'm going to give you an opportunity to release all that pent up emotion, loneliness, insecurity, negativity . . . and by practising what I teach you daily, you never have to go back to that bottled up state again," said Momo confidently.

The audience cheered in anticipation. Even Basho was intrigued by Momo's logic.

"First, I'd like you all to close your eyes and experience whatever negative emotion is plaguing you. It could be a sense of loss, of loneliness, of being unwanted—anything that's bringing you down or weighing heavily on your shoulders," said Momo. "Then hold those thoughts. Feel how they are affecting your entire body, mind, and soul." Momo paused.

"Now forget about everyone around you. You are alone in this auditorium. You are alone on this path. You are alone in this forest. You are all alone in this world . . ." said Momo in a sad voice for effect.

Momo waited for the sombre mood to settle in.

"Now, scream at the top of your voices and let it all out. Cry! Wail! Shout! Yell! As loud as you possibly can, and don't stop!" shouted Momo. Momo closed his eyes as well and led the way by letting out an agonizingly loud scream.

The audience followed suit. Kineosho, who was very self-conscious at first, started screaming too. Soon the entire auditorium was reverberating with cathartic screams—there were animal sounds of all sorts from frantic bleating and loud mooing to scary roars and piercing bird whistles. Even Viddi and Basho had totally lost themselves and were sounding quite mad releasing loud *Eeps* and howls.

The noise grew so loud that no animal could distinguish its own screams from the others. After quite some time, the deep voice echoed loudly over the crowd: "Keeping your eyes closed, slowly move to silence."

Gradually the crowd calmed down. Kineosho and many of the other animals felt their throats were raw from the yelling. Most of the sheep were panting with exhaustion. Then an incredibly calm silence floated over the auditorium.

Momo did not say anything for quite a while. He looked around the audience and appreciated the silence.

"Now, the following steps may be difficult for some of you — but just try as best you can until you become accustomed to it," said Momo eventually. "First, please keep your eyes closed and stay in absolute silence. Let your mind drift to happy thoughts." Momo paused again for a short while.

"Slowly, lift your hands, front paws, front hooves towards the sky as high up as you can. Keep those happy thoughts circulating in your mind," continued Momo. A few of the sheep and other animals fell over clumsily but most seemed to manage.

A fly on a nearby tree, who had accidentally opened one of his eyes, found the auditorium quite cultish at that moment. He quickly shut his eye and took his mind back to delivering fertilizer to Rocco's cabbit farm.

"This breathing exercise I am going to teach you now has been proven by our scientists to be extremely effective so put your all into it. First listen to what you're going to do, and then we'll do it together on my cue. I want you to quickly drop your elbows to your sides, exhaling as hard as you can through your nose as you do. When your elbows are down, repeat the chant *Yumana Yumana Yumana Yumana* as many times as you can. Do it until you feel like every ounce of air in your lungs is gone. Then, slowly raise your hands, front paws, front hooves again towards the sky. As you do, open your eyes slowly, look up at the sky and inhale deeply through your nose, until you cannot possibly inhale any more. Then close your eyes, and we'll repeat the exercise. Now, let's try it all together," said Momo as he raised his front hooves to the sky.

The audience waited for his cue and were only too relieved to lower their elbows quickly. They exhaled deeply and the wide variety of snorts and strange sounds that were emitted nearly made Kineosho and Viddi fall over trying to contain their laughter. Then, as instructed, the entire auditorium filled with a chant of *Yumana Yumana Yumana Yumana Yumana* . . . This gradually tapered off as the audience ran out of breath. Then they raised their hands again slowly, opening their eyes to look at the sky whilst they inhaled deeply, repeating the entire process.

"Continue this special breathing exercise," said Momo. "Each time you inhale, reflect on your happy thoughts and suck that positive energy inside you with your nose."

The animals continued this cycle at least fifty times before Momo asked them to lower their hands and be seated. "Please remain silent with your eyes closed and continue breathing normally now through your nose," said Momo. The audience obeyed.

"Feel the positive energy you have brought into yourselves percolate through your bodies. Maintain your happy thoughts," continued Momo after some time. After a long silence, Momo asked the audience to slowly open their eyes again.

"Now before you can see auras around yourselves and revel in them, you need to give each other a symbol of complete acceptance. I would like each of you to bow humbly to your neighbours and say: *I sincerely respect you, and accept you exactly as you are*," said Momo.

The audience obeyed and a murmur grew as they all did what Momo said. Kineosho felt a peculiar sense of calm when he did it—particularly when he did it with Viddi and Basho. The murmuring continued as the sheep said it to as many animals around them as possible.

By this time, Viddi, who had felt fantastic after the cathartic screaming and the first twenty or so breathing exercise cycles, was feeling quite bored and fidgety. As Momo continued with his positive affirmations and calming instructions, Viddi decided to open Kineosho's sack that had been on the ground next to her.

She started taking everything out. Out came Kineosho's first cabbit ear, mud from his near-death mountain adventure, his favourite green paint from Alia's art class, and a host of his other mementos. She also took out some of her personal mementos — a variety of flowers, a little hippo snot to remind her of Kilo's water cannon adventures, her lucky crocodile tooth from Rhino, and the little heart that Abu had sketched for her.

Viddi continued to rummage in the sack, until she gleefully pulled out the one remaining colourful frog. At that moment, Momo encouraged his disciples to bask in the bright, positive, and colourful auras around each other as the final stage of the therapy. Viddi looked around to see the bright colours and auras but saw nothing.

She looked at the frog, a little disappointed. The frog looked at Viddi, realising that he finally had the opportunity to escape if he were smart about it. He paused for a moment then whispered to Viddi: "I can show you some really lovely colours — the brightest you've ever seen, would you like that?"

Viddi nodded with excitement.

"Well, all you have to do is lick my back and then pass me on to that sheep next to you, and tell her to do the same," said the frog, pointing to the closest sheep to Viddi in the direction of the exit.

Viddi happily obliged and licked the frog's back all the way up to his head, and passed him on. Little did Viddi know that the frog she had just licked was one of those colourful frogs who secrete a powerful hallucinogenic neurotoxin on its back. Little did the sheep who happily imitated Viddi, and licked the frog before passing him on, know about anything. Really — she was quite a silly sheep and she didn't know much.

Most unfortunately though, little did the colourful frog know that the powerful hallucinogenic neurotoxin on its back doesn't play nicely with sheep. By the time the frog had been licked by the eighth sheep, Viddi was quite thrilled at the vivid colours and auras she noticed everywhere around her. The sheep, however, were going totally berserk. Some started headbutting their neighbours and others laughed uncontrollably while playing pranks on each other. The sheep started passing the frog in all directions instead of just towards the exit, and chaos ensued.

Except for Momo, everyone thought it was all very funny. The ruckus grew and Viddi soon found herself dancing on a deranged sheep's head. Kineosho and Basho could not contain their laughter.

A small mouse and Momo whispered something to each other. The mouse and two large hippos then stormed through the mad crowd, snatched Viddi off the sheep's head and sternly told Kineosho that they had best leave immediately. Viddi looked at the hippos sadly for a moment then proceeded to smile and happily pat the pretty, purple aura around them.

"Please leave right now!" said the mouse in the same deep voice that had echoed over the audience earlier. Kineosho burst out into hysterical laughter again, realising that the deep, super-charismatic voice had actually come from the little mouse. The hippos grabbed Kineosho and Viddi, and threw them out of the auditorium.

A few moments later, the hippos threw the colourful frog, Kineosho's sack, and their sack mementos out as well. The frog looked at Viddi who simply stared back at him and started clapping her hands. The frog grinned sheepishly and quickly leapt into a nearby bush with a chuckle.

They sat outside the auditorium for quite a while to recover from the experience and indulged in the odd mad giggle when they imagined what was still going on inside.

Viddi's psychedelic visions slowly faded and she sighed as everything returned to its normal state.

"Are you good?" asked Kineosho.

Viddi nodded. Both Kineosho and Basho smiled at Viddi, who looked like she was back to her cheerful old self.

"That really was great fun but this place . . . I'm quite tired now—I know exactly where I'd like to be . . ." said Kineosho.

Viddi and Basho both looked at Kineosho and nodded in agreement without saying a word.

"We should say goodbye to Uma and our other friends first," said Kineosho, smiling. He lifted Viddi, who was still feeling a little woozy from the frog lick, onto his back and they strolled back to the main clearing for the last time.

That evening, surprisingly, there was not much sadness as they exchanged goodbyes. Mofo and Rosco spiritedly told them about *Raptor*—the new rap therapy course that they were starting up. Milo looked as calm as ever and only asked that Kineosho wish Axolotl well if he met him on the other side.

Uma was a little more emotional, though not sad. "Remember, whatever you think or create in your mind is very real Kineosho," she said, dispensing her last bit of concerned advice. Kineosho nodded and hugged Uma tightly. "And don't go playing in any more mud!" she said with a laugh.

"I'll see you at home," whispered Kineosho to Uma as he turned around and headed towards the exit of the Third Path. Basho led the way and Viddi wrapped her arm tightly around Kineosho's neck. They did not look back.

❧ 34 ❧

Trial by demon

Basho looked around cautiously as they entered the Angel's Trident. The beautiful full moon glowed softly above the large clearing and there were few animals around. Basho nudged Kineosho to take the scenic route, avoiding the entrance to the second path. His last experience of a full moon there was not one that he cared to repeat.

Kineosho remembered his experience on the first path well, but for the first time since that day, he did not feel afraid about it. When they arrived at the entrance, they found the black bull playing some kind of game with the fluffy, brown-coated llama. They appeared engrossed and Basho whispered to Kineosho that it was probably best that they wait for them to finish instead of interrupting them.

The black bull thought for a while, looked at the llama and said:

"Another full moon, in the garden of no good —"

"— But also no evil, lest you be misunderstood!" replied the llama immediately with a smile.

"Ah Dolly, too good for me—I give up!" replied the black bull, shaking his head and spotting Kineosho waiting for them as he did so. He apologised for not having seen him earlier. The llama smiled when she saw Kineosho.

"Going home?" asked the llama in her familiar gentle voice.

"Yes," said Kineosho, as all three of them nodded.

"And with your jackal this time too," said the black bull, looking quite pleased with Kineosho.

"Thank you again for your advice about learning from the Second Path—it was most kind and helpful. Is there any guidance you can give us about crossing the river?" Kineosho humbly asked the llama.

The llama looked pensively at Kineosho. "No, nothing you haven't already been told. Although before you cross the river, you may find it interesting to look carefully at it. It's very deep," said the llama, giving Kineosho a gentle pat on his head.

The black bull looked at the llama and smiled as Kineosho thanked her.

"No baggage allowed," said the black bull to Kineosho, pointing at his magic sack.

Kineosho untied the sack and gave it to the black bull. He took a deep breath and nodded to Basho to start the journey. Viddi held tightly on to Kineosho as they all walked together through the dark entrance of the First Path.

When they had walked through the tunnel of trees, the scene was quite different to what Kineosho had seen on his first day-time visit. He had expected the darkness to take away from the beauty of the landscape but it did not. In fact, the river glistened in the moonlight and the banyan tree on the hill had an unusually warm glow that almost looked like a halo.

Kineosho thought back to the exceptionally positive plan he had hatched during the *Neuro-Linguistic Crystal Therapy* session with Toby. After his conversation with the axolotl though, he knew there was no way he would be able to cross the river without facing whatever it was he had left to face. Instead of heading to the river, Kineosho walked directly towards the banyan tree. As they walked, Kineosho described to Basho and Viddi what had happened on his first visit there. They both looked a little uneasy, but neither said a word.

When they reached the banyan tree, they all felt a sudden tiredness overcome them. Vivid memories of what had happened there earlier suddenly rushed back to Kineosho's mind. They seemed a lot more real and much worse than he had just described. For the first time since they had committed to do what they wanted to do, he felt a little nervous.

Basho immediately noticed Kineosho's nervousness. He was quick to reassure him that the past didn't matter and that whatever came their way, they would all successfully deal with it together. It was when Viddi patted his head and said that it would all be okay, and that they would be home soon, that Kineosho felt better. He gazed across the river and fond memories of home replaced his nervous thoughts.

Viddi and Basho soon dozed off under the tree. Kineosho looked at the full moon and the unusual glow of the tree one last time before closing his eyes. As soon as he did, his mind was swept away into darkness.

When Kineosho reopened his eyes, it appeared that dawn had not yet broken. He was glad to see Viddi and Basho still beside him. Their eyes had just reopened too. Kineosho waited to hear the voices in the night that he had heard before, but there was only an eerie silence.

As he stood up to suggest that they head towards the river, they all suddenly heard an enormous roar and what sounded like a stampede of animals coming towards them. Viddi was startled and immediately leapt onto Kineosho's back. She looked around and squawked out an anxious *Eep!* when she saw the dozens of black-bonneted moles storming towards them. Each of them wielded an ominous wooden staff. Twigs led them, and he looked furious. His head was still wrapped with the bright saffron turban that he had been wearing when they last saw him.

"There they are! Get them!" heard Kineosho. From the corner of his eye, he saw the foxes running towards them from another direction, their knives clanging against each other. Without any hesitation, Basho ran towards the river and Kineosho followed him blindly. His heart sank as he saw history being repeated, with even more adversaries against him. Basho continued to run as fast as he could towards the river. Kineosho followed as Viddi held on to him even more tightly.

Just when they reached the river, an enormous dark lion appeared in the distance. It stood in the only direction Basho could possibly run. It was much larger than Kineosho and its blood-red eyes were terrifying. The dark lion advanced slowly and Basho froze in his tracks. Suddenly, an evil-looking praying mantis leapt off its back and started walking towards Basho with a determined glare. Kineosho's attention was still glued to the vicious foxes running at them from the side.

Viddi, in the meantime, had been looking behind them at Twigs and the stampeding black-bonneted moles. "Ninja moles!" she whimpered into Kineosho's ear as she saw the staffs the moles were carrying. For the first time since that day, she remembered the beating they had both received from the ninja mice many moons ago.

No sooner had Viddi said that, than Kineosho swung around and saw each of the threats approaching them. Master Wu's words after the ninja lesson echoed in his head. "Slow it down in your mind and deal with each attack individually," he whispered to himself.

Kineosho immediately closed his eyes, took a deep breath, and focused on being aware of what was around him. When he opened his eyes and looked around, it was as though each of the threats advancing towards him had slowed to a snail's pace.

"Are you okay?" he asked Viddi and Basho, who did not seem to be affected by the slowdown. They looked shaken but nodded in reply.

Basho pointed at the large insect walking towards them. It was the closest creature in the attack.

"The Braying Mantis from the pond? What the—" thought Kineosho, before the mantis suddenly commenced his walk at his previous speed. His determined glare looked even harsher than before. As Kineosho stepped back, the mantis leapt towards him and let out an enormous roar in mid-air.

Viddi almost dislocated every bone in her neck turning around in surprise. When she saw that it was the Braying Mantis, she instantly leapt off Kineosho's back and started laughing at him. The Braying Mantis roared loudly again and this time Kineosho felt a little less perplexed. Viddi started cheering and tried to imitate the same roar but failed hopelessly. In fact, she sounded more like a little mouse trying to growl. Kineosho could not help but laugh. He roared as loudly as he could to show Viddi how it was done. The Braying Mantis roared again even louder and they all laughed. At that moment Kineosho recalled how upset and insecure he had felt at the pond and how right then, the same experience seemed so insignificant. He knew, as Basho had already known at the talent show, that his potential was far greater than his roar.

When he looked down at the Braying Mantis again, he was nowhere to be found. Instead, he saw the foxes running towards him at full speed. This time Kineosho was quick to react. He whispered something in Viddi's ear and to the foxes' surprise, he started running straight towards them. Viddi followed close behind. When Kineosho was close enough, he leapt over the foxes. The foxes screeched as they applied their brakes and turned around as quickly as they could. As soon as they did, they scrambled for their knives, getting ready to throw them at Kineosho.

After the foxes did their about-turn, their leader was farthest away from Kineosho. As soon as that fox had completed his turn, Viddi leapt onto his back. She tightened her legs around his neck and pulled his ears as hard as she could.

"*Ow!* Stop!" yelled the fox. The louder he yelled, the more Viddi yanked his ears. The other foxes immediately turned around to see what was going on. In that split second, Kineosho leapt into the pack and started beating their heads with his paws as hard as he could. There were foxes flying everywhere.

Viddi, in the meantime, was experiencing first-hand what it would have been like in a rodeo. The fox leader was doing an incredibly realistic impersonation of a wild bull trying to get a mad monkey off his back. Viddi, it turned out, was a cowgirl of note.

"Stop! Stop! Please stop!" yelled the fox, feeling like his ears were about to be pulled right off his head. Many of the foxes had run away already and the few that remained standing backed off. Kineosho signalled Viddi to come and stand next to him. She slowly let go of the fox's ears and climbed off, looking immensely disappointed as she did. The leader of the foxes did not move.

Kineosho leapt forwards and stood face-to-face with the fox. "Are we good?" he snarled ferociously. Even Viddi was startled.

The fox nodded with a sheepish grin. "*Erm . . .* sorry about that," said the fox apologetically. "You know, emotions get the better of me sometimes."

Kineosho let out a low growl and flashed his sharp teeth at the fox. "We're good! We're good!" said the fox as he backed away. "Good luck going home and all that," he added just before he disappeared with the remaining foxes into the darkness.

Viddi pointed to Kineosho's side, a little alarmed. He had not escaped unscathed. There were a number of cuts and bruises, but nothing serious.

"Kineosho!" yelled Basho suddenly. Kineosho quickly turned around to find Basho standing frozen, looking at Twigs and the dozens of armed black-bonneted moles. They were now stampeding ahead again at full speed.

"Tag again?" asked Viddi, but Kineosho shook his head.

"Too many of them and Twigs is too tall!" replied Kineosho, feeling some panic setting in.

"Aren't they supposed to be doing their full moon jackal-killing ritual today?" asked Basho nervously.

"Basho . . . you're right—they can't be here! This must be testing something else!" said Kineosho. His mind instantly flashed back to Master Wu's advice before he left the talent show and he whispered to himself: "Stupid, smart, strong, wrong . . . come on Kineosho—think—smart or wrong!"

Suddenly, he had an idea. "Quick, do exactly as I do," said Kineosho. He lay stomach-down on the ground at full stretch with his head facing the stampede. Viddi and Basho nervously did the same alongside him.

As soon as he could see that Twigs was close enough, Kineosho shouted as loudly as he could: "Stop! Please stop! Let me say something first . . . just a few words, please, Twigs?"

Twigs stopped right in front of him, as did his small army of black-bonneted moles.

"Say what?" snarled Twigs, extending his long neck down to face Kineosho on the ground. His army stood behind him, ready to inflict some serious damage with its wooden staffs.

Kineosho stood up, slowly. Twigs raised his neck, remaining face-to-face with Kineosho. "Well?" asked Twigs coldly.

"Actually, I wanted to ask you something Twi—" began Kineosho before being interrupted by Twigs.

"—it's a bit late for that!" snapped Twigs.

"Please forgive me for how things ended, and I accept that you have to do what you must. But something has been troubling me greatly since we left your home. Just hear me out, please, Elder Twigs?" asked Kineosho humbly. Twigs sneered back, and remained silent.

"I was just thinking about the story that Miss Karma told us on your beautiful lake shore. The one about the king of the pigeons, I cannot recall his name—" said Kineosho.

"—King Akbar," said one of the black-bonneted moles, promptly earning him a glare from Twigs and a few of the other moles.

"Yes—that's it, King Akbar. I feel we are in the same story here—with you as the noble and wise king, and these your loyal followers. And me, or rather us of course, the rogue pigeon," said Kineosho as he began to draw something in the river sand.

"Go on," said Twigs, a little intrigued about where Kineosho was going with the story and quite enjoying being identified with the noble pigeon king.

"When I heard the story about King Akbar, I understood the story from the rogue pigeon's point of view. I took away that in pressing times you have to be able to rely on yourself to survive.

Sometimes, you may upset others you care about in the process. The punishment for that would be loneliness, because you would no longer fit into the family," said Kineosho, continuing to draw in the sand.

"After the first story we heard about the monkey and the crocodile, Miss Karma took us around to show how various creatures interpreted the story very differently, depending on who they associated themselves with. I wanted to know how you interpreted King Akbar's story so that I may learn . . ." said Kineosho as he completed his drawing and looked up at Twigs.

Twigs peered curiously at the drawing. To his surprise, he saw a very similar image to the one they had created in the group *pawcollage* lesson with Curie when they were young. At first, he looked at Kineosho, a little confused, and then he realised what Kineosho had just cleverly done. He was trapped. He could not say anything to discredit Miss Karma's story. He could not offer the point of view of the rogue pigeon as Kineosho had already claimed that. He obviously could not offer the point of view of the hunter, or one of the pigeon subjects because he would have to relinquish his kingship. He was forced to adopt the view of the kind and forgiving king—otherwise, he would look royally foolish and inconsistent in front of his followers. The black-bonneted moles looked up to him quite literally, waiting for a response.

When Twigs saw the drawing he recalled how Kineosho had helped save him from embarrassment during the *pawcollage*. Twigs was smart enough to know that by posing the question to him, Kineosho had just given him a way to elegantly step down from his current position whilst still saving face with his black-bonneted followers.

Kineosho bowed his head in front of Twigs and the moles as he waited for a reply.

"I think you've learnt quite enough already, Kineosho," said Twigs with a smile. "Even King Akbar would be proud."

Kineosho smiled with his head still bowed. When he looked up, Twigs and his moles had vanished. Viddi wasn't sure what had just happened, but she was glad that the ninja moles had disappeared.

Her moment of relief was short-lived. Almost immediately after Kineosho had lifted his head, they heard a huge roar from behind them. It was louder than the Braying Mantis's and Kineosho's combined. They turned around and saw the dark lion approaching them.

"What should we do?" asked Viddi, beginning to panic. She had never seen anything quite so terrifying before. The dark lion was larger than Kineosho and its eyes were blood red. The earth trembled as it walked towards them and it seemed to look right through her, coldly.

"I don't know," whispered Kineosho. "Judging by what it did to me last time, though, I'm pretty certain it's not here to play with us!"

"What is it though?" asked Basho as he looked more closely. "There's something really strange about it."

"I have an idea!" said Kineosho suddenly. He whispered something in Viddi's ear and she nodded quickly in reply before leaping onto his back. Then Kineosho started to walk towards the dark lion.

"Bad idea! Bad idea!" said Basho to Kineosho, sensing that the creature was not what it seemed. He followed closely.

When Kineosho was close to the dark lion, he whispered to Viddi: *"Now!"* Viddi instantly leapt off his back and ran behind the dark lion. To their surprise, the ferocious beast turned instantly and swiped its paw at Viddi, sending her flying onto the river shore. It was almost as if it knew exactly what she was going to do. The dark lion turned to face Kineosho again and continued to walk towards him. Its red eyes glared at him even more angrily than before.

Kineosho roared as he saw Viddi lying on the shore. Every muscle in his body contracted. He could feel his claws dig into the river sand. On pure reflex, he leapt forcefully towards the dark lion's head. In mid-air, Kineosho could feel every ounce of power he was about to deliver with his claws. The millisecond before he was about to strike the dark lion, his focus was completely undivided.

When Kineosho struck, much to his surprise, the moment of impact did not materialise. Instead, he clearly saw his claws swipe right through the dark lion's head in slow motion as though it were just air. His intense momentum caused him to fall on his back and tumble painfully for quite a distance along the riverbank. Basho quickly ran around to Kineosho. They both looked at the dark lion's piercing eyes as it unleashed another furious roar. It did not move.

"What just happened? Did it move just before I hit it?" asked Kineosho. His shoulder ached from the fall. Kineosho cast a glance at Viddi, who had just about recovered from her unexpected flight.

"No," replied Basho. "And don't do anything until I figure out what's happening — there is something very odd here," continued Basho angrily as he took a few steps forward towards the dark lion. It did not move.

Basho cautiously looked up at the dark lion and when his eyes connected with its piercing red eyes, he suddenly felt everything fall into place. He heard part of the ferret's song from the talent show echoing in his mind. "An evil roar from behind . . . fiery eyes against a pitch black sky . . . what comes after that . . .

315

I turn around and what do I see, nothing but a reflection of—"
Basho turned around and looked at Kineosho, and then again at
the dark lion. He noticed that the dark lion had the same scar on
its side that Kineosho had after his fall off the cliff.

"Do you see it?" Basho asked Kineosho. Kineosho nodded in
disbelief.

"The song . . . how does it end?" asked Kineosho anxiously.

"Something about the game . . . to win this game, you cannot
play . . . for there is no way this beast . . . to slay," replied Basho.

"So somehow it's me . . . it knows everything I do, which
explains how it knew what Viddi was going to do. I cannot slay
it . . . I don't get it—what do I have to do?"

Kineosho and Basho slowly approached the dark lion, which
just glared back at them. It did not move. When Kineosho's
eyes met the dark lion's fiery eyes, his heart suddenly sank. In
an instant, he saw everything that he believed was bad about
himself. Hundreds of images flashed before him in the redness
of his dark reflection's eyes. The feeling of being useless in the
talent show, being foolishly proud after it, being insecure about
the Braying Mantis, being short-tempered and irritable with
friends, being arrogant during childhood games, and many others flooded through him. He fell to the ground before the dark
lion in shock. Neither Kineosho, nor the dark lion moved.

Viddi hobbled to them. She tugged gently at Kineosho's ear.
Basho looked at the dark lion and again at Kineosho. Then suddenly he yanked Kineosho's ear and slapped his face. "Snap out
of it! I know what you have to do . . . snap out of it!" he commanded as he slapped his face again.

Kineosho turned and looked at Basho.

"You can't fight it, you can't slay the beast, you can't interact
with it, you obviously cannot ignore it . . . there's only one thing
you can do, Kineosho . . ." said Basho.

"Accept . . . accept it—that's the only thing I can do," replied Kineosho as he looked back at the dark lion.

"I respect and accept you," said Viddi with a smile, glad that Kineosho had returned from his catatonic state.

Kineosho looked at Viddi and patted her on the head. "Yes, Viddi . . . exactly as you are!" said Kineosho, remembering Momo's line from their final adventure on the Third Path.

He stood up and looked at the dark lion's fiery eyes once more. He felt overwhelmed with emotion but he knew that this was an integral part of who he was. He found that he could not move, and even saying the words was unexpectedly difficult. Then, he looked across the river for a moment, and bowed his head.

"I sincerely respect you, and accept you exactly as you are," whispered Kineosho to himself. Then, he slowly raised his head and faced the dark lion, pausing as he looked into its fiery eyes. "*I sincerely respect you, and accept you exactly as you are,*" he said aloud. Kineosho could feel the melancholic lump in his throat subside as he said it. The dark lion dissolved into a gleam of light, which whisked itself away into Kineosho's body.

For a while, none of them said a word.

Kineosho looked around and the scene was peaceful once more. There were no foxes, crocodiles, crazed black-bonneted moles, or ominous dark lions.

"Home . . . let's go home," said Kineosho. Viddi smiled and climbed onto Kineosho's back sleepily. She was tired and soon passed out.

35

Goodbye baby steps

"The dark lion—when I was here the first time, it wasn't trying to attack me, I think it was trying to help me!" said Kineosho to Basho as they walked towards the river. Kineosho shook his head and sighed.

When they arrived at the river, Kineosho remembered what had happened the last time he had tried to cross it. "At least the moon doesn't have a wrinkly old face in the river this time," he thought to himself. "Still, it's probably best to be cautious with this place."

He asked Basho to wait behind him as he slowly dipped his paw into the river. Almost instantly, the same kind of violently powerful whirlpool that had appeared before formed around his foot again. It began to suck him into the river, startling Viddi who held on even more tightly to Kineosho's neck. He leapt backwards onto the riverbank in surprise and wondered why the river would still not let him enter.

"I don't understand," said Kineosho to Basho. "I mean, there's nothing else here . . . what do we still have to do?"

Basho shrugged.

Then Kineosho thought back to what the llama had said at the entrance. "Look carefully at the river before you cross, it's very deep," said Kineosho softly. He stared at the river and saw nothing except the calm, pleasant reflection of the full moon. Then he went right to the edge of the bank to see how deep the river was. He looked down and to his surprise, he could see the reflection of everything else except himself.

"Basho, I think you had better see this — there's no reflection of me in the river . . . it's weird!" called Kineosho. Basho walked up and stood next to Kineosho.

"What's weird?" said Basho, looking at the river, a little confused. "Your reflection is right there."

Kineosho looked down with Basho and he was right, his reflection was right there along with the moon and the stars. "It definitely wasn't there just a moment ago!" said Kineosho, quite puzzled. "Wait, step back a moment," said Kineosho.

As Basho stepped back, Kineosho's reflection in the water disappeared. Kineosho turned around and looked at Basho. "You're . . . you're not a jackal are you? You're a part—" started Kineosho before shaking his head, dumbfounded. "But I saw you — in the training with mom — at the river — the talent show — and you asked Twigs that embarrassing question at the Great Hall — and what about the initiation ceremony — you were there! Or was it all just—" Kineosho paused for a split second as it suddenly all came together for him. "—me?" he asked.

Basho shrugged with an innocent smile and immediately evaporated into a gleam of light that sped off into Kineosho's body.

"And you're not just a pretty face, are you?" asked a playfully sarcastic voice from behind him. Kineosho turned around quickly, almost slipping and falling into the river.

"Well you were told that things are not always what they appear to be, weren't you? So, now that you know who you are . . . you're lucky enough to get to ask me three questions," said the reflection of the moon in the river.

"About how to cross?" asked Kineosho.

"And the first answer is . . . *Yes*, or about whatever else you'd like to ask! But if you ask me that was a really silly question to waste it on!" laughed the moon. Then it was silent.

Kineosho growled at himself and then thought carefully about his two remaining questions.

After some time, he smiled and asked: "What do I need to do to cross the river?"

The moon smiled back at him. "You need to trust yourself fully," it replied smugly.

Kineosho looked at the moon, puzzled. He knew that he had only one question left to learn how to cross the river. He also knew that he had to be a lot more specific this time.

As he thought about it, he recalled how he had learnt to paint — he had first learnt how others did it, and then developed his own style. He thought for quite a while before asking his next question.

"How exactly did the last animal, preferably one that I knew, cross the river?" asked Kineosho finally.

"Well, she leapt off a cliff near the top of a waterfall, and bounced off a bunch of trampolines to the other side. One of the funnier ways really!" replied the moon with a chuckle.

"*The lemmings!*" thought Kineosho. "They didn't kill themselves after all . . . they really were just going home!"

"Anyway, bye now," said the moon quickly, and the moon seemed to become just the moon once more.

Thoughts rushed through Kineosho's mind. He remembered the lemmings with their funny dance and how confident they were about going home — there wasn't a doubt in their minds. They trusted themselves fully.

He heard Uma's voice roaming around in his head with her final words of advice, saying that everything he created in his mind was real.

He thought back to how Master Wu had levitated and moved the giant tree with his mind, and how he had told him that he had to learn to walk first. At that moment, he realised that Master Wu had meant it literally. He knew exactly what he had to do.

He stepped back a few paces from the river and closed his eyes. In his mind, he remembered the rhythm of the lemmings' peculiar dance-walk. He hummed the tune and repeated the steps on the spot, quite to the delight of the moon who had still been watching Kineosho.

A few moments later, Viddi awoke on his back and wondered what was going on with Kineosho's odd dance. She even asked him if everything was all right, but Kineosho appeared to be somewhere else.

Then, he stopped and walked to the edge of the river.

"Are we going home now?" asked Viddi sadly.

"Yes Viddi, hold on tight, all right?" replied Kineosho. She wrapped her long arm around his neck a little more tightly and looked across the river.

Kineosho closed his eyes, and took a deep breath. He cleared his mind of all distractions and focused on his path across the river. He imagined every step from start to finish.

Then he opened his eyes, and roared as loudly as he could. The sound of it echoed over the river and slowly died down.

Kineosho gazed across to his destination and slowly but without hesitation, he extended his right paw above the river. He rested his foot on the air above the water. Much to Viddi's surprise, as Kineosho shifted his weight onto that right paw, a solid clump of earth formed beneath it. It was suspended in mid-air and it did not budge.

Then Kineosho took his next step, and the same occurred under his left paw. Then he took his third step with his hind paw, and then the fourth. Each time a clump of earth formed beneath his paw as soon as he placed his weight on the air.

By the time he was ready to take his fifth step, the clump of earth had already formed for him to step on. Viddi held on tightly and looked at Kineosho in awe. Kineosho focused fully on the thought of going home, and walked. Every step he took thereafter felt like nothing out of the ordinary.

❦ 36 ❧

Home sweet home

Viddi held on tightly as Kineosho leapt onto the shore from the last suspended clump of earth above the river. They were both tired but sleep was the last thing on their minds. Kineosho turned around to look at the river and watched his makeshift bridge disappear into thin air.

"Are we home?" asked Viddi, holding Kineosho's ear. He nodded as he looked at the very spot from which he had dived into the river to swim across.

Kineosho savoured every step he took as they walked towards the clearing where Curie, Griffon, and Master Wu had shared so many stories with him. When they were close, he heard a vaguely familiar voice. It sounded as though it were telling a story.

"They edged closer curiously," said the voice. "But he still could not make out who it was. When they were close enough, they peered through the bushes to see if they could spot the storyteller. They only saw a large group of animals in a circle listening attentively. And then—" paused the voice with some drama.

"—he leapt into the centre of the circle, much to the surprise of everyone there," said Kineosho, as he suddenly leapt into the centre of the circle, surprising the audience.

For a moment, everyone was silent. Viddi, who had been dangling around Kineosho's neck after his leap, immediately rushed to Curie, giving her a big hug. It was as though she had relived every second of her experience in an instant. Then the entire clearing, including an ecstatic Abu, burst into manic applause.

Kineosho took a deep breath and looked around. The clearing was different and so were many of the faces there, but he felt as though he had never left. He recalled hearing his father's story from the same spot, after he had returned with Master Wu, victorious in their battle. Kineosho had expected to feel proud about his own story, but instead he only felt calm.

"Welcome back," said a deep voice next to him. Kineosho turned to his side and saw Griffon standing there proudly. It had only just sunk in that Kineosho had returned. Master Wu stood beside him, looking as pleased as a one-eyed kung fu mouse could possibly look.

"—and they all lived happily ever after," whispered a vaguely familiar voice softly behind Kineosho.

He turned around slowly. The elegant leopard he saw gave him a gentle, knowing smile. Kineosho looked into her eyes, and could do nothing more than smile gently in return.

❦ The End ❦

mystic tree

❧ **Personal Message from the Author** ☙

Thank you for reading my book, and I hope you enjoyed it. If you did, please would you be kind and take a moment to leave a quick review at your favourite online retailer. I would sincerely appreciate your time to do so, and it would make me happy to know what you liked the most.

To listen to the songs in this book, read free short stories about Kineosho and his friends, share your thoughts about this story or your own journey, or to get in touch with me directly, please visit http://www.kineosho.com/

Thanks again, and enjoy your day!

Pratish

www.ingramcontent.com/pod-product-compliance
Lightning Source LLC
Chambersburg PA
CBHW032052090426
42744CB00005B/178